The Redneck

Manifesto

Jim Goad

SIMON & SCHUSTER

Simon & Schuster
Rockefeller Center
1230 Avenue of the Americas
New York, NY 10020

Copyright © 1997 by Jim Goad

SIMON & SCHUSTER and colophon are registered
trademarks of Simon & Schuster Inc.

Designed by Leslie Phillips
Manufactured in the United States of America

10   9   8   7   6   5   4   3   2   1

Library of Congress Cataloging-in-Publication Data
Goad, Jim.
The redneck manifesto / Jim Goad.
p.   cm.
Includes bibliographical references.
1. Rednecks—United States—Social conditions.
2. Rednecks—United States—Economic conditions.
3. Working class whites—United States—Social conditions.
4. Working class whites—United States—Economic conditions.
I. Title.
HD8072.5.G67   1997
305.5'62—dc21   97-7865   CIP
ISBN 0-684-83113-9

Acknowledgments

Angry White Male gratitude is due to those who inspired me while working on this book, those who selflessly provided research tips or advice, and even those who tried their best to help and failed horribly:

Phil Anselmo • Jim Blanchard • Nick Bougas • Alan Brabson • Ivan Brunetti • G. Lynn Burch • Lisa Carver • Ray Crowe • Francisco Martin Duran • Lorin Ferguson • Donna Gaines • Jane Greenhow • Rick Hall • Rob Hardin • Mark Hejnar • Michael A. Hoffman II • Scott Huffines • Phil Irwin • Darius James • Jeff Kelly • Alan "Hellstomper" King • Hollister "Gun Fag Manifesto" Kopp • Jeff Koyen • J. Keith Layne • Jessica Morgan • Michael Moynihan • Annalee Newitz • Karen Niziolek • Adam Parfrey • Randall Phillip • Dickie Joe Reed • Chip Smith • Peter Sotos • Steve Svymbersky • Sean Tejaratchi • Jesco White • Diane and Richard Willman • Matt Wray • Leroy Wright

Just don't ask for any favors. And if you didn't spot your name, well, maybe it was on purpose. Thanks also to all the critics who've unwittingly provided their own heady brand of perverted inspiration.

May white-trash blessings fall like snowflakes on those in the publishing industry who've risked their reputations: Charlotte Sheedy, Neeti Madan, Chuck Adams, Cheryl Weinstein, Trish Todd, Bob Mecoy, Ted Landry, and Andy Hafitz.

Sloppy inbred kisses to all the members of my family with whom I'm still on speaking terms (hi, Sis). And, naturally, a trailerful of cracker affection to Igor, Eggy, Percy, Bjorn, Flavia, and Debbie.

No thanks to anyone else.

*Dedicated to everyone who lives
between New York and L.A.*

Contents

"You're writing about white trash? Well, I hope you don't make fun of 'em like the rest of the media does."
—A guy who still lives in my old neighborhood

1

White Niggers Have Feelings, Too

Don't you just hate 'em? Every gap-toothed, inbred, uncivilized, violent, and hopelessly DUMB one of 'em? Jesus, how can you *not* hate 'em? There's no class of people with less honor. Less dignity. No one more ignorant. More gullible. They're a primitive breed with prehistoric manners, unfit for anything beyond petty crime and random bloodletting. Their stunted, subhuman minds are mesmerized by cheap alcohol, Lotto fever, and the asinine superstitions of poor-folks' religion. They stop beating their wives just long enough to let 'er squeeze out another deformed rug rat. They scatter their hand-me-down genes in a degenerative spiral of dysfunction. They breed anencephalic, mouth-breathing children. Vulgarians. All of them. Bottom feeders. They really bring down their race.

Luckily for you, I didn't specify which race that is. If I'd been talking about black trash, I might be lynched. If I was talking about white trash, I'd merely be another torchbearer in an ongoing national lynching. The difference between vile racism and precision satire all depends on the nigger's color.

Day after cotton-pickin' day, we are invited to hate white trash. Our media machines and their huddled suckling masses show scant pity for the redneck. Our magazines and sitcoms and blockbuster films are crammed with slams of hicks and hayseeds and hillbillies and crackers and trailer scum. Through relentless exposure to images of lowlife undesirability, we are led to sniff disdainfully at the sour stench of

15

retrograde Eurosweat. Gradually, we come to believe that working-class whites are two-dimensional cartoons—rifle-totin', booger-eatin', beer-bellied swine flesh. Skeeter-bitten, ball-tuggin', homo-hatin', pig-fuckin', daughter-gropin' slugs. We learn to laugh at—and fear—their zit-scarred visages and stupid, filmy eyeballs. We chuckle at the crank-shooters and fart-huffers. The chip-tossers and snake-handlers. The bouffanted hausfraus and ducktailed loggers. The hairy-assed were-wolves who occupy trailer parks out near Superfund cleanup sites. The obese, curler-wearing women standing unashamed in orange bikinis, their sloping boobs slung over cesarean scars. Their unwashed, uncom-prehending kids with cavity-peppered chartreuse teeth. The scaly, pale-gray skin of buck-toothed men who inhale turpentine and punch the fuck out of anyone smarter than they are. Skull face after skull face of dull-brained peasantry. Rolling landfills of curdled whiteness. Cat piss and dirty diapers. Crusty dishes in the sink. Yellowy armpit stains on white T-shirts. Millions of smelly white assholes stinking up the nation.

The stereotypes aren't new, just more persistently cruel of late. The Dumb White Bumpkin has always been a stock figure in the American dramatis personae. But fifty years ago the depictions tended toward the benign and comical, from Li'l Abner to Ma and Pa Kettle. As our perceptions of a lily-fisted white hegemony started to fracture, the caricatures became meaner, yielding the murderous crackers in *Easy Rider* and the ass-fucking genetic disasters from *Deliverance*.

Cartoon people. These days, we hardly ever see the redneck as anything *but* a caricature. A whole vein of human experience, of poten-tial literature, is dismissed as a joke, much as America's popular no-tions of black culture were relegated to lawn jockeys and Sambo caricatures a generation or two ago. The redneck is the only cardboard figure left standing in our ethnic shooting gallery. All the other targets have been quietly removed in deference to unwritten laws of cultural sensitivity. We no longer have Stepin Fetchit, but Jim "Ernest" Varney still rears his ugly po'bucker head. Instead of Amos 'n' Andy, there's Beavis and Butt-head or Darryl and Darryl from *Newhart*. White trash are open game. The trailer park has become the media's cultural toilet, the only acceptable place to dump one's racist inclinations.

To buttress this wild, implausible-sounding contention, I conducted a short, pseudoscientific study of how the mainstream press handles the race-specific terms of "nigger" and "redneck." Mouse in hand, I clicked my way through an internet search of the *Detroit Free Press* archives from 1987 through the first six months of 1995, plus a more limited probe of the *San Francisco Chronicle* from August 1994 to May 1995. The search yielded one hundred and seventy-three occurrences of the word "nigger" compared to a hundred and fifteen instances of "redneck." Due to limitations in my internet software, I was unable to search for phrases such as "white trash," but it seems reasonable that "redneck" and "white trash," as well as "cracker," "honky," "hillbilly," and "hick," occurred with sufficient frequency to achieve at least a rough numerical parity with "nigger" and its synonyms. But it isn't until one analyzes how the slurs are handled—as well as who's doing the slurring—that the raw numbers begin to have any meaning.

First, the rednecks . . .

Redneck: 115 Hits

These citations can loosely be divided into the following categories:

THOSE CONTEMPTIBLE REDNECK CLOWNS . . . 39 HITS

✳ Rednecks are depicted as psychotic and repellent ("a fat, sloppy, redneck moron"; "an oleaginous redneck"; "a twisted, sneering, redneck maniac"; etc.).

✳ Rednecks are stereotyped as alcoholic lushes ("a beer-swilling redneck"; "beer-suckin' redneck"; and six instances of the phrase "redneck bar").

✳ Rednecks are portrayed as worthy targets of ethnic satire ("redneck humor" and the current surfeit of "You might be a redneck if . . ." jokes).

✳ Two references in this category linked rednecks to those old sex-pathology standbys, inbreeding and incest.

REDNECKS AS FOREIGNERS . . . 26 HITS

✳ The redneck experience is treated as something other-worldly, isolated from the mainstream both geographically and ideologically ("far-flung redneck burgs"; "a rustic, redneck South"; "redneck territory"; and "a redneck city in Texas").

✳ The redneck boondocks are consistently portrayed as enemy locales from which any sensible person should flee. After fleeing, the rehabilitated redneck is observed apologizing for his roots ("Lily's husband, Ralph, has climbed up from his redneck background . . . to spite his socially superior wife"; and "I was a product of the redneck area where I was raised, and I've tried through Buddhism and EST to support another side of myself").

YOU ALREADY KNOW WHAT A REDNECK IS . . . 22 HITS

✳ These citations are telling in their lack of descriptiveness, for they tend to assume that the reader's mind is already embossed with stock images of what constitutes a redneck. The stereotype is presumed to be so fully fleshed as to need no explanation ("redneck women"; "a redneck drill sergeant"; "redneck ecstasy"; "a great redneck walk"; etc.).

REDNECKS AND ETHNIC IDENTITY . . . 28 HITS

✳ The word "redneck" is used by whites as a defiant self-descriptor (REDNECK AND PROUD license plates; song lyrics that state, "They call me a redneck/I reckon I am").

✳ In five instances, blacks are quoted using the word to describe lowlife whites. This, interestingly, is never viewed as racist.

✳ Rednecks are fingered as the primary source of prejudice ("a redneck Klansman"; "a bigoted redneck"; "redneck racism"; etc.).

✳ Finally, in only six out of a hundred and fifteen total hits, the term "redneck" is scrutinized as possibly being a racial slur. Six out of a hundred and fifteen—less than five percent of the time. The other hundred and nine times that "redneck" is used, it's done with the unblinking certitude that slurring rednecks is an OK thing to do.

Not so the niggers.

Nigger: 173 Hits

"Nigger," of course, occupies a cranny far beyond "fuck" in our Pantheon of Unutterables. Predictably, EVERY TIME that "nigger" surfaced, there was some implied or overt repulsion with the word's usage. The "N" word is universally condemned as an "ugly gutter epithet," an "obscenity," and "the filthiest, dirtiest, nastiest word in the American language." The "nigger" data is perhaps best analyzed when split into three categories:

WHITES SAY "NIGGER" . . . 133 HITS

✳ Many of these references involved well-publicized racial bloopers by Great White Dopes such as Ted Danson, Marge Schott, and Mark Fuhrman. Several others reported on controversies and lawsuits arising after public officials or other injudicious Caucasians uttered "nigger."
✳ A full hundred and nine of these citations discuss the trauma experienced merely by being *called* a nigger, likening it to a "verbal lynching" that in several instances leads directly to violence. In seven cases, blacks are seen as justified in assaulting someone after being labeled a nigger by a lighter-hued human.

BLACKS SAY "NIGGER" . . . 33 HITS

✳ Blacks use "nigger" self-referentially, an inverted reclamation of a word others had used to disparage them. It's identical to how some poor whites stubbornly refer to themselves as rednecks.
✳ In eleven instances (more frequently than the ten times they refer to themselves as niggers), blacks put the term in

whitey's mouth. In other words, they accuse whites of saying "nigger" without any evidence that they actually had ("What? You never seen a nigger before?"; "They still look at you like you're a nigger"; and "A black man with a million dollars is a nigger with a million dollars").

✳ Blacks reject the term outright ("There's no such thing as a nigger"; "I've never been a nigger, so the word has never bothered me"; etc.).

✳ Blacks acknowledge that whites' usage of "nigger" has seriously waned ("Nobody comes out and calls you a nigger anymore"; "You don't hear the word 'nigger.' No one ever says that anymore"; and "No one ever called me a nigger").

"NIGGER" OCCURS NEXT TO AN ANTI-WHITE SLUR ... 7 HITS

✳ A black man who was kicked off a bus after the white driver said, "Let the nigger walk" complains of his treatment at the hands of "that redneck driver."

✳ A black activist who objects to being called "nigger" while at college asks, "Why should I beg some cracker to integrate me into his society when he doesn't want to?"

✳ In reviewing a street fight where whites and blacks traded taunts of "nigger" and "honky," the commentator only bemoans the fact that "nigger" was used.

✳ A white schoolteacher insists he "never, ever said 'nigger' around students" and underlines his assumed open-mindedness by adding, "I call whites 'white trash' if they're trashy."

White devil that I am, I saved the most damning statistic for last: In every occurrence of the word "nigger," the writer was quoting someone *else's* usage of it. But in eighty out of the hundred and fifteen instances of "redneck"—more than two of every three times the word popped up—it was the WRITER using "redneck" as a noun or adjective to degrade low-class whites. Think about it—no writer on any American daily newspaper would be able to say "nigger" without getting fired. But if the neck's red, the light's green.

The 1989 edition of *Webster's New World Dictionary* mirrors this semantic double standard. Its one-word definition of "nigger" (Negro) is followed by a fifty-eight-word disclaimer:

> USAGE—originally simply a dialectal variant of Negro, the term *nigger* is today acceptable only in black English; in all other contexts it is now generally regarded as virtually taboo because of the legacy of racial hatred that underlies the history of its use among whites, and its continuing use among a minority as a viciously hostile epithet....

Compare its definition of "redneck":

> a poor, white, rural Southerner, often, specif., one regarded as ignorant, bigoted, violent, etc.

Note that *Webster's* doesn't argue with the depiction of rednecks as "ignorant, bigoted, [and] violent." Nor does it mention that persons who use the word "nigger" often regard their targets to be ignorant, violent, and sometimes bigoted, too. While nothing short of apologetic in its use of the "N" word, *Webster's* is nearly conspiratorial in its loathing for the redneck.

Those rednecks must be pretty horrible people.

We've all heard that white trash is "the worst kind of trash," usually uttered without a droplet of irony by persons who consider themselves strident antiracists. Now, smack my white ass into a melanin-starved pulp, but this sounds awfully contradictory to me. I thought the First Rule of Racial Etiquette was that no one should be permitted to insult a group to which they don't belong. Yet blacks, Jews, Asians, and Hispanics—and, most significantly, rich whites—can say "redneck" or "white trash" with impunity. In fact, such utterances are usually considered somewhat ballsy and heroic, as if David had slung a two-pound rock at Goliath's bullying forehead.

In order to avoid the appearance of racism, the defenders of such slurs hasten to note that they aren't referring to *all* whites—just the white trash. And they'll rush to add that you don't have to be poor to act like white trash. I can only counter that white bigots have for years insisted that they don't hate *all* blacks—just the ones who act like niggers. And you don't have to be poor to act like a nigger, either.

Multiculturalism is a country club that excludes white trash. Its refusal to view terms such as "white trash" and "redneck" as race-specific and class-specific lends itself to a mountain of contradictions that would be comical if they weren't potentially dangerous. In their putsch to redress past grievances, the trash-bashers will expound endlessly about white-trash primitivism while ignoring some unpleasant realities about modern-day Africa. Dumb manifestations of American blackness are explained away as "culture," while white trash's peccadilloes are blamed on stupidity. If a black doctor seems embarrassed by scrotum-clutching gangsta rappers and sweaty black preachers, he's branded a race traitor and a sellout. But if a white lawyer seems ashamed of ball-scratching hillbillies and sweaty white preachers, it's a perfectly understandable distaste. If a white guy handles poisonous snakes to prove his faith in Jesus, he's a dope. But if a black guy sacrifices live chickens to appease voodoo gods, it's respected as a valid cultural expression. It's OK to mention Caucasian inbreeding, but not African-American teen-pregnancy rates. You can rag on trailer trash, but not ghetto scum. You can make fun of truck drivers, but not lowriders. Third World infomercial Stop the Hunger poster babies live in poverty because they were somehow forced into it, while rednecks have no one but themselves to blame.

I'm not going to deny that a lot of trailer-park rednecks are stupid. And, in the egalitarian spirit, neither will I hide from the fact that a lot of ghetto blacks and barrio Hispanics are as dumb as aquarium gravel. Certainly, the cracker class is ignorant of many things. But Hutu tribesmen aren't?

Contradictions. The steaming liberal revulsion for white trash evaporates under the high-friction heat of its own illogic. The liberal class analysis crumbles when viewed under the light of . . . well, the liberal class analysis. This "analysis" willingly understands the economic imperatives behind urban street gangs but not rural moonshiners; it embraces Crips and Bloods but not the Hatfields and McCoys. It "celebrates diversity" yet consistently frowns on the experience of the white working class. Somehow, white workers always seem to get factored out of the multicultural equation, a hue too pale for their rainbow coalitions. White-trash pathologies are almost never seen as a response to environmental factors, while the behavior of impoverished non-Euros is always viewed this way. There's no shortage of socio-illogical alibis for any other group's aberrant acts; with white trash, it's seen as some form of innate rottenness. If you're going to argue that rednecks simply don't have the "right stuff"—that they breed violence, stupidity, and other undesirable character traits—you're wandering into a eugenical argument and undermining any pretense toward liberalism or egalitarianism. If you embrace equality, sooner or later you'll be forced to hug white trash, and don't blame me if you can't handle the smell.

To justify the ideological *Anschluss* against white trash, one would have to establish that hillbillies wield an unholy degree of power. As leftists have argued for years, the only true racists are people with the power systematically to oppress others. And this is where the alt-pundits and lib-babblers fail in their assault on rednecks. They speak of white trash and white privilege as if the terms were interchangeable. Because most corporate executives are white males, they mistakenly conclude that most white males are corporate executives. They simultaneously depict white trash to be as dumb as oak sap, yet able to pull off an intercontinental conspiracy that enslaved most of the melanin-rich world. They flimsily assert that people who can't afford indoor plumbing somehow have a chokehold on the pipelines of global wealth. Rednecks are portrayed as the embodiment of white power, when the only time they're likely to encounter a powerful white man is when the boss barks at them down at the factory.

The epic-style trappings of redneck kitsch, given any degree of honest scrutiny, can only be seen as the fantasies of the powerless, not the powerbrokers. As a reaction to their inarticulated weakness, white trash develop a runic system of Wagnerian overstatement: monster trucks, nitro-burning funny cars, seven-foot wrestlers, messianic Elvii, heavy-metal bombast, and slasher-movie notions of male potency. And, ultimately, their fantasies are actualized in large-scale wars where the white-trash believers are shipped off and gobbled up like pearly fat hamburger meat.

23

While compiling my notes for this essay, I began to wonder if a day could pass when I wouldn't hear someone talk shit about white trash. So I attuned my fuzzy rabbit ears to the radio and TV. I focused my piercing rodent eyes on newspapers, magazines, fanzines, and the internet. Not one day clicked by without encountering angry fulminations against inbred yokels or at least a condescending Billy-Bob caricature. And I'm still waiting.

So why am I perturbed by all the trash-bashing?

Because they're talking about ME.

For the longest time, I didn't want to admit it. Realizing that you're white trash is like being diagnosed with cancer: First comes denial, then a "lashing-out" phase, then grudging acceptance. If you're fortunate, you'll be able to turn the bad news into something good.

Being white trash is akin to cult membership in that you don't realize what's happening until you get away from it. The neighborhood of my youth seemed perfectly normal . . . until I left it. Just like all other rednecks, I gathered my belongings into a red-and-white checkered tablecloth, tied it to the end of a stick, and set off for the big city. After being called white trash—what was it?—sixteen or seventeen thousand times, I started to think that the city slickers might be onto something. It was gradually painful, yet eventually glorious, for me to admit they were right: I come from a class of economically disadvantaged white people. But I'm not asking for food stamps. I don't even want forty acres and a mule. A little sympathy for the redneck would be nice, though. Otherwise, my mutant hillbilly brethren and I will have to kill you.

Like Marie and Donny Osmond, I'm a little bit country, a little bit rock 'n' roll. I'm equal parts city slime and country vermin. My mother was urban Philly garbage; my father was rural Vermont scum. Together they fled to a concrete Dogpatch five miles outside the City of Brotherly Love to live the half-baked consumerist dreams of post-World War II suburban trash. I am the direct product of miscegenated, cross-pollinated trash.

In block after block of brick tract housing, a Levittown-style Lego bummer, our neighborhood was a repository of working-class ruffneckism. The cheap houses, featuring basement dens proudly paneled in low-grade plywood, always smelled like methane and rotted fruit. Toe-nail clippings and balled-up boogers lurked beneath the sofas. The men were very hairy and dumb, while the women were somewhat hairy and dumb. I remember portly men in grass-stained T-shirts fistfighting on their front lawns. I recall Christmas trees being knocked over as drunken families slugged it out. My eyes get all misty as I think of gum-snapping teenage girls who wrote phone numbers on the kitchen wall and hoped for some speed-dealing biker to give them a gold-plated ring, a one-bedroom apartment, and a litter of babies.

Genetically, my neighborhood was evenly split between wops and micks, with nary another ethnicity apparent for miles. You were either a freckle-faced jig-dancer such as myself or an olive-hued dago. The Irishmen on our block did little to dispel the stereotype that their breed was a besotted lot of pug-nosed fuckups. Snarling Popeye characters were everywhere. A shillelagh-wielding passel of cirrhosis-ravaged leprechauns in brown work pants, shiny black shoes, and white socks. A rarely tilled potato field of unschooled, flinty-eyed, barbershop-smelling, alcoholic human shamrocks. Although my mother's ethnic canvas was also speckled with British and Scottish, and my father was a ragged quilt of Dublin, London, and Quebec, in our neighborhood we were considered Irish. Therefore, we drank and stayed angry.

It was the Italians and their bleedingly gaudy manifestations of papism that gave our neighborhood the tang of city-tenement trash. The Italian families I knew tried to mask their just-off-the-boat, low-dog social status with tinsel mountains of store-bought glitz. Walking into one of their homes was like strolling into the Liberace Museum. Beveled ceiling mirrors. Chintzy statues of naked, laurel-crowned water boys. Clear plastic slipcovers and golden shag carpeting. Sun-day-afternoon dinners at friends' houses with thin, sugary spaghetti sauce and a hot, air-conditioner-exhaust cloud of Roman sexual guilt. Rotund, pathetic Pagliaccis. Always a scarf-swaddled, half-deaf grand-mother wearing thick stockings that led down to swollen, old-world ankles. Impossible virginity and a thinly disguised führer in the Pope. They'd revel in the bloodlust of full-color, ultragory antiabortion tracts our church distributed in the vestibule outside Sunday Mass. The Ital-ians seemed otherworldly and much more theatrical than the Irish.

They seemed almost black. And for no other apparent reason than the fact that we reached America's shores first, we considered ourselves eugenically superior to them. The dagos were our niggers.

Trash starts at home, and my aesthetic soup bowl has always been smothered with a fat ketchup splotch of white-trash flavoring. This is thanks mainly to the cultural tutelage of my older brother. Back in the mid-sixties, he trained me to keep my bowels awash in lard-soaked, hot pepper–spiked Philly junk food. I ate smashed-'n'-burnt scrapple and learned to mangle my diction. I gobbled hoagies crammed with deadly lunch meats and strained to fart on cue. My brother took me to the drag races, hipped me to the flesh-melting gore of EC Comics, and made sure I knew all the words to "Greasy Grimy Gopher Guts."

One summer night in 1965, a year or so before the government sent him to Vietnam with a gun, he let me tag along for a triple feature of slasher flicks at the local drive-in. Thirty years later, I still remember those films. The first, *Color Me Blood Red,* was about a psychotic painter who killed women and used their blood to match his desired crimson tint. The last movie on the bill, *Blood Feast,* concerned an Egyptian caterer who extracted human body parts from mostly live subjects to prepare a feast for the goddess Ishtar. Strong stuff for a four-year-old's eyes, but really not much worse than what my father was doing to my mother and older siblings at home.

Consanguinely sandwiched between *Color Me Blood Red* and *Blood Feast* was the redneck-revenge epic *Two Thousand Maniacs!* The film is set in the mythical Southern town of Pleasant Valley (pop. 2,000), said to have been decimated by conquering Union soldiers in 1865. A hundred years later, the massacred villagers resurrect themselves and capture six Yankees as sacrificial offerings for their centennial celebration. While the Yankees mutter in their hotel rooms about the mysterious hospitality of Pleasant Valley's "backwoods Daniel Boone" and "overblown Daisy Mae" denizens, a britches-clad hayseed named Rufus rhapsodizes about how "classy" one of the female Northerners had behaved earlier. "By tonight, all that class is gonna be drained out of her, Lester," he drools to his sidekick. Sure enough, the woman's arm is axed clean off of her body that afternoon . . . and barbecued at a banjo-pluckin' hootenanny later that night. Her boyfriend's limbs are fastened with rope to four horses, who rip his bean-pole frame in four directions. The next day, another Yankee woman is crushed under a massive boulder called "Teeterin' Rock." Her beau is forced into an open barrel spiked on the inside with nails and then rolled down a hill, puncturing him to death. As I stared at the giant, bloody screen and all the hooting redneck caricatures, I said to my brother, "They remind me of the people where Grammy lives."

I was referring to Grammy Goad, our paternal grandmother, who looked and dressed almost identically to Granny Clampett from *The Beverly Hillbillies*. Grammy lived and died in Windsor, Vermont, my direct connection to country trash. The people of Windsor also reminded me of the characters on *Petticoat Junction, Green Acres,* or any of the other Cracker Comedies from the sixties. But economic pressures simmered behind the laugh track. Since Grandpa Goad, the town drunk, abandoned Grammy with four boys to feed, she made money by cooking for lumberjacks. Thoughts of her peanut-butter fudge, salt pork, jelly biscuits, and "yaller" gravy still make my saw-toothed mouth water. I'll probably never taste cooking like that again, for there will never be white people like that again.

Our family would typically spend a chunk of every summer up in Vermont, either at Grammy's, Aunt Berle's, or Uncle Junie's. Are THOSE names redneck enough for ya? We'd sleep as snug as tater bugs in splintery old shacks with rusted screen doors. Clean, wood-redolent air contrasted nicely with Philly's gag-spew. A rotted covered bridge spanned the Connecticut River, over to New Hampshire's sinsemilla-green hills. While my uncle was off slaving at the local Goodyear factory, we Goad kids would chase stray dogs or hunt tadpoles. Sometimes, Vermont was nearly perfect. Its loggers and earthworm salesmen were the friendliest and most honest people I've ever met. They never learned to be ashamed of what they were.

I wasn't so fortunate. I don't remember being explicitly instructed, but I somehow sensed that I wasn't supposed to be proud of my yokel kin in Vermont. This instinctual shame perhaps first saw blossom when I began attending grade school. The local Catholic youth indoctrination camp, Holy Cross Elementary School, sat at the crossroads between the blue-collar/redneck Clifton Heights and white-collar/whitebread

Springfield. I was from Clifton Heights. Springfield had a country club with a golf course; Clifton Heights had corner bars with dartboards. The men in Springfield drank cocktails; the men in Clifton drank their lives away. Springfield had college deferments; Clifton had Vietnam casualties. Springfield was happy, orderly, and quiet; Clifton was loud, sloppy, and miserable. The men in Springfield were allowed to fuck up a hundred times; the men in Clifton, only once. When you turned twenty in Springfield, life was only beginning; that's when life ended in Clifton.

The Springfield boys would scoff at Clifton as if it were Harlem, and their class-based condescension initially surprised me. I spent my early youth thinking I lived in the center of the universe, only to realize it was the other side of the tracks. I had grown cozily accustomed to a two-tiered social hierarchy—the omnipotent working Irish and the skeevy working Italians—only to learn that I was someone else's nigger.

While driving through Springfield in our bottlefly-green Chevy Impala, I remember Mom and Pop pointing at huge, razor-cut lawns and houses that seemed as big as Graceland. They mentioned that these were middle-class houses, and I wondered what class that made us. I wasn't really sure why other neighborhoods were more affluent than ours, only that they had somehow strayed from our flock. When my father did plumbing work for the owner of the bar where he drank, we drove out past Springfield onto a rolling estate. The place even had a private stream artificially stocked with sunfish. While my father scraped shit out of the bar owner's copper pipes, I swam in the backyard pool with the man's son. Up until that time, I didn't know that some people had pools in their backyards. We didn't even have a backyard, we had an alleyway.

While my father acted like Mussolini at home, he was an eager bellhop around his wealthy client. I remember seeing the bar owner pull out a two-inch-thick clump of bills and start peeling off individual notes for dad. My father just stared at the money in the man's hands. So deferential. Accordingly, I behaved with unusual politeness around my swimming playmate and didn't splash him once. I never acted that way around the kids in my neighborhood.

I slowly learned to disown my roots. Media images of white trash began to repel me. Country singer Porter Wagoner seemed to embody everything I was starting to hate about my white-trash posterity. Why, I'd leap through a hoop of flamin' turnips if Porter wasn't the ugliest human I'd ever seen. Standing there alongside impossible-breasted hillbilly belle Dolly Parton on his mid-seventies syndicated TV show, stiff and stiltlike in his rhinestone red peacock suit, wearing a gilded pompadour on a head thinner than a peanut, Porter Wagoner made me feel ashamed.

The last time my parents dragged me up to Vermont, it was the summer of '78, right before my senior year in high school. Since I had fully ingested the faux-nig blues of the Rolling Stones and the muddied politics of an FM-radio generation, my paternal kinfolks' skeet-shooting, pond-paddlin' ways embarrassed me more than ever. For my "What I Did on Summer Vacation" speech in English class that fall, I lampooned the "Goad Clan," painting my Vermont relatives as crude hillbilly wolverines. It drew gales of snot-nosed guffaws from the mostly female class members, young poetic girls who all looked like Ben Franklin.

Class consciousness was becoming somewhat of a full-time obsession for me. I entered college a little too late to enjoy being white, and just in time to be blamed for what dead white people I'd never met had done. It didn't matter if my ancestors had installed plumbing in the pyramids—I was still the oppressor. I fit in with neither the preppy butterbuds nor the henna-haired spider-rockers, opting instead for the unconscious white-trash gesture of retro rockabilly. And no matter how much deodorant I wore, I still gave off *eau de garbage blanc*. My girlfriend of the time, whose father snagged a quarter-mil a year drawing blueprints at home, initially told me she thought I was some poseur from the suburbs. She, with her high-acreage home and summer classes in Paris, was indubitably punker than I. She encouraged me to read *Ms.* magazine and to acknowledge my role in her systematic oppression. At one point while we were shacked up together, she griped that she was tired of living "hand-to-mouth." I didn't know why she was complaining, for I had always lived that way. Then, when she had flown back to Pittsburgh to get more money from daddy, I drove a cab in the snow to earn my half of the rent.

For it wasn't until I started to WORK for a living that I realized being white trash wasn't something to be ashamed of. . . . It was something to get angry about.

I hated my parents as people, but I've come to appreciate their social predicament and how it may have fed their bitterness. Both Mammy and Pappy used to browbeat me with Great Depression horror stories. My father—who loved to read—was forced to quit high school in order to help support his brothers and mother, selling chocolate milk to rock-quarry miners. My mother told of ceaseless weeks sipping thin gruel and wondering if she would starve. Both wore tattered clothes because of other folks' untethered speculative greed. These "other folks," as you might surmise, aren't the kind who are likely to be called "white trash." And then, as the Depression was ebbing, these same other folks sent my father into Germany with a rifle, offering his life to protect military-industrial interests beyond his comprehension.

For as long as I'd been alive, the old man worked eighty-hour weeks —forty wearing a hard hat under the harsh refinery flames of Gulf Oil, and forty as a plumber, allowing rich white families' shit and rust and termite spray to seep into his blistered redneck hands. To help meet the bills, my mother and sister worked as country-club waitresses, scooping up the half-chewed egg-salad sandwiches of wealthy white women. Although a crabby prick, my father was a reasonably bright man, seemingly suited to something better than plumbing or oil-rig work. Part of it, I can't help feeling, is because no one ever expected him to be anything better. As he realized he'd never get any further than shoveling shit or refining oil, he started acting like trash. He became a slave to booze and racetracks and cigarettes and coffee and stomach remedies and short, intermittent blasts of desperate violence.

The bacon-addled old coot died long before my 1987 Las Vegas marriage inside a Tropicana Mobile Park trailer home. The man who tied the knot was the Reverend Walker Goad, whose name we found in the white pages. Suffering the same lack of ancestral perspective as many American whites, I wasn't even sure of the ethnic origin of "Goad" or when the first Goads came to America. Walker, a big bald linebacker of a reverend, amiably explained that the name was British. He said the first Goads in America were convicts shipped over from

England to work their jail sentences as indentured servants on plantations. In other words, my ancestors were white slaves. After slavery
ended, these were the people who became the hill-scrubbers and corn-
crackers, the assembly-line insects and truck drivers, over three hundred years of hopeless shit jobs dripping down on my head.

If Walker's statements were true, that would give me an entirely
different heritage from wealthy whites. It would mean that my ancestors were niggers in the U.K., and they haven't stopped being niggers
here. Is it fair to say I was born with the same chances as Thomas
Jefferson? Or even a well-heeled Taiwanese expatriate or a Kuwaiti
immigrant? Trash-bashers haven't seriously pondered such questions,
arguing fallaciously that the rednecks had their chance and blew it.

About three A.M. every morning, I rip myself from sleep like a fetus
aborting itself. Sometimes I have to smack myself in the face to assure
I won't nod off again. Another ephedrine tablet, another mugful of
shit-thick coffee. My ass squirts blood from all the speed variants I
imbibe to stay awake and work. I'm often such a fatigued dishrag, I'll
just stare at my notes for hours. But I can't afford to close my eyelids.
I'll try to write until around seven, when me and the missus get ready
for work. She's a typist in a steel mill. I do pre-press work in a print
shop. In the early evening, I try to squeeze a few more written words
out of myself before I drop. And then I instinctually awake myself
again at three A.M. I'm pulling two full-time shifts, just like the old
man did. If I didn't work a day job, I'd starve. And if I didn't write at
night, I'd die.

On my way driving to work, I take a shortcut through a well-tended
suburban quadrant that reminds me a lot of Springfield. Heavy fortifi-
cations. Tall cubist bushes. Lawn sprinklers chugging in arrogant circles. White women in white sweatshirts, white shorts, white anklets,
and white tennis shoes waiting at the roadside for a bus to whisk their
marshmallowy children away to prep school. At work, I'm doubly
reminded of class differences among whites. My boss has hired his
wife and daughter to answer phones, eat doughnuts, and file their nails
while I toil for eight hours without stopping. As my limbs robotically
perform their blue-collar mambo, my mind drifts back to all the jobs
where I've taken orders from trust-fund ferrets with half my brains and

31

a hundred times my money. Those bloody stints as busboy and french-fry chef and taxi driver and shoe-store clerk. The times when I slept in my leaky car and let my teeth rot because I couldn't afford a dentist. The part-time gig at an alternative weekly newspaper where I listened to the limo-libs constantly dumping on white trash, silently enduring their barbs as if they were telling polack jokes and didn't realize I was Polish. So sometimes on my way to work, I fantasize about those rich white women and their children bleeding all over their white clothes.

Because it was always the people in THEIR neighborhood who were the primary trash-bashers. Because poor blacks remind them of their sins, they refrain from nigger-bashing; because poor whites remind them of their successes, they shit on rednecks and laugh. What should I call the nontrashy Caucasians? White Gold? The Valuable People? The true profiteers of white imperialism? These are the same class of folks who create negative media images of white trash, the writers who use "redneck" as an adjective. They disparage white trash much as one insults an embarrassingly drunken relative. And in so doing, they shunt nonwhite resentment away from themselves and toward white trash. It's some sort of guilt projection, almost like a father who rapes his next-door neighbor and then blames his son for the crime. For it isn't the Ivy League multiculturalists who serve as cannon fodder in our wars, it's the niggers and rednecks. It isn't the condo-owning East Village social theorists who die of black lung, it's the West Virginia miners. The incessant media disgust for white trash may be, consciously or not, a mechanism for richer whites to scapegoat poorer ones. It's an easy, effective, divide-and-conquer stratagem. For most of America's history, they worked at getting the rednecks to blame the niggers. For the past thirty years or so, they've encouraged the niggers to blame the rednecks. This is for certain: If the niggers and rednecks ever joined forces, they'd be unbeatable. But the people in their neighborhood don't want it that way.

So it chaps my hide to read a syndicated newspulp column by someone named Tad Friend, who seems to have built a career on decrying white trash as if they were genital lice. In an article called "White Trash Nation," Tad warns us of a "white-trash epidemic," disapprovingly snorting that

the shame of white-trash behavior . . . is neither a delightful plastic
flamingo on the front lawn of American culture nor a glimpse of
existential freedom. True trash is unsocialized and violent. True
trash is one long boiling tantrum, primed to explode. True trash is
the terrible twos forever.[1]

What Tad neglects to mention is that true trash probably couldn't
afford the tuition at the college where Tad's parents sent him. True
trash was busy enjoying all the wondrous physical and mental pathologies you never see on *The Beverly Hillbillies*. True trash was worrying
about that one wrong move that would render them homeless. True
trash was living on tuna fish and ramen noodles and macaroni 'n'
cheese and dying young because they couldn't afford all those doctors.
True trash was wrangling with the cramped, toxic rage of knowing it
will never get any better. True trash had no time to be witty or creative
or graceful. True trash was working two jobs and still falling behind.

True trash is also something that has outlived its usefulness to the
trashmakers. As the global village becomes something more real than
a vague McLuhanism, white American workers are just another cheap
labor pool. Actually, not that cheap at all compared to the wages that
Malaysians and Dominicans will accept. White trash are industrial
waste rendered in human terms. Racial Edsels. Genetic effluvia, crumpled milk cartons on the slagheap of progress.

But beyond some Bilderbergian economic conspiracy, there's a simpler reason that white collars hate white trash—rednecks were the
ones who beat them up in high school. That's usually the only time
white-collar white liberals were forced to mingle with white trash.
High school was probably the most egalitarian social experiment they
were ever required to make, and they haven't stopped running from it
yet. Because that's an oft-overlooked form of white flight—away from
one's roots. The redneck reminds them of what they used to be . . . and
were lucky enough to escape. It's a deep-rooted ancestral antipathy. In
white trash, rich whites see the crude Norse demons they like to think
they've "civilized" out of themselves.

So they've made white trash the pinnacle of uncoolness. But such
things have a way of changing. I fear a looming wave of Mock Trash,

already hinted at in campy white-trash fashion spreads in vapid national glossies. Starting somewhere around the time of Norman Mailer's "The White Negro," bored white art students infused their empty lives with the "authenticity" of the black experience. Could claiming identity as Okie-whites be the next rage? If there's anything more ironic than white teenagers pretending to be black, it's white teenagers pretending to be white. The fake blacks are sometimes called "wiggers"—should we call the fake whites "nudnecks"? Don't be shocked if you see a bumper crop of phony Tex 'n' Edna types refurbishing old Winnebagos and wearing Elvis outfits, emulating white trash in a perverse form of minstrelsy. They'll empty a whole can of postmodern Cheez Whiz atop their white-trash homage, making sure you don't think for a second that they're actually embracing these people or their lifestyle. As usual, they'll gobble up the stylistic trappings and discard the experience as if it were a banana peel.

As white poverty balloons, the redneck jokes keep coming. But real trash doesn't get upset. It gets violent . . . right? Out in the trailer parks, they seem to be preparing for some kind of Second American Revolution. Under the current wet Prozac blanket of multicultural media appeasement, working-class whites are denied any identity besides a guilt rap. Their resentment isn't to be trusted. So don't act surprised when they form an identity merely on being hated and scapegoated. As opportunities for unskilled labor vanish, white trash is likely to get nasty. And politicized in ways that will make you squirm. These "paranoid, right-wing lunatics" are right about this—the rest of the world IS out to get them. No wonder they scamper through forests in camouflage, lashing out at the hidden enemy. No wonder their class resentment is manifest in the big shit-blowup of fertilizer bombs. There are no dreams left for white trash. But all this inbreeding and bad nutrition and cheap beer and biker-gang crank have given us an evolutionary advantage. All these soul-smashing jobs and all the rich-white condescension have backed us into a corner. And, like the slum rats you've always said we are, we just may strike back. It takes a lot to rouse our anger, but don't push it. America's next large-scale ethnic skirmish may be intraracial—white trash vs. white cash.

Personally, I can't squeeze any time in my busy schedule for political extremism. Nor for political moderation. But I do feel more comfortable living around white trash. It's not quite what I'd call brotherhood, but definitely a sense of shared experience. I tried living the big-city multicultural thingie for twelve years, only to realize that most of multiculturalism's proponents—rich white people—didn't want me. So I moved to a neighborhood that is redneck, blue-collar, white trash. Low rent. Low class. Lowlife. Truckers, welders, meth dealers, pit bulls, rotted picket fences. An old, faded-pea-soup-colored suspension bridge spans the Willamette River, over to Forest Park's sinsemilla-green hills. Almost identical to Vermont, but on an entirely different coast. Of all the neighborhoods in Portland, this one—St. Johns—is most notorious for its high white-trash quotient. Yet more blacks and Mexicans live here than in most parts of the city. For economic reasons, the trash—be it black, brown, or white—have always lived side by side in America. It's the Gold Card whites who've always paid to segregate themselves, leaving the rednecks, niggers, and spics to fight over day-old cookies.

You might call me a cynical peddler of grease-monkey chic, a class separatist with an aesthetic predilection for trashy manifestations of white workers' anxiety. But that's REALLY hard to fit on a button. So it's fine if you call me a redneck. I won't cry. I make no apologies for living in a festering cauldron of the displaced and deformed. I find their most repugnant qualities to be wildly attractive. As I see it, their scabs and bruises and missing teeth are unconscious class-rooted fashion statements. On my block, arteriosclerotic women walk around shaped like early models of the A-bomb, their pale, flabby legs jiggling under the rare summer sun. Teen mothers with black eyes and track marks on their arms push baby carts and stop to chat with meth dealers who ALSO have black eyes. Retarded kids are everywhere. I sit on the splintery front porch of my cheesy Oregonian love shack and watch these people struggle to escape their ugliness, only to be recaptured by it again and again. This is far, far away from the hipsters. This feels like home.

Once you go trash, you never come back. The current climate offers me nothing but self-denial, so I'm comfortable living in the past. It's like coming out of the closet—I've come out of the trailer. I embrace

35

the shame. I wallow piglike and palefaced in a landfill of my peers. I'm proud to be an endangered species, a latter-day saint of the Caveman Diaspora. Now I'm cheering for the Two Thousand Maniacs to lynch a few Yankees. And I listen to Porter Wagoner almost daily. Am I hurt when I'm called white trash? No, somehow I'm emboldened. I'm a phoenix rising from the garbage. Forever plebeian. If it ain't trash, it ain't shit.

2

Feudal Existence

The Roots of Eurogarbage

Here's where I step into my history-teacher shoes. I'd really rather hock loogies at telephone poles than try to revise history, but the tunnel-visionary myopia of popular notions about American whiteness forced me off my ass and onto the soapbox.

Written history, like the missionary position, is an act executed from the top looking down. Most historical texts bear the distinct accent of people who talk with silver spoons in their mouths. So here I am, with seven cavities dotting my choppers, saddled with the dubious task of rewriting American history. I've been thrust into the role of cultural archeologist—a trash digger. I come with a chip on my shoulder and a sledgehammer in my hand, ready to bust some ideological kneecaps. I'm here to fist-fuck you with the facts.

History itself is an endlessly unfolding S&M novel. History is much more sick, bloody, and unjust than historians will ever let on. When they finally get around to writing some *real* history, we'll all need medication. It'll be too depressing.

The history books were written by dead white men, to be sure, but by RICH dead white men. And it STILL looks bad for the rich guys. Throughout history, the rich have been only a tiny statistical percentage of all whites. During the Dark and Middle Ages, untold millions of Euro-peasant bones turned to white dust beneath the soil, deprived of the only promise ever made to them, an afterlife. What sort of history would they have told if they'd been given the chance to speak?

We've had the Negro Question. The Jewish Question. The Irish Question. Finally, the Redneck Question. Whence the redneck? How did these mule-toothed, lobster-faced, thick-browed, daughter-fuckin', pappy-suckin', sheep-schtuppin', chaw-chewin' cretins get here? While we are encouraged to chuckle at their simpleminded degradation, we are never compelled to ponder their ancestry. White trash HAD to have come from somewhere; I mean, they didn't just pop outta Jed Clampett's ass last week, right?

Po' white trash, along with the planter-elite entrepreneurs who brought them here, is the immigrant group with roots deepest in this country. They were working the plantations in big numbers before the first major shipments of African slaves. And yet, po' white trash is likely to be the social group in America least aware of their ancestry.

I'll accept the premise that white trash currently exists in America. But that dredges up two more questions—how did they get here, and how did they get trashy? And which happened first—getting here or getting trashy? So with apologies to Alex Haley, these next two chapters will serve as an ersatz *ROOTS* for rednecks. Just as all the food you eat goes through a tortuous decomposition process before it emerges out the other end as a long string of mushy turds, I'll demonstrate how the "system" turned human beings into trash. It won't be pleasant, but the sanitation business never is.

Being white trash in America is mostly perceived to be a personal attitude rather than a socioeconomic situation. It is thought to be a choice rather than a predicament. Here a chicken, there an egg. Are hillbillies barefoot by choice, or because they couldn't afford shoes? Are they toothless because of bad fashion sense, or because the nearest dentist is a hundred miles away and too expensive? The gooey sputum rainstorm of anti-redneck imagery is aimed at things beyond mere character deficiencies, unless you count toothlessness as a moral weakness. Most anti-redneck imagery, consciously or not, points to a SITUATION behind the ATTITUDE. It makes fun of someone not for anything they've done, but merely for where they come from.

To some, claiming that our popular imagery is hostile to rednecks might seem as preposterous as saying that the danged Nazis ain't getting a fair shake, either. There exists, I daresay, a myth of redneck power in this country. As my bloodshot, squinty, suspicious eyes see it, one of the primary problems is semantic: People confuse "good ol' boys" with the "old boys' network." I've often heard the terms used interchangeably, or one term used where the other would have been appropriate. This blunder occurs with such frequency that the phrases are thought to be synonymous.

This is a mistake of megaton-sized proportions. In confusing the good ol' boys with the old boys' network, the redneck beer belly gets mistaken for the capitalist fat cat. As defined for my purposes, the good ol' boys and the old boys' network are at loggerheads. The good ol' boys are rock quarrymen; the old boys' network are Rockefellers. The old boys' network represents the entrenched elites whose white talons have been wrapped around a disproportionate percentage of wealth and power for thousands of years. The good ol' boys are the guys in aluminum trailers and rusted-out trucks who keep wondering when they'll finally get a chance to join the old boys' network.

The 'neck-haters habitually argue that rednecks are merely disgruntled reactionaries fearful about losing their power at the hands of noble, triumphant, liberally uplifted Third World peasants. I arise from the murk like the Loch Ness Monster and snap back angrily that rednecks never—neither here nor in Europe—had anything that may properly be called a grip on power. Well, if you mean "power" in the sense of being able to beat up interlopers in their neighborhood, then yes; if you mean "power" in terms of the ability to send soldiers overseas, no. Power to commit petty burglary, yes; power to tax, no. Power to shoot someone with a flintlock pistol, yes; power to drop nukes, no. Power to distill whiskey, yes; power to declare it illegal, no.

But to some minds, the trailer park and Capitol Hill are indistinguishable. Media depictions of Bulging White Evil rarely discriminate between the dirt-poor cracker and the wealthy slaveowner. The lack of distinction has led to the impression that he's one and the same dude. This still-pervasive pop-cult fable of a classless white America is founded on the rickety assumption that all American whites are blue-blooded greyhounds who burst out of the starting gate with equal wealth and opportunities, and that poor white trash must have squandered their fortune on bathtub crank and slot machines. In dealing with rednecks, blame-the-victim is the normative mode. The human breed *Redneckus Americanus,* for all his alleged nigger-hatin' ways, has become our National Nigger.

I kid the niggers, of course—I'm pummeling you, dear scrumptious reader, with the word "nigger" merely to make a point about relative sensitivities to foolish li'l vowel-consonant clusters. People allow the liberal use of "redneck" while making the utterance of "nigger" assume blasphemous proportions.

Why the double standard? It's simple: PERCEIVED HISTORY OF OPPRESSION.

People tend to excuse trash-bashing with, "Oh, well, their historical experience has been entirely different from that of African-Americans." Like the spiny blowfish that they are, they'll puff up their cheeks and spew out melodious lukewarm airstreams about how rednecks haven't had remotely the same history of poverty, suffering, and exploitation as American blacks. From their exhaustive research of TV movies and free alternative weekly newspapers, they've concluded that it's IMPOSSIBLE for a white American male to be oppressed, however the fuck they define oppression. For they *know* the white-boy hegira has been one huge, monolithic, coconut popsicle of skin privilege, and that any white guys who didn't make it in this country must have been stupid. When they talk about "equality," it's phrased strictly in racial and gender terms, as if white males ever had true equality among themselves, as if the white-male experience in America has been one uninterrupted vanilla holiday.

And most importantly, they'll remind you that all rednecks came here VOLUNTARILY and that Europeans have NEVER suffered the degradation of slavery, neither here nor in Europe. Forgive them, Lord, for they have no idea what the fuck they're talking about.

Cognitive dissonance is a mutha. People won't want to admit they've been wrong about all this. Realizing you're wrong is like enjoying a buttery bowlful of noodles only to discover a long, greasy, curly hair at the bottom. Denial is a river that usually flows in but one direction—denial of that which is too horrible to admit. People rarely deny the unspeakably beautiful. What can I tell you? Some people want justice; others want blow jobs. Most just seem to want to go to sleep and forget about it all.

Open your peepers. It only hurts the first time. Pull the camera back . . . just a bit . . . and the picture takes on a different shape. My intent is not to downplay the guilt you already know about, merely to infer that there's a lot more guilt than you may have suspected.

I will meekly attempt to prove that by the current rules, "redneck" is a bigoted term. By the current rules, the media's uninterrupted campaign of redneck-roasting constitutes hate speech. By the current rules, rednecks are a victim class rather than an oppressor class. And then I'll explain why the current rules are full of shit.

The redneck as commonly understood is an American entity, but the paradigm, the archetype, the blueprint, the model, the freakin' socially evolutionary antecedent to the American redneck was the European peasant in all his costume changes throughout the Dark and Middle Ages. The groundwork for a small group of white elites to disparage and abuse a large mass of the white rural dispossessed was laid at least a thousand years ago and possibly earlier.

So when they say "the white man," I say, "WHICH white man?" Let's pop open a can of air freshener and demystify this privileged-white-male thing, shall we? The question is begged—have any white people suffered at any time during the planet's history?

My answer is a quick, flat, self-righteous YES. In fact, MOST white people in America could probably lay some claim to ancestral oppression, if that's your idea of a good time. Most white people—certainly a higher percentage than are descended from slaveowners—have ancestors who were slaves at one point or another in history.

Once upon a time, all the members of the old boys' network were slaveowners. And all the good ol' boys were slaves.

Long ago on Europe's windswept, blood-splattered plains, there was no such thing as government, nor really something such as "class" as it's currently understood. People roamed alone or in packs. Those who roamed alone typically fell prey to those who roamed in packs. And the bigger packs ate up the little packs. It's doubtful that this was a utopian existence. Life was brief, gory, disease-ridden, and unrewarding. Then again, you could set your own hours. And when men killed each other, they almost always had to look each other in the eyes.

By necessity, these loosely organized clans either became stronger or were ripped to pieces by blood-slurping, skull-impaling invaders. Tribally based hunting/gathering societies were absorbed—almost always via force—into a web of centralized agricultural slave-states. Men who hunted animals had their freedom stolen by men who hunted men.

Under the Roman Empire, barbarians were the rural trash of their day. The word "pagan" is derived from the Latin *pagus,* meaning "country," and Romans used it disparagingly to describe country dwellers. Likewise, "heathen" originally meant those rural types who lived under cover of the heath. Both "pagan" and "heathen" are thus ancient verbal ancestors of "hillbilly."

Roman writer Ammianus Marcellinus described the Huns as "a race savage beyond all parallel. . . . They are certainly in the shape of men, however uncouth. . . . [They] utter all kinds of terrific yells. . . . Like brute beasts, they are utterly ignorant of the distinction between right and wrong." [1] Sounds like hillbillies to me.

After touring Britain, Julius Caesar wrote about clans of "inland nonagricultural people" whom he dubbed *interiores.* These bizarre, non-Romanized tribes were said to have painted their skin blue with a plant-based dye and were called "Picts" by Roman observers (from *pictus,* meaning "painted"). The Picts are thought by some to be the progenitors of Celtic mountain folk in Wales, Scotland, and Western Ireland. Gothic tribes apparently had several nicknames for the Picts, all of which translated into "petty" or "nothing." The Picts were contemptuously referred to as "Blue Legs" by other chroniclers. Britain's ruling tribes, who lived above ground in wooden houses, called the cave-bound Picts "mansion-dwellers," which may be the first ancient synonym of "trailer trash." Others noted that among the Picts, "each woman was with her brother," possibly the first historical antecedent to modern inbreeding jokes.[2] The Romans probably laughed at the Picts in the same way that New Yorkers laugh at hillbillies.

But Rome, for all its power, was never entirely safe. Its ever-

changing borders were always rimmed with ultraviolent posses of re-
morseless killers. The decapitating hordes just beyond the emperor's
clutches had always been a problem. The Romans eventually turned
from a war of attrition to attempted assimilation. Then came monetary
bribes in a pathetic effort to scratch the barbarian itch. Then came
the Visigoths, Vandals, and Ostrogoths, smashing Rome to tiny little
pieces.

Mamma Europa was where landfills of white trash first started piling
up. And after Rome fell, one could hardly find a better garbage can.
Modern Western European history is commonly thought to have arisen
from Rome's ashes. But—oof!—what a painful birth. Rome's collapse
hastened a New World Disorder. They didn't call 'em the Dark Ages
for nothing. Europe was killing itself again and again and again. Invasion. Massacre. Plague. Famine. Cannibalism. Infanticide. Chopping,
hacking, torching, looting, stomping, crushing, raping, eviscerating.
Lawn jockeys in the form of heads on sticks. War, war, war, war, war,
war, war . . .

And then, only smoke and quiet. Europe was a vast charred mud-
bowl, moonlike and dead. Giant black holes had been poked through
the continent, swallowing everything downward. A contemporary car-
tographer called these depopulated areas "solitudes." [3] Where life
hadn't been completely smothered out, there were black walls of mis-
ery. "The world seems near its end," [4] cried Pope Gregory I.

Some were lucky enough to spare their skulls from the truncheon by
beating a path into the hills and woods. Since this marked the first
large-scale exodus of white peasants from a wretched society, it might
be fair to label these refugees Europe's first self-conscious hillbillies.

Down on the plains, the upheavals had thrown Europe's peasant
populations into the air like a million ants off a picnic blanket. When
they landed back down, all the old Roman plantation owners had their
throats slit, and power was seized by those with the biggest arms and
heaviest clubs.

Like the Greeks and Romans before them, the barbarians kicked ass
and took slaves. Barbarian slave codes allowed for the removal of
almost anything you could chop off a human body, including genitalia.
If a slave wasn't tilling the field to the satisfaction of his Ostrogothic

master, he risked the removal of both arms. Duke Rauching, a Frankish nobleman, was said to have gotten his rocks off by watching his slaves extinguish burning torches between their legs. Thieving male slaves in Britain during the Dark Ages were stoned to death, while female slaves accused of theft were burned alive. In 1410, a Venetian slave code allowed for bodily torture of female slaves suspected of practicing sorcery against their masters. Italian slaves found guilty of poisoning or plotting against their owners had their eyes poked out, their lips and noses amputated, and their flesh ripped apart with red-hot pincers. Such atrocities often took place in city streets or public squares as a warning for other slaves and rebellion-minded peasants.

Throughout antiquity, European slaves were bought, sold, and traded for livestock. Irish female slaves during the Dark Ages were reckoned to be worth three milk cows. Under the Frankish kings, anyone found guilty of murdering or stealing someone else's slave was obliged to repay the owner a horse or its monetary equivalent. In Anglo-Saxon Britain, a murdered slave's owner was entitled to a compensation of eight oxen.

And let's not forget the Slavs. In ancient times, the Slavs were so commonly identified as being a slave population, the very word "slave" arose as a bastardization of "Slav." Check the dictionary if you don't believe me. Mostly captured by neighboring German tribes as part of the krauts' timeworn rape-and-pillage routine, Slavic slaves became just another commodity—like furs, wax, spices, and honey— on international markets. For centuries, Venetian slave traders kept pumping captured Slavs into the harems and plantations of Syria and Egypt.[5] Think of it—lily-white Slavic types imported as slaves and eunuchs to both the Middle East and the Dark Continent of Africa. And lest you think I'm talking about something that happened thousands of years ago, the Italian white-slave trade with Egypt continued until at least the 1400s, only two centuries before Africans were forced onto boats headed for the New World.

The urge to enslave is truly color-blind. Africans were imperialistic; they just weren't very good at it. The one-way-street view of white imperialism tends to forget that the African empire of Carthage temporarily held a portion of Europe and sent conquered white warriors into

Northern African slavery. We also gloss over the fact that African Moors invaded the south of Spain in the eighth century and ruled there for roughly five hundred years, sending untold numbers of white Christian slaves into Egyptian and Mediterranean bondage. You may have heard of the disastrous, ill-advised Children's Crusade of 1212, in which European youth by the thousands streamed southward to recover the Holy Sepulcher; the rarely quoted punch line to the story was that many of the hapless kiddies were seized by Moslem slave drivers and sent to Egypt.

Things weren't much better at home. Almost everyone was a serf. The serf was bound to the turf. So let's talk about serf . . . and turf. The peasant was a piss-ant. A peon was somebody to pee on. Life for the peasant was unpleasant. The serf was poor and uncouth, having no manners and no manors. The serf was white. He was also trash. And I'm sure that after hoeing the field all summer, his neck was red. He was toothless, dirty, and smelly, too. And he was fundamentally voiceless. And universally thought to have DESERVED his status.

Feudalism, like all forms of government, arose as a protection racket. And just like all forms of government, you found yourself needing protection from the protectors. The lord-to-serf equation was the traditional master-to-servant, pitcher-to-catcher, male-plug-going-into-female-receptacle relationship. The difference between barbarian invaders and feudal lords was that the lords killed you slowly, and they did it for your own good. The lords were long-haired mosquitoes in flowing robes, sucking the land and the peasants dry. As one observer put it, "The lords seek to fleece and devour their subjects."[6] To the lords, the serf was little more than human manure used to fertilize his agricultural holdings. It was good to be the lord.

The word "serf" is a French term derived from the Latin *servus,* meaning "slave." The Romans had referred to their nonurban peasantry as *servi rustici,* or "rural slaves." Medieval texts frequently used the terms "peasant," "serf," and "slave" interchangeably. Serfdom was comparable to slavery in all the important senses: Serfs worked on giant agricultural plantations for the lord's sole benefit. From birth until death one remained a serf, or as a German saying phrased it, "the air alone makes serfs."[7] A serf's children were automatically born into serfdom. Serfs were not permitted to leave the plantation, and if they did, the lord could legally recapture them. He was also allowed to beat, whip, rape, and murder his serfs with impunity. Serfs were forbidden to buy, sell, or own property, although they could be bought and sold themselves. Serfs weren't allowed to own weapons; several contemporary texts referred to them as "the unarmed people." Serfs were segregated from the lordly class by a strict code of apartheid —they weren't allowed to marry anyone from the gentry or anyone outside the manor. As property, serf families were frequently split apart in legal transactions. The legal codes did not recognize serfs as human beings.

The big men were few, while the little people were plenty. Out of roughly a million and a half British inhabitants recorded in the Domesday Book of 1086, fewer than three percent are listed as free landholders.[8] The class pattern was the same throughout Europe—according to one historian, "Millions of men had thus found themselves subjected to the domination of a few thousand."[9] So in medieval times, only a fingernail-moon sliver of the white population could be said to have been privileged. The rest were slaves.

In England, members of the servile class were called "villeins" instead of serfs. The word had the same Latin root as "villagers." The modern English word "villain"—the BAD guy—is a direct descendant of a term used to describe unfree, exploited, oppressed, plantation-tilling white trash.

Medieval literature drew lines between "courtly" and "villein"[10]; between "princes" and "the vulgar"[11]; between "free" and "poor"[12]; even between "heroes" and "farmers."[13] The French had a slang term for their peasantry—*bouseaux*—from which is derived the word "bozo." Literally translated, *bouseaux* meant "cow turds."[14] French comic fables alleged that the serf was "a stinking creature, born from an ass's dung,"[15] and that he savored the shit heap's aroma. Another comic writer referred to peasants as "ugly brutes."[16] William of Breton identified four classes of humans: priests, knights, city-dwellers, and rustics, noting that only the rustic was "stupefied."[17] A stock literary character, the serf was uniformly portrayed as cretinous, shuffling, animalistic, and lazy. "The highlander," complained one writer, "never sits at ease at a loom; it is like putting a deer in a plough." [18]

To this day, most societies have derogatory terms for their peasantry. Israelis are said to poke fun at Yemenite shepherds. Russians, who used to call their peasants *moujik*s ("men of naught"), refer to their contemporary hicks as *zhlob*s. This same social type is called the *ah beng* by Singaporeans and the "yobbo" by Australians. In Bosnia, as constant artillery shelling forced mountain folk and their livestock down into Sarajevo's streets, city-dwellers recently complained about the onslaught of lowly, goatlike *papak*s.

The Great White Unwashed are usually portrayed as freely sensual —much more comfortable with bodily functions than the nobility— and stupidly, joyously, childishly satisfied with their lot. The peasantry is rarely, if ever, depicted as miserable. Medieval paintings of docile serfs at play are remarkably similar to the stereotyped toothy, banjo-playing, happy Sambo caricatures of black slaves in the American South.

But portraying the rustics as clownish boobs and clodhoppers has never entirely assuaged elitist fears that the yokels might one day beat their plowshares into swords and seek vengeance against their social betters. According to one feudal historian, "Advice to beware of the serf is commonplace in literature designed for the upper classes." [19] Cartoons drawn by elite hands have always presented the lower-class Everyman as a simpleton, yes, but a *dangerous* simpleton. England's King Henry I was said to have received three "nocturnal visions" in which bloodthirsty peasants assaulted him with "rustic implements." [20]

In medieval British literature, the peasantry was often symbolized by the fictional persona of Piers Plowman, an honest sort of Mr. Green Jeans who was tickled pink to be yoking oxen from sunrise until sunset. In French-speaking countries, a nearly identical mythical character was known as Jacques Bonhomme. In the Frogs' native tongue, *bon homme* means "good man," a precursor of "good ol' boy." French nobles disdainfully referred to their peasants as "Jacques" in the same way one might be called a "Bubba" today.

In 1323 and 1328, in the Flemish towns of Ypres and Bruges, respectively, Jacques Bonhomme shook off his mythic slumber and incarnated himself in peasants' uprisings known as the jacqueries. They featured the Angry White Males of their day. Led by two workers, one of whom was actually named Jacques, the jacquerie declared war on the wealthy and the clergy, only to be crushed by a coalition of bourgeois merchants and landed nobility. In northern France thirty years later, another jacquerie arose, said to be a hundred thousand French Bubbas strong, and they were beaten down mercilessly again. Twenty thousand French rebels were executed, and the surviving ones were punished with astronomical taxes. Another contemporary group calling themselves the White Capes demanded freedom from taxation. An upper-echelon scribe called the idea "a lunatic presumption," [21] foreshadowing current attempts to link tax protest with mental illness. The White Capes, predictably, were obliterated. Similar underclass uprisings occurred in Italy and Spain, with similar results.

The English Peasants' Revolt of 1381, essentially a rebellion against oppressive poll taxes and wage restrictions, was described by royal apologists as "thirty thousand devils" [22] who represented "the poor favoring the rustics." [23] Led by a soldier named Wat Tyler, the Peasants' Revolt preached the destruction of class hierarchy through the annihilation of the upper class itself. Via a brief lightning bolt of violent action, the rebellion seized control of London for roughly a day. Appearing before royalty amid a throng of street rebels, Wat Tyler made a conscious display of guzzling a throatful of beer in a manner deemed disrespectful to the Crown, and he was stabbed to death by one of the king's agents. Wat Tyler was a martyred forefather of the belching, beer-bellied, government-hating redneck. In the chaos that ensued after Tyler's murder, the rebellion was snuffed. Leaders of the revolt were executed. The main difference between peasant violence and kingly violence was that royal officials heard confessions before beheading their victims.

All this social violence occurred against a backdrop where a tiny germ had beheaded most of Europe. The bubonic plague, a bacterium borne by fleas on rats, sucked the life from twenty-five million Europeans. Human bodies writhed and rotted atop heaps of smoldering waste, their half-alive flesh picked at by wolves and crows. Combined with decimating famines and near-constant wars, Europe sank to a state not unlike the barbarian miasma of a thousand years prior. Bruised and bleeding peasants vainly searched for food amid dirt and dry weeds.

When Europe staggered back toward stability, an ominous process with the benign-sounding name of "enclosure" began uprooting peasants from the land. The same nobles who had once demanded that peasants remain *chained* to the manor were now evicting them. Wealthy landowners, realizing their holdings would be much more profitable as privately run superfarms, began fencing off—enclosing —these areas and booting out tenants en masse. Amid the agricultural expanses the British referred to as the "commons," the commoners were no longer wanted.

And if the peasants were going to be thrown off the land, it only made sense that they be blamed for it. "The poor in Northamptonshire," wheezed one royal lickspittle, "dwell in woods and deserts and live like drones, devoted to thievery, among whom are bred the very spawn of vagabonds and rogues." Rural areas were described by King James I as "nurseries and receptacles of thieves, rogues and beggars." England's countrified poor were seen as a detriment to the nation's exploding economy. "The poor increase like fleas and lice," wrote John Moore in 1653, "and these vermin will eat us up unless we enclose." [24]

Enclosure's net effect was to turn rural peasants into urban beggars. London's population, a trifling sixty thousand or so in the early 1500s, had exploded nearly a thousand percent by 1700. The urban economy was unable to absorb the massive human injection. London became a Caucasian Calcutta, stinking with open sewers and a wretched, filthy, volatile, sore-covered, crime-prone proletariat.

The Crown responded by making poverty a crime in itself. Foreshadowing the whipping of black slaves in America, British law allowed for beggars to be whipped until blood trickled down their bare white skin, tortured for the "crime" of asking for food. Debtors' prisons arose, where one could be tossed into dark, moldy dampness for LIFE merely for being unable to make ends meet. Other malnourished Londoners were imprisoned in dehumanizingly regimented workhouses, which the Crown claimed was an act of beneficence.

Royalist writers, perhaps cognizant of peasants' revolts from centuries prior, came to label their rootless urban mass as "the mob." London's urban trash were also called "the profane vulgar," "the mean multitude," "the rout and scum of people," the "schismatic rabble," "the meaner, ignorant sort of people," "the base and obscure fellows of the world," "the rascals and very sink and dunghill knaves of all towns and cities," and "men with no shirts." [25]

But as destitute as London's underclass was, they could take a sort of bitter consolation in one fact: They had it much, much better than the Irish. If you look at a map of Britain next to Ireland, you'll see a big puppy dog eating up a little one. In 1610, King James—the same cocksucker who colonized America—began sending shiploads of Scots to Northern Ireland. Although he claimed he was doing it "out of his unspeakable love and tender affection" for Scottish folk, it was actually an ingenious plan to subdue Ireland by social colonization rather than by military conquest.

When in doubt, blame the British. What the Crown did to the Irish is directly analogous to what it did to the American Indians. The Irish were thrown off their ancestral homelands. Their traditional Gaelic language and modes of dress were outlawed. Catholicism, which had been the national religion, was likewise forbidden. In the mid-1600s, priests who gave the last rites to a believer were themselves sentenced to death. The Irish were purposely starved, massacred, and enslaved, and their land was given to English and Scottish colonists. Catholics, who owned sixty percent of Ireland in 1641, owned only five percent a hundred years later.

The British had always considered the Irish to be a separate race. British literature customarily mentioned "the wild Irish" [26] and the "mere Irish." [27] They were consistently compared to ancient barbarians. A writer named Fynes Moryson accused them of rampant inbreeding and likened sleeping in an Irishman's house to venturing into a wild beast's cave. [28]

The British-controlled area of Ireland came to be known as the Pale, and those wild shamrock Irishmen who stampeded in alleged barbarity outside of it were said to live "beyond the Pale." The conquering British referred to these Celtic rebels as "woodkernes." The word "kerne" was synonymous with "lightly armed peasant." So "wood-kerne," meaning an armed peasant who lives in the woods, is a predecessor to "hillbilly." The woodkernes were said to be savage butchers given to ceaseless feuding and moonshining. Royal police chased them up into the hills with bloodhounds. Upon capture, woodkernes were casually shot in the head without trial.

As brutally as the Crown had treated the Irish, it was nothing compared to what a Puritan führer named Oliver Cromwell would do. After seizing power from the monarchy, Parliamentary Puritans bragged that they'd kill every Catholic in Ireland. When Oliver Cromwell and his New Model Army crossed into Ireland in 1650, there were roughly a million and a half inhabitants of Erin. When he left nine months later, more than FORTY PERCENT of Ireland's residents had been massacred, starved to death, or deported. "What Cromwell did," remarked one writer, "deserves to be ranked with the horrors perpetrated by Genghis Khan." [29] Over the next half-century, nearly a half-million Irishmen were enslaved, sent eastward onto continental Europe, and killed in the service of the French army.[30]

The British upper crust, who for generations had wondered how to dispose of their "surplus" population, also turned their gaze westward. They found a verdant new toilet in which to dump their social feces. It was called America.

51

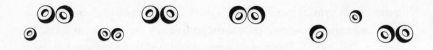

3

A Quick History of the White
American Underclass

(And an Even Quicker History of the Goads)

WHITE PEOPLE IN AMERICA. Yumpin' yiminy, whatta loaded concept. It has acquired the same sinister ring as "HIV in your bloodstream" or "radioactive waste in our water supply." There's a primitive, biblical, sins-o'-the-father notion that ALL American whites, by virtue of their birth alone, bear a stain on their souls for black slavery.

White guilt. Can't turn on the TV or radio without being bum-rushed with it. White guilt. After tubes and tubes of toothpaste, I still can't brush it off my teeth. White guilt. I tried to have an operation to remove the guilty tumor, but no doctor could help me.

I've finally figured out why I can't get rid of my white guilt. It's because I have none. Yet the guilt-merchants keep tapping at my door like court-ordered psychiatrists, insisting that I swallow the guilt pill. They chide me with increasingly patronizing tones that I must be too thick-skulled to grasp the doctrine of collective guilt.

Bend over and grasp THIS. I understand collective guilt better than you do. I'm willing to accept blame for whatever I've done, but I need PROOF, especially if I'll be forced to pay reparations. I won't accept it on hearsay. From my research, I can't find any ancestors who owned slaves, but more than a few of them seem to have been slaves themselves. So you can take your white-guilt la-dee-da, fold it into a paper airplane, and respectfully tuck it up your rectal canal.

It's ironic that American schoolbooks preach that all white people came here looking for freedom, when so many of them came in chains. Yet the "freedom angle" is the panoramic totality of received history as pumped into your cranium by school textbooks and multimillion-dollar TV period pieces. As riddled with Swiss-cheese holes as it is, our generalized impression of the white American diaspora runs something like this: There were no white slaves. All whites CHOSE to come to America. Only blacks were kidnapped, shackled, and sent here. Only blacks suffered through a harrowing "middle passage" across the Atlantic. Only blacks were beaten, whipped, sold on auction blocks, and forcibly separated from their families. Only black women were raped by slavemasters. Only blacks were brutalized by their masters to the point where they ran away.

Would you call me a naughty sprite if I proved that every one of those perceptions was wrong? Would you label me as Satan hi'self if I were to prove them erroneous not only in isolated, freaky-fluky instances, but as they apply to most whites who came to the colonies? Would you strike my name from the list of invited guests to your next wine-and-cheese gathering?

'Tis OK. I'm used to it. I'm a professional jerkoff. My surname is also a verb. To "goad," if you haven't caught on by now, means to incite, to prod, to annoy. Jim Goad—Jim the Annoyer.

Little Jim Goad went to a grade school, a high school, and a college where I was taught an incomplete version of history, probably something similar to what you were taught. You've likely heard of "indentured servitude"—maybe for about fifteen seconds. If history teachers mention it at all, the context is almost exclusively a comparison of how bad it WASN'T compared to black slavery. You might have the perception of indentured servitude as a benign, voluntary contractual arrangement like apprenticeship. After I left history class, I carried away the idea that a cabal of muckety-muck benefactors allowed white people to learn a trade in the New World and were so effusively benevolent that they even paid for their passage across the Atlantic. I pictured Ben Franklin teaching Oliver Twist how to run a printing press, or maybe Tom Jefferson instructing the Artful Dodger in Latin. It sounded like such a good deal, I wondered how I could sign up.

But alas, as Young Jim Goad reached adulthood, there was too much white trash around and too few explanations of their historical genesis to satisfy my tortured mind. So I asked myself: What were the historical circumstances that gave birth to me, a pasty glob of ivory-colored rubbish? I started probing my ancestry hoping not to find nobility, but peasantry. And it looks as if I've struck a gold mine of garbage.

About a year ago, I received a bulk-mailed sales pitch from an Ohio company for a limited-edition volume entitled *The World Book of Goads*. For $39.95 plus S&H, the book promised to trace my family surname's history. I ponied up the wampum and waited by my mailbox. The first two-thirds of *The World Book of Goads* has nothing to do with Goads; instead, it's a cheap historical rehash resembling my old grade-school textbooks. Pastel-drawn, *Reader's Digest*–style artwork portrays historical personages as better-groomed and happier than we all know they were. But almost in spite of itself, this section provides some valuable half-assed disinformation:

> Many early immigrants to America at this time were driven from
> Great Britain and Europe by religious motives. . . . The African-
> American is the only class which immigrated against its will.

No doubt you've heard it before. But it isn't true. A staggering percentage of early European "immigrants" to America were FORCED out of Europe for reasons that had nothing to do with religion. *The World Book of Goads* also states that Britain sent more than 120,000 convicts to Australia, a painful penal policy of which most Americans seem aware. But there's nary a chirp about the fact that Britain sent more than 50,000 convicts to America and only *started* sending them to Australia after we rebelled against the Crown.

Apart from such cockeyed history, *The World Book of Goads* contains a list of presumably every Goad family in America, along with mailing addresses. According to my assiduous calculations, sixty-one percent of American Goads live in the South and what I call the "Redneck Southwest," Texas and Oklahoma. Virginia and Tennessee are the two biggest Goad states, respectively. Another twenty-one percent o' Goads live in the Midwest. Fewer than one in five American Goad families live outside of these areas. So by satisfying the geographical prong alone, most of us Goads are rednecks.

The book devotes a scant three pages to "Early Goad Immigrants to America," but this alone may have been worth the purchase price. In 1635, the first year that my paternal ancestors are recorded as having reared their Goadly heads in the New World, five Goads surfaced in the American colonies or West Indies. Thomas Goad, fifteen, arrived in Boston. Another Thomas Goad, also fifteen, landed in New York. William Goad, eighteen, planted his Goad toenails on Virginia soil. In the same year, two other Goads arrived in Barbados: John, twenty-two, and William, twenty-one. Samuel Goad was sent to Barbados in 1654, followed by another Sam to "Barbados or Nevis" in 1661. A third William Goad (I remember the stinging schoolyard taunts of "billy goat," and my name isn't even William) alighted upon Maryland ground in 1674. And according to a cited source called *English Convicts in Colonial America,* a jailbird-in-exile named Thomas Goad was shipped here in 1766.

I toss and turn at night, sweatily tugging on my ultrafluffy Elvis blanket: Why only male Goads? Why did all of those male Goads come here alone, without their families? Why were these Goads so young? Why was a convict Goad sent here? And why did so many of dem Goads, dem Goads, dem dry Goads go to Barbados?

Frankly, I don't have solid answers. I don't even have solid bowel movements, OK? I can only speculate and expectorate. Most Goad families currently in the British Isles, according to *The World Book of Goads,* reside in the south of England. And most indentured servants in America had been plucked out of a shiftless, unemployed, potentially volatile group of lime-suckers from England's southern end.[1]

Although you wouldn't know it from gawking at your TV, nearly all current historians concur that the MAJORITY of whites who came to America in colonial times arrived in a servile condition. Most who specialize in researching indentured servitude agree that at least half, and possibly as many as two-thirds, of ALL white colonial immigrants arrived in chains.[2]

In Virginia and Maryland during the 1600s, the white-servant quotient was even higher. A study of Virginia from 1623 to 1637 showed that white servants outnumbered white freemen by three to one.[3] In Maryland at one point in the 1600s, the ratio was six to one.[4] As noted above, at least two Goads were sent to Virginia and Maryland during the 1600s. I'll play the odds and bet that at least a few of my colonial ancestors were brought here as bound servants. This doesn't count Tom Goad, the aforementioned convict.

Chances are as good, or even better, that some of those Barbados Goads were white slaves sold by Oliver Cromwell to the whip-crackers of huge West Indies sugar plantations. Barbados, a sweltering Hades closer to South America than North America, became a favored dumping ground of Cromwell's political enemies. He sacked so many of his opponents in this manner, the practice became known as being "Barbadosed."[5] Cromwell was said to have Barbadosed at least a hundred thousand of his politico-religious foes.[6] With one decree in 1651, Cromwell enslaved seven to eight thousand Scots and British Royalists he'd conquered at Worcester and sent them all clanging in chains off to the New World.[7] He also sent Irish survivors of the slaughter at Drogheda into slavery. In the 1640s, more than eighty-five percent of the estimated twenty-five thousand slaves in Barbados were white.[8] In 1653, an estimated half of all white Barbadians were Cromwell's political and religious slaves.[9]

Cromwell's son Henry helped run the white-slave racket from London along with daddy, and in 1655 Henry issued an edict which stated that although "we must use force" in seizing young Irish women as colonial laborers, it was "so much for their owne goode" anyway.[10]

Young Hank Cromwell had a point, if you agree that a rapid death from disease, overwork, or torture is for your own good. From nearly all accounts, the hundred thousand or so white slaves in the West Indies rarely survived the term of their indenture. You might say that the climate was hostile to the Caucasian constitution. Hundreds of thousands of dough-colored Brits, Scots, and Irishmen had been transplanted from their ancestral rain and freezing gloom onto the clay-baked furnace heat of the West Indies and American South. Their pale-white ankles were suddenly planted in tobacco fields, sugar farms, and rice swamps.

The acclimatization phase was known ominously as "seasoning." With the prick of a mosquito's proboscis, malaria was shot into their veins. Dysentery wormed a bloody swath through their intestines. Bone-melting fevers often boiled them alive. According to accounts from both Virginia and the West Indies during the 1600s, roughly EIGHTY PERCENT of white slaves/servants died within the first-twelve months after arrival.[11] Thousands and thousands of white servants, male and female, quietly perished in tropical squalor, their "seasoning" having rendered them crispy corpses.

Barbados was barbaric. Not only was the flaming equatorial heat inimical to the European metabolism, Barbadian slave drivers were said to be particularly cruel. One island commissioner reportedly petitioned Cromwell to switch over to black slavery, reasoning that since black slaves were a costlier, more permanent investment, the vicious overseers might "take more interest in their preservation and so work them with moderation."[12]

Some blacks in the West Indies are still said to retain vestiges of Gaelic language and culture. Music scholars have maintained that the odd mix of anger and rhythm engendered by commingling Irish and black slaves in the West Indies provided the cultural genesis of rock 'n' roll. But if the white slaves of Barbados still exist, it is only in words and music. They were almost all murdered by a blood-hungry system of human bondage. And some of them may have been my distant relatives.

It would be bad enough if Barbados had been an aberration, but it was only part of a much larger pattern of forced expulsion and enslavement that had arisen in the British Isles and parts of the German Rhineland. Starting in the late 1500s, legal entities in these areas had realized that the most efficient way to quell potential domestic trouble was to deport potential domestic troublemakers.

First came the recruiters. Pamphlets and posters. A greasy hand-shake, a wide-open smile, and a pocketful of lies about a sunny new land called America. There were boatloads of filthy lucre to be made by shipping human bodies to the New World, but your typical British recruiting agent might not state it that crudely. With a come-on pitch soaked in brassy ostentation and impossible promises, the recruiter of voluntary indentured servants was a sleazy used-car salesman who peddled human bodies as if they were rusty Ford Pintos. Like most swindlers, he worked first by persuasion, resorting to force only when necessary.

Apparently, force was often necessary. In England, the recruiting agents who were polite enough not to bop you on the head and drag you onto a slave ship were called "drums," because they restricted their activity to drumming up recruits. Those who slipped a mickey in your beer or overpowered you in a grimy alley were called "crimps" or "spirits." The spirit, perhaps accompanied by several other burly ghosts, would snatch his prey quietly and suddenly. If a person disappeared suspiciously, he or she was thought to have been "spirited away." According to historian Richard Hofstadter, the spirit was someone who "waylaid, kidnapped, or induced adults to get aboard ships for America. . . . Often their victims were taken roughly in hand." [13] Gary B. Nash writes that the practice of "kidnapping and shanghaiing of drifters and drunks was endemic. Many unfortunate seaport dwellers awakened one morning with a head-splitting hangover to find themselves in the hold of a ship headed westward across the Atlantic." [14]

A British folk song from the era conjures the chilling subconscious havoc wrought by the spirit gangs:

> The night I was a-married
> And on my marriage bed
> There come a fierce sea captain
> And stood by my bed stead.
> His men, they bound me tightly
> With a rope so cruel and strong
> And carried me over the waters
> To labor for seven years long. [15]

Adults weren't the only whites being kidnapped and sold into colonial slavery. Forcible seizure of homeless and orphaned children was widespread. It was commonly known as "kid-nabbing," later mangled by the Cockneys into "kidnapping." Hundred of thousands of British kids were nabbed into slave work not only for colonial plantations, but also into forced domestic child labor for Britain's smoke-snorting industrial machine.[16]

Because kidnapped men, women, and children were assigned forged contracts of indenture—or, in several cases, no indentures at all until they arrived in the New World—it's difficult to gauge what percentage of white indentured servants came here against their will. In *The Mind of the South,* W. J. Cash guesses that "the greater number" of indentured servants "seem to have been mere children or adolescents, lured from home by professional crimps or outright kidnapped." [17]

As with black slaves from Africa, white slaves from Europe were being kidnapped and shipped overseas not for reasons of unvarnished human hatred, but because it was profitable. When all the horrors are peeled away, the spirit business was precisely that—a business. Without a strong profit motive, the wholesale seizure of white flesh wouldn't have occurred. "One could kidnap a man at random in the alleys of London and be sure of a ready sale for him in the South," writes Thomas J. Wertenbaker in *The First Americans.*[18] An ad in a 1784 New York newspaper refers to a still-vibrant "traffick of white people," [19] and an 1829 judicial decision notes that "it was formerly a considerable business to import Irish and German servants." [20]

Although the spirit was himself frequently drawn from London's lower classes, he was merely the hired gun of higher-ups so insulated by their wealth—merchants, judges, shipowners, and New World planters—that they could afford paying others to do their dirty work. Amazingly, kidnapping was in many cases a legally sanctioned practice. A 1618 parliamentary bill allowed for constables forcefully to nab all orphaned children over eight years old and to detain them in prisons awaiting shipment to colonial plantations.[21] Other laws allowed for the bodily capture of debtors and criminals. A 1652 Commonwealth law permitted officials to identify "begging or vagrant" subjects and cause them to be "seized on and detained" in order to be schlepped in shackles to the colonies.[22] Similar initiatives arose throughout the British Isles as local officials realized it was cheaper to sail their lumpen proles westward than to continue doling out poor relief. Hoping to send their underclass en masse to New York, the Scottish Privy Council in 1669 issued orders for local officials to round up "strong and idle beggars, vagabonds, egyptians, common and notorious whoores, theeves, and other dissolute and lousy persons." [23] It was a new, and sparklingly effective, method of taking out the trash.

An estimate published in 1670 alleged that ten thousand British subjects had been kidnapped that year.[24] A pamphlet issued ten years later reckoned that ten thousand Brits were still being captured per year, every year.[25] If those stats are reliable, this would total a hundred thousand British kidnapping victims in the 1670s alone. In the history of slavery in America, fewer than four hundred thousand black slaves were imported.[26] For all the bad rep Amerikkka gets about black slavery, it probably received no more than six percent of all African slaves shipped to the Western Hemisphere.[27] (Psst—blame Brazil.) Making only mild extrapolations from these British kidnapping estimates, and surmising that roughly ten thousand whites were also abducted yearly for a forty-year run all told, the total of unwilling white immigrants brought to America would equal or surpass the number of Africans forced here against their will. And this estimate is probably low, as indentured servitude flourished for over two hundred years, not forty. And I'm not counting the fifty or sixty thousand convicts dragged over here in the 1700s.

So even though the popular belief is that NO whites were shipped to America against their will, it's highly possible that MORE whites were brought here unwillingly than blacks. It ain't a competition, but it sure complicates the picture.

Once nabbed by a spirit gang, newly enslaved white kiddies and adults were often detained in rat-filled prisons awaiting the next available ship. En route to the vessel, they were publicly dragged through the streets in chains, with all the whipping, branding, pomp, and ceremony normally attendant to such displays. In other instances, they were chained down in the ship's hold pending departure.

Then came the middle passage, which often proved as traumatic and lethal as it had for African slaves. Like the British, the Germans were engaged in uprooting and ass-booting their peasantry. German "new-

landers," the continental equivalent of the British "drums" and "spirits," peddled false hopes and empty dreams to German Palatines, many
of whom had been rendered vulnerable by political shifts in *der Vater-
land*. Gottlieb Mittelberger, a German church organist who in 1750
paid for his passage on a six-month embarkation from Nazi-land to
Philadelphia, wrote with keening outrage of newlanders who had
promised heaven but delivered hell. Once upon the choppy seas, passengers began realizing they'd been duped:

> During the journey the ship is full of pitiful signs of distress—
> smells, fumes, horrors, vomiting, various kinds of sea sickness,
> fever, dysentery, headaches, heat, constipation, boils, scurvy, can-
> cer, mouth-rot, and similar afflictions. . . . In such misery all the
> people on board pray and cry pitifully together. . . . But most of all
> they cry out against the thieves of human beings! Many groan and
> exclaim: "Oh! If only I were back at home, even lying in my
> pig-sty!" Or they call out: "Ah, dear God, if I only once again had
> a piece of good bread or a good fresh drop of water. . . ."

Mittelberger wrote of dead women and babies being tossed into the
ocean foam. He describes passengers as constantly scraping lice off
themselves. The drinking water was salt-infested, and the food—what
existed of it—was

> very black, thick with dirt, and full of worms. . . . [T]oward the end
> of the voyage we had to eat the ship's biscuit, which had already
> been spoiled for a long time, even though no single piece was there
> more than the size of a thaler [thimble] that was not full of red
> worms and spiders' nests.[28]

Despite the atrocities that Mittelberger's eyeballs absorbed, he was a
paying passenger and received first-class treatment compared to the
German servants chained below deck with stale air, scant light, and no
freedom of motion. And as soul-snuffingly dismal as Mittelberger's
voyage was, one commentator says, "There is no reason to think it
particularly unusual." [29] In 1731, the *Love and Unity* sailed from Rot-
terdam to Philly with an estimated one hundred fifty German Palatines,

all but thirty-four of whom died before reaching the City of Brotherly Love. Food became so scarce that scalpers were SELLING rats and mice to the highest bidder.[30]

Likewise, the British slave ships were often little more than floating coffins. Duncan Campbell, an English merchant who shipped white convicts to America until the Revolution broke out, chalked up a ten-percent middle-passage death rate as a "moderate loss."[31] One historian calculated that between ten and fifteen percent of all white bondsmen "commonly died during the voyage."[32] Others peg the overall death quotient as murderously higher.

During a 1638 voyage to America, nearly three-quarters of an estimated three hundred fifty passengers died before arrival. One of the ship's survivors had written, "We have thrown overboard two and three for many dayes together."[33] In 1720, a third of the passengers croaked aboard the *Honour.*[34] The next year, roughly forty percent of those on the *Owners Goodwill* died on the way over here.[35] On the 1768 voyage of the *Snow Rodney,* food became nonexistent—passengers resorted to chewing their own shoe leather.[36] The 1741 passage of Belfast's *Sea Flower* took four months and killed nearly half of the one hundred six humans aboard. During the trip, six human cadavers were gnawed at by famished passengers-cum-cannibals.[37] Water was so scarce on the *Justitia*'s 1743 London-to-Maryland jaunt that transported felons resorted to drinking their own urine. Almost a third of the ship's human cargo died at sea. The vessel's commander, like most provisions-embezzling ship captains caught up in the trade, picked the dead convicts clean of their belongings. He proclaimed that he was "Heir of all the Felons that should happen to dye under his Care."[38] Nice guy.

In 1771, another *Justitia*—maybe the same boat—arrived in Virginia with its Caucasian cargo. "Just arrived at Leedstown," ran the *Virginia Gazette* ad, "the Ship Justitia, with about one hundred Healthy Servants, Men Women & Boys. . . . The Sale will commence on Tuesday the 2nd of April."[39]

The *sale*?!? Surprise, surprise, Gomer Pyle—white indentured servants were sold to the highest bidder, exactly like black slaves. In 1625, a British merchant claimed that in Virginia "servants were sold here up and down like horses." [40] In 1755, Maryland's governor echoed the livestock simile: "The planters' fortunes here consist in the number of their servants (who are purchased at high rates) much as the estates of the English farmer do in the multitude of cattle." [41] Transported convict William Green recalled the auction process: "They search us there as the dealers in horses do those animals in this country, by looking at our teeth, viewing our limbs, to see if they are sound and fit for their labour." [42] Potential servants were often quizzed to determine their temperament and overall eagerness to be treated like shit.

As with Africans, white families were frequently broken apart and sold to different bidders. At auctions, white servants were often purchased in bunches by men known as "soul drivers," who'd chain groups of newly arrived white slaves together and herd them on foot through rural areas, selling them at a profit. "We were driven through the country like cattle to a Smithfield market and exposed to sale in public fairs like so many brute beasts," griped one white servant. [43] "They drive them through the Country like a parcell of Sheep untill they can sell them to advantage," sneered another. [44]

An indentured servant was legally "the property of his Master," as phrased by West Florida's Governor Johnstone in 1766. [45] A South Carolina bill introduced in 1717 argued that "the ownership of one white man" should be a prerequisite for State Assembly membership. [46] A 1757 Pennsylvania court ruling declared that a white servant named Thomas Teaffe was indeed his master's "property." [47] White servants were listed as property on tax returns alongside livestock, the chattel next to the cattle.

As property, white servants were bought, sold, traded, and inherited like any other disposable goods. One boy was traded by his master for two deer, much to the amusement of his fellow servants. [48] In 1657, a female servant's owner swapped the degraded lassie for a pig. [49] Many white servants were bartered for tobacco. [50] John Rolfe, one of Virginia's early elite luminaries, commented in 1619 that white servants were being exchanged to settle gambling debts in card games. [51] Living servants were often indistinguishable from inanimate commodities, as evidenced in this 1765 comment from a Philadelphia entrepreneur:

"[T]he chief articles that answer here from Ireland which can be bought are Linnens . . . Beef, Butter, Men, Women & Boy Servants." [52]

Few indentured servants could properly be called apprentices, unless you think that "learning" how to pick tobacco or clear swamps or remove tree stumps is a valuable educational experience. The whoppin' majority of indentured servants were used as field hands on Southern estates and Northern farms. [53]

White temp-slaves had few legal rights. They couldn't vote or sit on a jury. [54] They couldn't marry without their master's permission, which was often denied. [55] Female servants were forbidden from becoming pregnant, even if their masters had raped them. [56] It was his word against hers. And her penalty didn't stop with a bloody good bull-whipping and an extra coupla years tacked onto her servitude. By Virginia law, her bambino itself was born into slavery until the age of thirty-one. [57] Back then, thirty-one years constituted most of a lifetime. In 1765, Virginia curtailed its out-of-wedlock baby-slavery laws to twenty-one years for white boy trash and eighteen years for white girl trash. [58]

White servants were often whipped *à la* Kunta Kinte. So-called "privileged" white skin was brutally ripped open on plantation after plantation. "I have seen an Overseer beat a Servant with a cane about the head till the blood has followed," remarked an observer, "for a fault that is not worth speaking of, yet he must be patient, or worse will follow." [59] In 1624, white servant Elyas Hintone was bludgeoned to death with a field hoe by his master. [60] A Massachusetts servant named Marmaduke Pierce was also pummeled into eternal darkness by his master, who went unpunished. [61] A New England couple was acquitted of murder in 1666 after the mistress had chopped off a servant's white toes, causing a slow death. [62]

Female servants often fared worse than men. The same Virginia slavemaster who whacked out Elyas Hintone's headlights had regularly whipped his female slave Elizabeth Abbott to the point where "her flesh in some places was raw and very black and blew." [63] Abbott ran away into the forest, where she died of flesh wounds and weakness. In 1663, murdered white female servant Alice Sanford was so viciously abused, her dead body was described as having been "beaten to a jelly." [64] Another white girl was whipped to death by her overseer, Mistress Ward, who was found guilty by a jury but only fined three hundred pounds of tobacco.[65] White servant Elizabeth Sprigs complained in a 1756 letter that she'd been "tied up and whipped to that degree that you'd not serve an animal. . . . Nay, many negroes are better used. . . ." [66]

Under such conditions, suicides proliferated. A Scottish ex-servant commented that "some of these poor deluded slaves, in order to put an end to their bondage, put a period to their lives." [67]

Physical torture of white servants was so pervasive that the law began to take notice. A 1642 Virginia statute remarked how "the barbarous usuage of some servants by cruell masters bring soe much scandall and infamy to the country in generall." The law went on to prohibit the private burial of servants because masters frequently were "guilty of their deaths" and tried to hide the bodies.[68] A 1717 law in South Carolina mentioned "barbarous usage of servants by cruel masters." [69] Thirty years later, a Maryland coroner who was alarmed at all the bruised corpses whizzing through his office bemoaned the "rigorous Usage and Ill-treatment of Masters to Servants." [70]

But for the most part, the law wasn't much kinder than the individual slavemaster. Whipping a disobedient or runaway servant was legal if performed under the direction of a judge, who presumably liked to watch. Up to thirty-nine lashes were allowed in Maryland; masters were only forbidden from "excessively" beating their servants.[71] A South Carolina servant who had run away twice was ordered in 1671 to "be stript naked to his waiste, and receive thirty-nine lashes upon his naked back." [72] As late as 1785, Virginia's legal code allowed for uppity white servants to be "corrected with stripes." [73]

Indentured servitude was harsh enough that servants frequently ran away, and colonial newspapers were crammed with classified ads from masters trying to reclaim their white-skinned property. These runaway ads first appeared in the early 1600s and lasted into the late 1820s. Servants are commonly described as bearing whip marks and burned scar tissue, with their attitudes deemed as "saucy," "proud," and "impudent." [74]

Upon capture, white servants were routinely whipped and then penalized with extra time added to their bondage. Statutes and court decisions mandated that runaway servants have their ears cut off, that they be branded with red-hot pokers, or that they wear leg irons and metal neck collars called "pot-hooks." Virginia law provided that servants who had run away a second time be "branded in the cheek with the letter R and pass under the statute of incorrigible rogues." [75] Captured runaway servants in Virginia were also obligated to serve two extra days for every day they had escaped. [76] In Maryland, the ratio was ten days to one. [77] In South Carolina, it became an extra *year* for every week a servant had absented himself. [78] There are recorded runaway penalties of five, seven, ten, and even fifteen years. [79] Runaway white servants were such a pervasive problem, the U.S. Constitution proclaimed that those "held to Service or Labor in one State . . . escaping into another . . . shall be delivered up."

Some have estimated that as many as half of all white bound servants, throughout the two-hundred-plus years the system was legal in America, never survived their term of indenture. [80] If you have any residual doubts that this was a merciless system that chewed up humans and spat out cadavers, consider that these dizzying mortality rates occurred among a population comprised mostly of teenagers whose typical term may have been seven years.

Yeah, Mister Charley, an indentured servant's life was just a long, gluttonous pig-feast on that triple-scoop smorgasbord of lily-white skin privilege and sterling cultural entitlement. I wonder what a white slave of two or three hundred years ago, after being whipped, shackled, beaten, raped, starved, infected, or impregnated, would have thought of the currently fashionable SoHo/boho doctrine of white-skin privilege? They'd probably want to kill every writer in New York.

The latter-day guiltmongers just can't face the reality of WHITE SLAVES. But in colonial times, the words "servant" and "slave" were used interchangeably. For a fuzzy fifty years or so after Jamestown's settlement, there was hardly any distinction between white and black forced laborers—the system of racially defined, legally endorsed black chattel slavery didn't blossom in any significant numerical sense until late in the 1600s. According to one historian, "There is no doubt that the earliest Negroes in Virginia occupied a position similar to that of

the white servants in the colony." [81] A 1641 law provided for all disobedient servants to have their skin branded, regardless of its color.[82] A
1652 law in Providence and Warwicke (later Rhode Island) mentions
"blacke mankind or white" servants.[83] A 1683 Pennsylvania law contains the phrase "no Servant White or Black." [84] So there's a strong
chance that if some of those Goad "immigrants" from the 1600s were
indentured servants, they sweated in the fields alongside blacks. And
you STILL want me to pay reparations?

During a 1659 parliamentary debate on the white-servant trade to
the colonies, legislators used the word "slaves" rather than "servants." [85] A Virginia law of 1705 mentions the "care of all Christian
slaves," Christian being a contemporary euphemism for European.[86] A
scribe for *London Magazine* wrote in 1751 that a British convict
shipped overseas became a "slave in America." [87] A colonial observer
of Virginia convict laborers said, "I never see such pasels of pore
Raches in my Life . . . they are used no Bater than so many negro
Slaves." [88] A 1777 screed protesting the indenture racket claimed that
a white servant's body was "as absolutely subjected as the body or
person of a Negro, man or woman, who is sold as a legal Slave." [89] In
the 1820s, Karl Anton Postl commented that nonslaveowning whites
"are not treated better than the slaves themselves." [90]

White indentured servants frequently referred to themselves as
slaves. In 1623, Virginia servant Thomas Best wrote that "Master
Atkins hath sold me for a £150 sterling like a damn'd slave." [91] A
white servant named Robert Perkins said that his bondage featured "all
the Hardships that the Negro Slaves endured." [92]

Modern historians would agree. Howard Zinn states that "white
indentured servants were often treated as badly as black slaves." [93]
Eugene Genovese claims that "in the South and in the Caribbean, the
treatment meted out to white indentured servants had rivaled and often
exceeded in brutality that meted out to black slaves. . . ." [94]

The reason for this was nothing as retardedly ethereal as human
hatred. It was the same reason that people beat the shit out of a rent-a-
car more readily than a car they own in toto. "The Negro," argues
historian James Leyburn, "was a permanent piece of property and must
be conserved; the servant was a temporary investment to be exploited

to the full." [95] In 1770, Annapolis customs surveyor William Eddis reasoned that black slaves, as "property for life," were "almost in every instance, under more comfortable circumstances than the miserable European, over whom the rigid planter exercises an inflexible severity." Eddis observed that whites, as temp-slaves, were "strained to the utmost to perform their allotted labour. . . . There are doubtless many exceptions to this observation, yet, generally speaking, they groan beneath a worse than Egyptian bondage." [96]

Apparently, some black slaves saw it the same way. "I'd rather be a nigger," ran a popular plantation song, "than a poor white man." [97] Elija Henry Hopkins, a black ex-slave from Arkansas, said that "in slavery times, a poor white man was worse off than a nigger." [98] Black slaves were known to tell anti-Irish jokes to amuse their owners, who often placed the Irish on a social tier below Africans. "My master is a great tyrant," ran one of the barbs. "He treats me as badly as if I was a common Irishman." [99] In 1855, when landscape architect and travel writer Frederick Law Olmsted asked a steamboat shipmate in Alabama why the Irish were performing more dangerous work than black slaves, he received this verbal shrug: "Oh, the niggers are worth too much to be risked here; if the Paddies are knocked overboard or get their backs broke, nobody loses anything." [100] I recall the line from *Blazing Saddles:* "Alright, we'll give some land to the niggers and the chinks, but we DON'T WANT THE IRISH!"

Buried at the bottom of the white-slave trash heap were the white convict laborers. Convicts were different from indentured servants in that they were thought to have *deserved* their bondage, whether they actually did or not. White convicts were possibly the first group in America to be verbally likened to trash. A British author dubbed them "offensive Rubbish." [101] Another called them "the Vermin of Society." [102] A Boston writer referred to them as "Excrescences." [103] In 1751, the *Virginia Gazette* decreed that the only way for Britain to "show a more sovereign contempt" for the colonists would be to empty their toilets on America.[104] Ben Franklin offered to send rattlesnakes to Britain in trade.[105]

White convict laborers had dribbled into the colonies throughout the 1600s, but they may have comprised as much as a quarter of ALL white colonial immigrants—free or bound—in the 1700s.[106] During the period in which Thomas Goad was transported to Maryland, convicts comprised an estimated forty percent of everyone who entered that state from overseas. One in five of these Maryland convicts bore a sentence of fourteen years to life.[107] You heard me—white slaves for LIFE.

British convicts began arriving here in large lumps—an estimated fifty thousand during the 1700s[108]—after Parliament's passage of the Transportation Act in 1718. The law provided that convicted felons could be "transported" overseas as slave laborers. Convict-slaves were frequently referred to as "transports." Transportation was viewed second only to the death penalty in severity. According to one historian, convict deportation became "Britain's foremost punishment after 1718." [109] It was considered preferable to hanging, but far worse than being whipped or branded. A British judge in 1741 concluded that a thief whom he'd convicted didn't qualify as "an Object of mercy and therefore I ordered him, instead of being burnt on the hand, to be Transported for Seven Years."[110] Convicted felons often begged for whipping or burning instead. A thief named Mary Stanford requested to be hanged rather than be banished overseas.[111] To the average British subject of the day, America represented a savage, frightening wilderness, more Siberia than Disneyland.

Most transported British convicts were not violent criminals. As one writer tells it, "Grand larcenists made up the majority of transports. . . . The typical malefactor cast for transportation, then, was a young male labourer driven to crime by economic necessity." [112] Grand larceny was defined as theft of anything worth over a shilling. The average unskilled worker's daily salary at the time was barely more than a shilling. Let's say your average unskilled worker today makes seven dollars an hour, which translates into fifty-six smackolas for a full workday. Therefore, grand larceny back then constituted the theft of anything deemed worth more than fifty clams in modern currency.

Many, if not most, of the transported convicts may have done nothing more "criminal" than being poor. Convict transportation flourished during a period when one in ten citizens was starving in the best of times, and nearly half went hungry in the worst of times. British

69

subjects were being hanged for stealing bread. One could get the noose merely for plucking fruit from a rich man's estate.[113] One man received a seven-year banishment to America for stealing a lamb after being tormented by the "Cryes of his familey for Bread, at a tyme, when he had it not to give them." [114] In 1771, a starving pregnant woman was banished to America for stealing a large basin of soup.[115] This case, far from an exception, was described by one researcher as "fairly typical." [116] There were even rumors of some workers being enslaved merely for asking that they be paid.[117] And there's evidence that public officials frequently convicted innocent persons in order to get monetary kickbacks from slave traders.[118]

By ridding themselves of the poor, the British saved money on jails and public welfare. As one writer explains, convicts were "pickpockets and thieves who were worth more to the Crown on a New World plantation than dangling from a rope." [119] The Crown typically paid merchants five pounds to transport a convict overseas. In London, the business was cornered by a few wealthy companies. A merchant on the colonial side remarked that "the Sales of the Convicts run up amazingly in a little time." [120] Convicts generated much more income —although not for themselves—than was possible in foggy old England. It was estimated that a convict's personal upkeep cost between thirteen and fifteen pounds yearly,[121] while his labor during the same stretch could generate from fifty to one hundred fifty pounds of income for his owner.[122] Taking the lowest possible estimate—that of a thirty-five-pound-per-year profit for the master—and multiplying it by seven years, one arrives at a MINIMUM profit of two hundred forty-five pounds for the convict's owner. Not a bad profit on a convict who may have only stolen a shilling. The slaveowner's financial return was possibly FIVE THOUSAND times the monetary amount originally stolen by the convict. Who was stealing from whom?

Economics. That's all it was, is, or ever will be. Racism is only a smoke screen, a cynical diversionary tactic. Once you understand that, the rest is easy.

Whites comprised the majority of colonial slave laborers through most of the 1600s.[123] Black slaves reached a numerical parity with

70

white servants sometime late in that century or early in the 1700s.[124] The idea of racial supremacy had little to do with the gradual shift from white to black slavery.

Throughout the time span of white indentured servitude, African slaves-for-life had always been much pricier than British temp-slaves. In the 1690s, black slaves were still selling for twice or three times the cost of white servants, but the megaplanters began a slow tilt toward black slavery. The reason for the shift was economic rather than racial. "The profit motive alone favored the substitution of black labor for white," argues historian Edwin J. Perkins.[125] In England, it had become common knowledge that the servant trade was not the smiley-faced "Join the Navy and see the World" program promised by the drums and crimps. To attract new "volunteers," the colonies had passed laws protecting white servants' rights. The plan backfired, as it rendered their upkeep more expensive. The supply of white servants diminished as more African markets opened up, cementing the shift toward black slavery.

Planters were also said to have perceived blacks as less criminal and more docile than their hell-stompin' white-trash co-slaves. A final reason for the transition from white slavery to black is so nose-crushingly obvious that it's often overlooked: Blacks were visually identifiable by their skin color. They weren't so much *hated* for it as they were *identified* by it. According to a commentator in 1735, the problem in recapturing runaway white servants had been the difficulty in sussing out "whether they were Servants or not"; blacks, however, could "always be known and taken into Custody." [126]

So it was the rich white man's money and law—not the poor white man's unregenerate hatred—that favored black slavery over white in-dentured servitude. Yes, the intensification of slavery pushed the poor black man down; what's rarely acknowledged is that it also squeezed the poor white man out.

Ebony midget Spike Lee raises a hellish funk about emancipated black slaves having been cheated out of the "forty acres and a mule" promised by their alleged liberators. He even named his film company after that broken promise. Spike's right that black ex-slaves were

71

cheated, but I wonder if he realizes that white ex-slaves were also routinely defrauded of their fifty acres and a hoe. Shit, he probably doesn't even *know* about white slaves.

Upon release from bondage, white servants were legally entitled to "freedom dues." The popular myth is that most servants received a fertile chunk of sod and lived happily ever after. This is an outright falsehood, as most states granted no land whatsoever as part of their freedom dues. Maryland was an exception. But a study of approximately five thousand white indentured servants in Maryland during the 1670s reveals that only a quarter of them inherited the fifty-acre headright; in fact, a higher number of them had died in bondage than had received land.[127]

Instead of land, most white ex-slaves were promised only clothing, tools, and/or a pittance of cash. A 1700 Pennsylvania law provided only for two suits, an ax, and two hoes.[128] The hoes, we are to presume, were gardening tools instead of prostitutes, unless "weeding" and "grubbing" were sexual euphemisms in colonial America. In the mid-1700s, Virginia's freedom dues for newly released servants amounted to a one-shot cash payment of three pounds, ten shillings.[129] In North Carolina around the same time, freedom dues were a trifling three pounds.[130]

So how far could a white ex-slave go on three pounds sterling? Would he be able to purchase livestock, land, or slaves—in short, any of the things that brought financial security, especially in the South? Fat chance, liver-lips. For the freed indentured servant, "the statistical probability for rising to even middle-class position was very slight," writes one historian.[131] The most commonly cited guesstimate, provided by indentured-servitude specialist Abbot Emerson Smith, is that only one in ten white ex-slaves would "wax decently prosperous." Smith reckoned that maybe another one in ten would achieve some measure of self-sufficiency. Eight of ten servants, however, either "died during their servitude, returned to England after it was over, or became 'poor whites.' "[132] A Maryland priest observed that "white servants, after their terms of bondage is out, are stroling the county without bread."[133] Governor Bradford of Massachusetts lamented that "by one means or another, in 20 years time, it is question whether ye greater part be not growne ye worser." [134] In South Carolina, Frederick Law Olmsted commented that "the poor white people, meaning those, I suppose, who bring nothing to market in exchange for money but their labor . . . are worse off in almost all respects than the slaves." [135]

Because they had been forbidden from marrying or starting families during their term of bondage, freed white servants often led fractured social lives upon their release. Perhaps the only thing positive about black slavery was that it gave blacks a sense of community. This was not afforded to the white ex-convict. He drank and died alone. And because he was now a "free" laborer in a slave-based economy, he had priced himself out of the market. There was nowhere for him to go but down (economically) and out (geographically).

Virginia's Governor Spotswood also noted that many ex-servants, banished from the Southern economy, had "settled out on the frontier." [136] Poor white trash started occupying America's frontier in more than one sense of the word.

4

The View from Outside

How Rednecks Became Aliens

Poor Southern whites, obviously, have not been lucky in their portraiture. If not seen as vicious redneck brutes, they have often as not been figures of fun. . . . Just as rednecks seem to be the last remaining identifiably ethnic villains, so hillbillies appear to be the last acceptable ethnic fools. . . . [T]he derogatory lower-class types, redneck villains and comic hillbillies, serve the same "mudsill" function as they did when some ladies and gentlemen of the antebellum South found that thinking in terms of these types allowed them to think comforting things about themselves. —John Shelton Reed, *Southern Folk, Plain & Fancy*

Many hillbillies in the mass media are there to make the normative middle-class urban spectator feel better about the system of money and power that has him or her in its grasp. Someone is always beneath us, lending proof that the twig on which we stand is really the rung of a ladder leading upward to something we must defend with our lives. . . . [T]he urban majority is growing further and further removed from real rural experience and hence is freer to dissociate the hillbilly as a purely comic cartoon, something to be safely and unambiguously dispensed with rather than something symbolic of the banished rural memory that will not stay banished. —J. W. Williamson, *Hillbillyland*

Yoo-hoo, all you spics, spooks, slopeheads, beaners, greaseballs, coolies, kikes, krauts, wetbacks, dotheads, spearchuckers, and camel jock-

THE VIEW FROM OUTSIDE

eys—d'ya think you'd be able to recognize an ethnic slur when you heard one?

Sure you could. And though the type of hateful sow bucket who spews such filth might deny allegations that his lingo constitutes "hate speech," you'd probably feel hated nonetheless. It's understandable.

So why shouldn't certain pale-skinned bipeds bristle when outsiders snipe at rednecks, hayseeds, bumpkins, crackers, hillbillies, pecker-woods, Bubbas, yokels, lintheads, shit-kickers, and poor white trash?

Any way you slice the liverwurst, it still seems like bigotry. But the 'neck-negaters, the trash-compactors, the hill-bullies, excuse their fire-breathing with an inventive alibi—"WE can't be bigoted—RED-NECKS are the bigots." It's like, "He hit me FIRST, mom!" They deflect attention from their own prejudices by hating the haters, all in the name of love.

Nice try. Still sounds like hate to me.

One of the chief denunciations about rednecks is an alleged bundle of psychological "fears" that lead them to demean anyone different from them. But flip the pancake over: Isn't this precisely why most people demean rednecks—for being DIFFERENT from them, as measured by most known indexes of social difference?

People seem to need an "other." It appears impossible for societies to conceive of an "us" without an antagonistic and constantly threatening "them." Call it the scapegoating mechanism. A black box beeping inside the heart's cockpit. A recalcitrant obsidian chunk of bigotry. An irredeemable fleck of hatefulness. Everybody hates somebody sometime. What the world needs now is hatred, bitter hatred. I don't mean it needs *more* hatred or *less* hatred—it simply needs the hatred it has always needed.

What constitutes a negative bigoted stereotype? Usually a combination of signifiers—tagmarks—whether biological, behavioral, geographic, or cultural. A *visual* signifier based on inherited biological traits is often paramount, such as slitted chink eyes or fat nigger lips or a red neck on an ice-white body. Bigoted caricatures frequently allege genetic regressiveness, as in the subhuman slopehead, the ape-like junglebunny, or the inbred hillbilly. Behavioral traits are blamed on accidents of birth—chinks are born neurotically organized, niggers are born lazy, and crackers are born stupid. Stereotypes often mention bacterial problems—chinks boil alley cats, niggers smell bad, and toothless hillbillies get dirty feet from walking barefoot to the out-house. Some sexual dysfunction or aberration is frequently attributed —chinks fuck like rabbits, niggers fuck like monsters, and rednecks fuck their mothers. Stereotypes also imply geographical distance—the chinks live in either Asia or Chinatown, the niggers in Africa or the black ghetto, and the rednecks in the South or trailer parks. All such places are implicitly foreign lands to the one doing the slur-ring—if you joke about trailer parks, it's presumed that you don't live in one.

Our stereotypical, pop-up, cardboard-cutout, cereal-box redneck figurine is a Social Martian under all the prongs of bigoted stereotyp-ing: biologically (inbred, degenerated, momma-impregnating vermin and scum); geographically (xenophobic, backwoods, rustic, heath-dwelling, trailer-sheathed yahoos); economically (poor, barefoot, toothless, no-account, earth-scratching trash); culturally (gullible, su-perstitious, bumpkinesque rubes and throwbacks); and morally (cross-burning, baby-molesting swamp creatures and their slatternly wives).

When JumboTron movie screens smack your head on every corner with images of buck-toothed, straw-chompin', pellagra-stricken, swine-schtuppin' yokels, does it have the air of people poking fun at *themselves* or at *others*? The answer should be obvious to anyone but an urban supremacist—the mainstream consistently depicts the red-neck not as itself, but as a cultural weirdo. The redneck is the *watched,* not the *watcher.*

To stereotype is to erect a boundary between yourself and those you don't want on your side of the chicken wire. It's like grabbing one of those flashlight-thick felt-tipped pens, the kind whose volatile-fume blast gets you dizzy right after you pop open the cap, and drawing a thick LINE between YOU and THEM.

In 1728, a way-upscale Virginian named William Byrd II led a committee whose purpose was to draw a legally enforceable line be-tween the colonies of Virginia and North Carolina. Byrd's book of the same year, *Histories of the Dividing Line Betwixt Virginia and North Carolina,* made it clear that he considered the two states to be not only

76

distinct geographical and legal entities, but different states of mind as well. If you a look at a map of Virginia straddling North Carolina, the states look like complementary sides of a Rorschach inkblot, split evenly across a horizontal line.

Socially, Byrd hovered among the creamiest of the early eighteenth-century crop, having inherited massive Virginian acreage from his uncle. He multiplied his wealth by trading in skin—the furs of dead animals and the bodies of white and black servants. He worked his land, and all creatures great and small upon it, toward his own advantage. To Colonel Byrd, Virginia was a glimmering gemstone reflecting his own opulence.

Below the dividing line, however, was a whole 'nuther ball o' grimy wax. North Carolina, drawn south of Virginia, was a zone of negative value that Byrd derisively dubbed "Lubberland." The foreign inhabitants, whom Byrd called "Lubbers," were typified by the near-savage white frontiersmen of the Carolina backcountry, a lazy set of yawners and ass-scratchers, "indolent wretches," wrote Byrd, who "loiter away their lives through aversion to labor." [1]

The Lubbers upon whom Byrd spat tobacco juice were uniformly poor people, many of them former indentured servants and ex-convicts scattered like white silt throughout the backcountry's interstitial pockets and faraway meadows. As the wealthier speculators—men of Byrd's ilk—consolidated their grip over tidewater government and land, they established a two-tiered economic system of wealthy white landowners and propertyless black slaves. The poorer class of whites were hurled westward by the gale force of economic winds.

While Byrd blamed these Lubbers for sitting around and doing nothing, the truth was that there was nothing for them to do. The plantation system, concocted and exploited by Byrd-brains, had tossed a growing class of poor whites onto the worst land in the colonies, dead tundra largely unsuitable for farming. Land divorced from the geographic and economic "mainland." Land still largely under the control of red-skinned Native American "aliens." In the early colonial west (still east of the Appalachians), the degraded "Lubber" types often fetched arrows with their rib cages. Eastern planter types such as Byrd frequently mentioned "planting" settlements of poor whites out west to serve as a sacrificial buffer zone against the Injuns.[2] But instead of blaming the Lubbers' degraded situation on himself or the system that enriched him while it ignored them, Byrd shifted the blame over to the Lubberly side of the line. He pinned their poor condition on their alleged lousy work habits, their "disposition to laziness."

The Carolina backcountry seems to represent an important early cultural dividing line in redneck popular iconography. The people that Byrd labeled "Lubbers" were also called "buckskins" by eighteenth-century observers of the backwoodsman's tendency (by necessity) to garb himself in animal pelts. Then as now, most writers came from the elite classes, and tidewater scribes who invaded the backwoods to observe primitive whites cavorting in their natural state were said to have used the term "buckskin" derisively.

North Carolina Governor Gabriel Johnston in 1737 described his own state's upcountry Lubber and buckskin types as "the lowest scum and rabble . . . [who] build themselves sorry hutts and live in a beastly sort of plenty." Like Byrd, Johnston blamed frontier conditions on the gutter morality of the frontiersmen themselves, claiming they were "devoted to calumny, lying, and the vilest tricking and cheating; a people into whose heads no human means can beat the notion of a publick interest or persuade to live like men."[3]

An Anglican missionary named Charles Woodmason essayed into the Carolina backcountry during the 1760s, and in two holier-than-thou passages may have inaugurated the white-trash stereotypes of inbreeding and bare feet. Woodmason found frontier people

> swopping their wives as Cattel, and living in a State of Nature, more irregularly and unchastely than the Indians. . . . No Shoes or Stockings—Children run half naked. The Indians are better Cloathed and Lodged. . . . They were as rude in their Manners as the Common Savages, and hardly a degree removed from them.[4]

A 1783 observer from Georgia, commenting on the strange new breed of white cavemen crouched on the colonial fringes, was to mention a term that had greater longevity than either Lubbers or buckskins:

> The Southern colonies are overrun with a swarm of men from the western parts of Virginia and North Carolina, distinguished by the name of Crackers. Many of these people are descended from convicts that were transported from Great Britain to Virginia at different times, and inherit so much profligacy from their ancestors, that they are the most abandoned set of men on earth. . . .[5]

The etymology of "cracker" is disputed. In Britain during the 1600s, the word was synonymous with "bomb"—as in "firecracker"—and came to describe a person with explosive anger or who made a lot of noise. Many historians trace the word's American usage to the phrase "corn-crackers" (remember "Jimmy crack corn, and I don't care"?), because pounding, or cracking, corn was one of the few ways for the early piney-woods dwellers to squeeze out some food for themselves. Another explanation is that "cracker" is a truncation of "whip-cracker," a phrase invented by Southern city folks to label Georgia and Florida's rural cowboys, who drove their oxen and mules over grazing lands with a sadistic whip crack.

Modern American blacks, who seem to use the word "cracker" more than anyone else, might argue that the cracker's whip was that of a slavemaster instead of a cowboy. During the mid-1800s, American blacks had gradually begun to favor "cracker" over their earlier hate-whitey slur of choice, "po' buckra," which was a mangling of the word "poor" and an African word which meant something along the lines of "honky devil."

The economic signifier "poor" likewise pops up in the phrase "poor whites," said to have become part of the American vernacular during the 1700s. This phrase has a revelatory history, having shifted over the years from "poor whites" to "poor white trash" to merely "white trash"—in shunting the emphasis from "poor" to "trash," one's attention is diverted from economic explanations toward behavioral and genetic alibis.

At the start, "poor whites" were perceived as economic aliens, a light-skinned underclass distinct from the white aristocracy. The elites' contempt for their poorer prodigal brethren was observed and often regurgitated by blacks. In *My Bondage and My Freedom*, Frederick Douglass comments that even slaves knew trash when they saw it:

> A free white man, holding no slaves, in the country, I had known to be the most ignorant and poverty-stricken of men, and the laughingstock even of slaves themselves—called generally by them, in derision, "poor white trash."

Poverty—whether material, cultural, or intellectual—came to be the hallmark of poor white trash. In an 1857 essay entitled "The Poor Illiterate Whites of the South," Southern abolitionist (and self-described son of poor white trash) Hinton Rowan Helper blamed plantation slavery for impoverishing both black slaves (inside the system) and poor whites (who were banished outside of it). According to Helper, the poor whites were afforded scant privileges for their skin color:

> It is quite impossible, however, to describe accurately the deplorable ignorance and squalid poverty of the class to which we refer. The serfs of Russia have reason to congratulate themselves that they are neither the negroes nor the non-slaveholding whites of the South. Than the latter there can be no people in Christendom more unhappily situated. . . . Many of them grow up to the age of maturity, and pass through life without ever owning as much as five dollars at any one time.[6]

Beyond their economic pauperdom, Helper saw in the South's poor whites a poverty of mental capacity, religious sophistication, and moral restraint:

> Thousands of them die at an advanced age, as ignorant of the common alphabet as if it had never been invented. All are more or less impressed with a belief in witches, ghosts, and supernatural signs. Few are exempt from habits of sensuality and intemperance.[7]

Such sleazy, slutty, steamy, stinking, slimy, white-trash "sensuality and intemperance" invariably led to the birth of a familiar stereotype, that of the ultrafecund cornpone Earth Mother. She pops out babies as if she were an estrogen-injected rodent, littering her rocky rural front yard with a "half-dozen of dirty, squalling, white-headed little brats," in the harsh words of antebellum Alabammy writer Daniel Hundley. His 1860 opus *Social Relations in our Southern States* featured an entire chapter called "Poor White Trash." Hundley charted their trashy lineage back to colonial America's indentured servants and convict laborers. But rather than realizing that destitute forefathers may lead to impoverished descendants, Hundley echoed William Byrd and blamed poor whites for not being self-starters:

> They are about the laziest two-legged animals that walk erect on the face of the Earth. Even their motions are slow, and their speech is a sickening drawl . . . while their thoughts and ideas seem likewise to creep along at a snail's pace. . . . [They show] a natural stupidity or dullness of intellect that almost surpasses belief.[8]

Like the Virginian Byrd, the Alabaman Hundley was drawn from the South's elite planter class—a man in the center of things—who described poor white trash as living in "hilly and mountainous regions . . . far removed from the wealthy and refined settlements." Places such as Hundley's, for instance.

Despite Hundley's contention that hillfolk and poor white trash were essentially the same group, his era's common semantic tendency was to distinguish the highland "mountain whites" from flatland "poor whites." This wasn't to imply that mountain whites weren't poor, it was just an added geographic dimension. By default, "poor whites" came to designate any cracker/trash types who didn't live in the mountains. To this day, "white trash" is perhaps the least area-specific of all the terms used to designate a despised white American class—it would be proper to use it for a New Yorker, perhaps even a Manhattanite, whereas you'd be stretching it to call him a cracker, redneck, or hillbilly.

The hills. What a cheap, easy metaphor to represent a cultural wall. As opposed to "poor white trash," the term "hillbilly" is perhaps the *most* area-specific of all the phrases our society uses when it really means to say "white nigger." Hillbilly, like nigger, was a term invented by outsiders, resented by the hillbillies and niggers themselves. As used by those who didn't live in the hills, the term "hillbilly" gradually replaced "mountain white" during the tail end of the 1800s. It also outlasted terms such as "sand hiller" and "pine-lander." Originally spelled "Hill Billy" (or "Billie"), it described a goofy mountain Everyman, your average Billy from the hills. It's akin to calling someone a Ghetto Leroy. A contemporary synonym of Hill Billy was Country Jake. Other rural pejoratives are similarly constructed from the first names of imaginary males who supposedly represent *all* country menfolk—the word "hick" comes from a now-obsolete variant of the name "Richard," and "rube" is a rural abbreviation of "Reuben." Other similar designations, such as "hayseed," point directly to a rural life. And "yokel" would seem to designate a farmer type, one who bears the yoke.

It's generally thought that the word "hillbilly" first surfaced in print in the *New York Journal* of April 23, 1900:

> A Hill-Billie is a free and untrammelled white citizen of Alabama, who lives in the hills, has no means to speak of, dresses as he can, talks as he pleases, drinks whiskey when he gets it, and fires off his revolver as the fancy takes him.[9]

"Yahoo," another common designation for rural boobs, was coined by Jonathan Swift in 1726's *Gulliver's Travels*. The narrator describes himself as going "up into the country, resolving to deliver myself to the first savages I should meet." He quickly finds them in the despicable Yahoos, "who appear to be the most unteachable of all animals." Swift, who must rank as some sort of hillbilly-literature prophet—he beat *Deliverance* by nearly two hundred fifty years—described the "execrable Yahoos" as a species that had derived from solid lowlander stock but had "retired to the mountains, and degenerating by degrees, became in process of time, much more savage than those of their own species in the country from whence . . . [they] came."[10]

Whereas the hillbilly and yahoo pointed to a place on the map, "redneck" could be said to designate a place in the *heart,* most commonly an attitudinal aneurysm pulsating with suicidal stubbornness and poisonous hatred. The word "redneck" is based on a physiological trait—after all, Asians and Africans don't get red necks from planting turnips by daylight—but I suspect that the stinging pain of a sunburned Caucasian neck symbolizes a propensity toward unreasonable anger, of "seeing red." On our national palette, the color red has always betokened a potentially violent alien. How else to explain the other major cultural "threats" from the past—the Red Man, the Red Army, and invaders from Mars, the Red Planet?

The word "redneck" signals a low economic status—wealthy landowners never had to plow the fields until their clammy white necks bubbled into a lobster red. But in its early usages, it more often connoted the self-conscious contrary stance of a rebel. The underlings of Scottish chieftains who practiced guerrilla warfare against the British had been known as savage, rebel-yelling "redshanks."[11] White slaves in the West Indies and American South were called "redshanks" or "redlegs" due to their inherited need for #42 sunscreen.[12] The term "redneck" seems first to have been used to describe religious heretics in northern England.[13] In America, the earliest printed occurrence of "redneck" is said to be from *Southern Tour,* an 1830 travel book by A. Royall, who applied the term to Presbyterians living in Fayetteville, North Carolina.[14] At the time, Presbyterians were an oft-maligned religious minority, and the term "Presbyterian" was used synonymously with "Scotch-Irish," meaning the hard-kneecapped former Ulster Scots who formed much of the frontier population. And during 1921's "Battle of Blair Mountain," newspaper reporters referred to striking West Virginia miners as "rednecks" because they wore red scarves to symbolize solidarity against the coal-company police.[15] So by these Presbyterian/coal-miner derivations, a redneck is a rebel, someone who opposes established authority such as the Pope and the cops.

Whereas "white trash" may describe an economic or behavioral impediment, and where "hillbilly" suggests a geographical handicap, the word "redneck" above all implies a reactionary mood. Although the term was invented by outsiders to describe soil-tilling low-class white nobodies, the word's stiff-spined rebel obstinacy made it the term most frequently embraced by the aliens themselves. To this day, "redneck" connotes defiance—stupid or otherwise.

A redneck, as I define it, is someone both conscious of and comfortable with his designated role of cultural jerk. While hillbillies and white trash may act like idiots because they can't help it, a redneck does it to spite you. A redneck is someone who knows you hate him and rubs that fact in your face. A hillbilly doesn't know he's a clown, and he's happy; a redneck knows he's a villain, and he likes it. In the same way that stubborn mules are often able to make their owners look like asses, the redneck has the troublesome capacity to make ironic sport of the greater public's repulsion/fascination with him.

This self-consciously mischievous ability to turn the world upside down is evident in the earliest white-trash fictional types to emerge in American literature. "Arkansas Traveler," a popular song during the 1840s, came to represent a template in the national gallery of comic situations. Some form of the Arkansas Traveler–type vignette should be familiar to the reader—a city slicker, lost out in the country, chances upon a hayseed character who lazily languishes outside a dilapidated shack or farmhouse. Through a series of shrugged shoulders and evasive, zenlike, "Ya cain't get thar from here" answers to the city boy's honest inquiries, the country clown effects a role reversal. He places the dunce cap atop the urban intruder's head. The Arkansas Traveler situation seems an indelible element of America's fablery and need not be situated in the South—growing up, I remember the hayseed character always being played by New England farmers with Yankee-bean accents.

The rural bumpkin who outwits the urban invader became a fixed player in America's mythology around the same time that the toothy Negro minstrel became a recognizable type. The idiot-savant country boob is comparable to the "trickster" type in African folklore, usually an anthropomorphized animal whose mocking mental cunning extricates him from threatening situations. Although not a Negro, Bugs Bunny is a trickster.

Redneck tricksters, those butts of insult who are able to twist the punch line around until it boomerangs back onto the joke teller, flooded

84

the mid-1800s literary school known as Southwestern Humor. What's now known as the Deep South was at that time a frontier area called the Old Southwest, a free-range red-clay tableau inhabited by earthy white savages who habitually ate the earth itself. "Clay-eaters" was a term often applied to far-flung denizens of the unsettled South. Clay-eating, called geophagy by science geeks, has been a perennially documented practice. Men ate it to increase virility, while women chewed it to enhance fertility. Although clay-eating was once common among both black and white Southerners, the stereotypical clay-eater is invariably a white person.

Ransy Sniffle, who by appearing in Augustus Baldwin Longstreet's 1835 book *Georgia Scenes* rates as one of American fiction's first redneck tricksters, was a clay-eater. So was Yellow-legs, the Eddie Haskellesque prankster in J. J. Hooper's 1845 *Some Adventures of Captain Simon Suggs*. Yellow-legs needled straight-man Suggs to the point where Suggs threatened a whupping:

> I'll kick more clay outen you in a minute than you can eat in a month, you durn'd little, dirt-eatin' deer face.[16]

Sut Lovingood, an eastern-Tennessee redneck hell-raiser created by writer George Washington Harris, was not specifically a dirt-eater, but he was a gunk-wallower nonetheless. As rendered in 1867's *Sut Lovingood: Yarns Spun by a "Nat'ral Born Durn'd Fool,"* the shit-strewn Lovingood homestead resembles the real-life rural dirt farm described earlier by Daniel Hundley—animals and excrement are everywhere. Baby machines Hoss and Mam Lovingood (who provided the literary sperm 'n' eggs for Pappy and Mammy Yokum, Ma and Pa Kettle, Snuffy and Loweezy Smith, the elder Clampetts, etc., etc.) blessed their baby Sut with a dozen-and-a-half brothers and sisters. All of them lived amid literal farm animals, primitive creatures stewing in their dirty country juices.

Sut realized he was an idiot—admitting his brains were "mos' ove the time onhook'd" [17]—but like the Three Stooges, he used his hoi polloi wiles to disrupt the hoity-toity's costume ball. Sut Lovingood, like Ransy Sniffle and Yellow-legs, was a shit-disturber. After all, these characters were only fictional marionettes who mirrored the prejudices and fears of their creators, all of whom looked down on them from some implied superior vantage point.

As a fictional stereotype, the poor white originally entered the national consciousness with a hillbilly clown puppet on one hand and a redneck villain puppet on the other, a cultural foreigner with a limited ability to achieve and a massive capacity to destroy. He walked a tightrope between amusing the audience and murdering it.

In the low-rent dinner theater that dances through our collective skulls, the redneck still plays two roles—laughable idiot and horrifying villain. This is analogous to the watermelon-slurping Sambo clown who might also slit your throat and rape your daughter one day. Laughing at a hillbilly is a way of wishing the hillbilly won't get the last laugh.

In the War Between the States, the South attempted to make itself into a foreign land. The North didn't permit the South to do so. The North won the war. Ever since then, the North has made the South into a foreign land.

Having conquered the region through force, having sliced off its economic *cojones* and eaten them for supper, the mouthpieces of Northern supremacy began concocting ways for the South to feel continually ashamed. Post–Civil War literary renderings of the ex-Confederacy, almost all of them issuing from Northern pulp houses, gave us the primitive South, the isolated South, the backward South, the devilish South, the benighted South, the horrible South, the lynch-rope South, the guilty, guilty South.

The major media have never been concentrated in places where cotton grows. The redneck ethos, by and large, has been propagated by those with an absentee ownership in rednecks' cultural heritage. In the 1850s, the South was said to house only a tenth of the nation's publishing companies;[18] as recently as 1981, the region was issuing a scant three percent of America's book titles.[19] After the Civil War, the old urban/rural, elite/poor axis was given the added dimension of North/South, which roughly translated into heaven/hell. Everything south of the Mason–Dixon Line became Lubberland.

In a vituperative 1917 New York *Evening Mail* essay called "The

Sahara of the Bozart," Maryland crank H. L. Mencken offered one of history's blackest jeremiads against Southern culture (or lack thereof). Mencken, that rare bird who managed to be both anti-Southern *and* anti-Semitic, at least begrudged the Jews some contributions to civilization; conversely, he found the South to be "almost as sterile, artistically, intellectually, [and] culturally, as the Sahara Desert." Mencken blamed the South's cultural poverty not on slavery, but on the poor white trash who, he alleges, rose to prominence after the Civil War wiped out the antebellum planter swashbucklers. Mencken was wrong —except for a few nicks and bruises, the Southern gentry had survived the Civil War relatively unhurt (if supplemented by a new class of invading Northern gentry). But by Mencken's time it had become customary to blame white trash for all the area's problems.

The Civil War created a new form of cultural apartheid, a new us/ them split that has persisted into modern times. According to a 1966 study by Norval Glenn and Leonard Broom, cultural differences between Southern whites and all other American whites were greater than the cultural divide between American whites and blacks overall.[20] The Yankees and rednecks are more different from each other than the honkies and niggers. Whereas antebellum comical character sketches had prepared the country to mock a social *type,* the Civil War had given America a whole fucking *place* to hate. The South has become America's cultural nigger rendered in geographical terms.

That which we fear most, saith the Mountain Man, is that which we don't know. The other. The outsider. The alien. The furriner. Appalachia is often viewed as the South in the extreme, a distilled South, what tar heroin is compared to a poppy-seed muffin. To the late-1800s travel writers who crept Dr. Livingstone–like into Appalachia hoping to harvest enough exotica to appease bored city reader-dweebs, the area appeared as a sealed-off cultural aquarium hosting prehistoric life-forms. One writer referred to the mountain folk as "our contemporary ancestors"[21]; another described hill culture as "caught like the shapes of lower life in stone."[22] William Wallace Harney stuck his nose into the Cumberland Mountains in 1869 and titled his subsequent essay "A Strange Land and Peculiar People."[23] The narrator of an 1878 fiction piece describes Virginia's Blue Ridge Mountains as host to "another world and another race of human beings." [24] A Chicago sociologist described the Southern mountains as "a retarded frontier." [25] To the urban invaders of Appalachia, these "contemporary ancestors" represented several uneasy contradictions—they were internal foreigners; cavemen in a modern world; trash surrounded by wealth; genetic defectives in a world teeming with equality. Perfect aliens. In 1913's *Our Southern Highlanders*, Horace Kephart wrote that Southern mountaineers had become "ghettoed in the midst of a civilization that is as aloof from them as if it existed on another planet." [26]

Even today, Northerners (meaning all non-Southerners, even Southerners who hate the idea of being Southerners) haven't rid themselves of the need to feel superior to "the South." And when they say "the South," they seem to mean only "poor Southern whites" and carefully sidestep a moral condemnation of any blacks or affluent whites who just may happen to live down there. A movie reviewer for *Time* magazine belittled the "Deep (read shallow) South." [27] In the *New York Post,* Murray Kempton bewailed "the imbecile optimism that is the curse of Georgians." [28] Headlines from the *San Jose Mercury-News* are condescending and cautionary: NASHVILLE WITHOUT ITS MAKEUP and HOW TO GROW UP SOUTHERN, IN SEVERAL UNEASY LESSONS. The *New York Times,* which in 1912 boasted a headline about "Ignorant Mountain Boys," [29] recently spoke of "fraternal backwoods idiots . . . with I.Q.'s well under 50." [30]

If one were to believe New York writers, the isle o' Manhattan is a crime-free lily pad of radiant social harmony, with all cultural evil quarantined out in the boondocks. In a 1994 *New York Times* op-ed piece called "The Hate Game," Bob Herbert snorts that when racist Southern demagogues spoke at rallies, "the crowds from the backwoods shacks and ramshackle farms would get so happy they could hardly contain themselves. They were better than somebody." [31] The point that is lost on Bob Herbert, and countless other urban supremacists like him, is that he obviously feels better than "the crowds from the backwoods." Everyone needs a nigger.

The way I look at it, anywhere more than fifty miles outside of New York and L.A. might as well be Texas. By class and attitudinal definitions, a redneck need not be from the South—the Nebraska corn-husker, the California desert rat, the Northwestern logger, and the Maine lobsterman all fit the type. But since mainstream America has designated the American South as the redneck homeland (even aliens need a place to sleep), a Southern accent often brands one a redneck whether one likes it or not. That's why would-be broadcasters from the South are required to take speech lessons to lose that foreign accent—our media moguls don't want anyone ever to fall under the impression that a Southern viewpoint is being represented. Dixie-hostile writers will often phoneticize Southern speech patterns when quoting some yokel they want you to perceive as ignorant—y'all knows whut ah'm talkin' 'bout—when to do the same with a black or Hispanic inflection would be considered an unbearable stereotype in these enlightened times.

But light implies darkness, and progressive souls seem to seek out their regressive counterparts. Southern historian C. Vann Woodward noted that the Northern nose-in-the-air attitude of immeasurable cultural superiority over Southerners is identical to the way in which Europeans deem themselves vastly more cultured than Americans.[32] In *Southern Folk, Plain & Fancy,* John Shelton Reed argues that Northern depictions of Southerners consistently take the shape of an "id stereo-type."[33] An id character's lack of self-control leads to sexual loose-ness, spendthrift carelessness, and inexplicable outbursts of sudden violence. That's why the id character, like the id itself, must constantly be kept in check by outside forces. Niggers were once id stereotypes in pop-culture representations. In response, American blacks have often come to perceive whites as *superego* stereotypes—cold, power-ful, arrogant, and prone to fibbing. Ironically, this is also the way that many Southern whites think of Northerners.

As America's id, Southern rednecks have been cast as the most primitive tribe on earth, the product of far more filth, stupidity, and bad genetics than any aborigine or Eskimo you'd care to name. The white-trash caveman is a hillbilly rendered as pale junglebunny, a club-swinger in place of a spearchucker. Why, the hookworms that invade his bloodstream through cuts in his bare feet are a higher life-form than the spermatozoa with which he impregnates his daughters.

Our hillbilly characters—even if books such as *The Bell Curve* offer contrary evidence—*have to be* the most mentally stunted clan on earth. They just *have* to be. The plot synopsis to "Hillbilly's Problem," an episode of TV show *Kids in the Hall,* demonstrates our need for a retarded redneck: "A hillbilly has some problems after his cow kicks him in the head." Our redneck stereotypes wander through life with their mouths hanging open, their eyeballs glazed over in a smacked-with-a-2-x-4 look of dissociative serenity. They come in two flavors: dumb and dumber, or, as was the eternal curse of Ernest P. Worrell's kin in *Ernest Scared Stupid,* they progressively grow "dumber and dumber and dumber" to the point where "if their IQs were any lower, they'd be houseplants."

Later in that movie, the camel-faced Ernest (the most visible modern-day descendant of Ransy Sniffle and Yellow-legs) bemoans the fact that his family comes from the "bottom of the gene pool." White-trash cretinism is a popular theme among outsiders and is usually blamed on the alleged "kissin' cousins" sexual perversity of rural folk. A late-1800s travel writer commented that mountain clans had "married back and forth and crossways and upside down till ev'ry man is his own grandmother." [34] To the mainstream observer, rednecks comprise less of a gene pool than a gene puddle. "You might be a redneck," ran one of Jeff Foxworthy's earliest redneck jokes, "if your family tree doesn't fork." And you can tell a Southern virgin, so the saying goes, when you see a girl who's running faster than her father and brothers. A 1936 scholarly paper titled "Mental Deficiency in a Closely Inbred Mountain Clan" demonstrates that degenerate bumpkin DNA was not merely a vein of humor, but also a school of serious research. [35]

After World War II and the cloud of ashes that Hitler left over Europe, the idea of eugenics—that human genes could dictate positive or negative traits—acquired a status akin to a forbidden religion. To aver that Asians or Jews might inherit intelligence, or that blacks and Hispanics might breed stupidity, has become a cultural mortal sin. There remains one lily-white exception to our eugenics-are-quackery folk religion, and that is the inbred hillbilly. Then, and only then, are the old moth-eaten, genetically deterministic theories dusted off and given new credence. With the hillbilly, eugenics magically become good science, not pseudoscience. One would never mention breeding as it applies to the situation of nonwhites—the fact that breeding is mentioned *at all* shows an attempt to ascribe alien ethnic status. His bloodline degenerated like the mangiest junkyard dog, his DNA a few rungs shy of a double helix, the inbred hillbilly serves a multicultural melting-pot society's need for an ethno-eugenic alien.

This isn't to suggest that I think there are no white-trash retards, or that stupidity can't be bred—what's important here is the self-styled sophisticate's *need* to see hillbillies as stupid. For all I can tell, literal degenerative inbreeding is possible among any race or class of people. But the fact that incestuous bloodlines exist hundreds or thousands of miles away should be of no immediate concern to an urbanite except as it serves a metaphorical need. The topic of inbreeding occurs with such frequency among white-trash stereotypes that its symbolic function begs analysis.

The clue may lay in the fact that early literary allusions to mountaineer inbreeding were also often accompanied by allegations that America's mountain folk, if comprising a regressive gene pool, at least possessed culturally clear waters. Most late-1800s ink-and-paper vultures who swooped down over the mountains made mention, somewhat jealously, that mountaineer life came closest to preserving old British folkways, that geographical isolation was a sort of cultural formaldehyde. Some even alleged that the trademark mountain drawl sounded more like English as the ancients spoke it than did the British accent of modern times.

The underside to deriding hillbillies for inbreeding may be a silent resentment that they had stubbornly OUTBRED, away from the stampeding urban juggernaut. The mainstream is itself an inbreeder, a powerful culturally homogenizing force that has rendered mall people in Massachusetts indistinguishable from mall people in California. The subtext to hillbilly inbreeding jokes is that hill people were too stupid to breed with the rest of us. Or, perhaps, they were simply a different species altogether and must be hated for it.

The irony is that history's most inbred clan has been the royalty, not the peasantry.

In another paradox, those who portray rural whites as biologically polluted also often depict them as morally pure. The disdain for hill-billy outbreeding often hides a wistful romantic attachment to a perceived mountain Valhalla, some clumsy conception of Paradise Lost. Most writers who muddy their ankles in white-trash degradation can't conceal their jealousy that the fictive Pygmalion aliens they've created display a stupidity that is so intense, it accidentally produces a primitive code of ethics. All too frequently to be coincidental, hillbilly jesters who are as stupid as the night is dark are also honest as the day is long. The city-dweller with a symbolic need to see the hillbilly as a de-brained clown constantly reassures himself that humans *gained* something when they left the hills and formed city-states, but he can't escape those nagging whispers that we also lost something in the civilizing process. He hears a faraway swamp frog croaking that "progress" may not always be headed in the right direction.

With urban royalists having cast the Southern white peasantry as "the other guy," they reaped literary gold by examining all the comic and tragic possibilities inherent in the city mouse/country mouse colli-sion. The literary, cinematic, and televised results never seemed to propose that these clashing cultures meet each other *halfway*. Instead, it was always phrased in terms of an invasion: "What would happen if we invaded the countryside?" or "What would happen if the country-side invaded us?" It was either the Douglases moving out to Green Acres or the Clampetts hauling ass into Beverly Hills.

When he was fifteen, a New England boy named Alfred Eugene Caplin invaded the South by hitchhiking his way down through the Kentucky hills. The strange breed of people there so impressed him that he started drawing cartoons of them while on his two-week trip. Ten or so years later, Caplin was living in New York, trying to establish a career as a cartoonist. Sometime in 1933 or 1934, while the country flailed desperately in the Depression's lowest pits, Caplin and his wife Catherine went to see a hillbilly revue at a Columbus Circle vaudeville joint. This type of hillbilly minstrel show was common at the time. Bands such as the Skillet Lickers and Seven Foot Dilly and His Dill Pickles played "hillbilly music" before it became known as country-and-western. They engaged in self-consciously bumpkinesque patter between songs and generally served the function of comical white niggers to amuse their cocktail-clinking urban audience. "They stood in a very wooden way with expressionless deadpan faces," explained Mrs. Caplin years later, "and talked in monotones, with Southern accents. We thought they were just hilarious." [36]

What was odd about such traveling white-nigger shows was that the clown hillbillies were usually played by *real* hillbillies who knew that their audiences would never accept them on their own terms. By playing up the clown angle, they self-consciously traded their humanity for the privilege of being embraced as cartoons.

Alfred Caplin had invaded the Kentucky hills, and in the form of a traveling bumpkin act, the Kentucky hills had invaded Alfred Caplin's Manhattan. As cartoonist Al Capp, he gave the world *Li'l Abner,* a global emblem of the cultural war between Dogpatch and Gotham.

Abner Yokum of Dogpatch, Kentucky, is described by a 1934 promo ad as "six feet three of hill-billy, who doesn't know what it's all about but who thinks it's a lot of fun, anyway." Slack-jawed and in tattered clothes, the early 1934–35 Abner plodded barefoot through Dogpatch's foreign hardscrabble, bragging that "Ah allus gits along wif other dumb animules." The animules in Dogpatch often take human form, and, like wild animules, they can be dangerous. Abijah Gooch is a real Piltdown man, and with his big nose and poor posture, he resembles Nazi hate cartoons of alleged Jewish defectives. And like degraded Jewish cartoons, the repellent Gooch wants the blonde—he's always on the verge of raping the busty-but-brainless Daisy Mae. The most frighteningly prehistoric character in Dogpatch is the ironically named Hairless Joe. Like a bald man named Curly or a fat man named Tiny, the joke about Hairless Joe is that he's a huge ogre who's almost completely *covered* with hair—his nose is the only part of his face not obscured by the hirsute blanket. He can count up to five, but that's about it. His stupidity is matched by his threatening size—Joe seems about twelve feet tall and carries a wooden club as big as most humans. A minor figure who lingers in the background of these early *Li'l Abner* strips, Joe reminds us that Dogpatch is a potentially dangerous place.

Most of the comedy from Capp's early panels came when Abner found himself trapped in Manhattan. Abner's New York aunt, the Duchess of Bopshire, had a dirty secret—she was really a Dogpatch girl named Bessy Hunks, a self-hating hillbilly who had fashioned herself into a phony city lady. The Duchess of Bopshire's cosmopolite friends sniffingly refer to her déclassé houseguest Abner as "mountain trash," a "big ape," and "that deliciously, divinely dumb, hill-billy!"

But idiot Abner is also an innocent, whereas the city slickers are either liars (like the Duchess) or financial swindlers (like all of her friends). Al Capp seems to suggest that while mountain life may have been laughably backward, city life might be despicably advanced.

The implications of this *pescado*-out-of-*agua* comic scenario were identically duplicated in TV's *The Beverly Hillbillies*. Whereas Abner had left Appalachia for New York, the Clampetts loaded their Ozark jalopy and ooh-doggied their way into Beverly Hills. And, like Abner, they meet dishonest city characters driven insane with the lust for moolah. Jethro Bodine, like Abner Yokum, may be a big magnolia stump of stupidity, but he's ethically purer than Mr. Drysdale. That's the essential hillbilly contradiction—ethically pure, if ethnically polluted.

The Beverly Hillbillies, of course, was not written by hillbillies. Most of the viewers who made it one of TV's highest-rated shows ever were probably not hillbillies, either. What's interesting is that most Americans were likely to take the hillbillies' side *against* the city creeps, even while perceiving the hillbillies as alien invaders. Although urban America allowed itself to criticize city values by wearing Granny Clampett's glasses, as it were, the fantasy only lasted half an hour— urban Americans may have wanted to learn something from hillbillies, but they certainly didn't want to *become* hillbillies. This is analogous to the white guy who collects blues records but doesn't want his daughter to marry a Negro.

The Beverly Hillbillies and other sixties yokel sitcoms signified "a broader pattern of cultural imperialism," according to writer David Whisnant.[37] In his book *Crackers,* Roy Blount, Jr., called the show "an atrocity that would never have been perpetrated as late as the sixties on any other ethnic group. Would you call a television program 'The Bel Air Bagel-Eaters'?"[38] No shit. Who would play Granny Clampett —Auntie Semitic?

The Gomer Pyles and Clem Kadiddlehoppers who brushed up against city sophistication were a staple of sixties television. Although always a primitive character, he is not always an innocent. Sometimes, he's merely a pest, someone who makes us feel glad to live in the city. When "two hillbillies from Kentucky" named Pop and Moose Mallory invade 1313 Mockingbird Lane on *The Munsters,* hollering things such as "hoo-wee!" and "land o' Goshen!" the appalled Munster family begins devising ways to evict their unwanted guests. When Moose drools, "I declare, you're purtier than a bucket full o' hog livers!" at Marilyn, her squirmy response makes it clear that she does not consider Moose a suitable breeding partner. Even though they come from a line of Draculas and Frankensteins, the Munsters are not nearly as way-out as the hillbillies. Likewise, when the Flintstones' Bedrock cottage is invaded by the pipe-puffing, musket-shooting, yee-hawing Hatrock (AKA Hatfield) clan, the Cro-Magnon Flintstones and Rubbles can't wait to get rid of these strange creatures who are more primitive than they are.

In a 1966 episode of TV's *Lost in Space* entitled "The Space Croppers," Dr. Smith gets entangled with a group of "space hillbillies" who grow plants that feed on human flesh. A recent independent comic book bore the title *Yuppies, Rednecks, & Lesbian Bitches on Mars.* In 1992, the Walt Disney Company was working on a cartoon project called *Silly Hillbillies on Mars.*

These fictional hillbilly invaders started cropping up during a period when literal hillbillies were invading American cities in large numbers. More than two million 'billies left the Southern hills from 1940 to 1970, squeezed out of the mountains by automation in the mining and timber industries. They were sucked into Rust Belt cities by the promise of assembly-line employment. In a similar pattern during the 1930s, nearly a half-million so-called Okies pulled up roots from the barren Dustbowl and headed for Cal-i-forn-eye-ay.

Article titles such as "The Hill-Billies Come to Detroit" (1935), "Down from the Hills and Into the Slums" (1956), "Hillbillies Invade Chicago" (1958), "Chicago's Hillbilly Ghetto" (1964), "Displaced Southerners Find Chicago an Impersonal Haven" (1964), and "Appalachia Transplanted" (1971) mildly suggest that the hillbillies were not always welcome.[39] Urban natives contemptuously called *all* white Southern migrants "hillbillies" whether they had come from the hills or not, and the word served as a put-down on both class and ethnic levels. Even though they were white, these hillbillies were treated as a distinct ethnic group, huddled together in "little Kentuckys" on the seedier side of town. Out west, these ghettos were called "little Oklahomas."

Urban whites reacted to invading hillbillies in a manner almost identical to the "there-goes-the-neighborhood" attitude stereotypically applied to new black neighbors. "Those places were ruining the neighborhood, running the property down," wailed a xenophobic Chicagoan regarding the hillbilly slums in the late 1940s.[40] "Those people are creating a terrible problem in our city," bitched an Indianapolis resident in the mid-1950s.[41] Even a Chicago municipal judge warned, "You'll never improve the neighborhood until you get rid of them."[42]

A Wayne University survey quizzed native Detroiters in 1951 about what sort of "undesirable people" they thought were "not good to have in the city." Respondents chose the group that researchers labeled "poor Southern whites, hillbillies" over "Negroes" by twenty-one to thirteen percent.[43] In "Hillbillies Invade Chicago," Albert Votaw repeats the sentiment that Southern migrants presented a worse "problem" than blacks:

> The City's toughest integration problem has nothing to do with Negroes. It involves a small army of . . . migrants from the South —who are usually poor, proud, primitive, and fast with a knife. . . . [Their] sex habits—with respect to . . . incest and statutory rape—are clearly at variance with urban legal requirements. . . . On the job they are said to lack ambition. . . .[44]

As with their earlier Lubber brethren, hillbilly poverty was blamed on their alleged laziness. But there's evidence that they were victims of both housing and job discrimination. One landlord boasted that he'd "rather rent to a Negro, a Mexican, or a Filipino than to a white person from the South."[45] A social worker explained that migrant hillbillies were "discriminated against because they are rural people whose ways and mannerisms seem foreign to an urban people."[46] In *White Southerners,* Lewis Killian cites a case where "in seven of fourteen industrial plants studied, officials stated openly that they would hire white Southern workers only when they could not get anybody else."[47] Killian also quotes an employer from the late 1940s:

> I told the guard at the plant gate to tell the hillbillies that there were no openings. The guards could tell which ones were from the South by their speech.[48]

The Kentucky hillbilly who eagerly boasted, "I'm a-goin' to Dee-troyt!" often found that Dee-troyt wished he'd stayed in Kentucky. And the Okie who'd hoped for better days out in California often found himself a despised outsider, too. According to author Henry Shapiro, hillbilly migrants who enter urban areas "become aliens in a strange land and among a peculiar people."[49]

With all these dad-gum *real* hillbillies invading the cities and driving property values down, the "Ma and Pa Kettle Go to the City" motif didn't seem nearly as funny anymore. One rarely sees this comic theme used these days. Likewise, travel writing and screenplays that in the past had an at-least-occasional tendency to portray rural areas as Edenic frolicking grounds were becoming more likely to portray a Savage South, a Heart of Darkness in which all human evil dwelt. This change occurred over the sixties and seventies when making fun of nigs became forbidden. Since the hate was no longer permitted to be spread around, America poured all of its hate and evil down the redneck's red throat.

Deliverance (1972) is roughly as kind to hillbillies as *Triumph of the Will* is to Jews. It's not the first of the hillbilly horror movies, merely the one that has . . . um . . . *penetrated* the national psyche most deeply. And when someone says *Deliverance*—soo-wee!—they usually only mean *that* scene, the one where the suspenders-wearing tumors-with-legs pump rancid gobs o' hillbilly cum up Ned Beatty's city-boy bumhole. The message that most Americans gleaned from *Deliverance* seems to be that wandering up into the hills is to risk a bloody anus. It's far better to stay in the city. In fact, the trouble didn't start until the city boys strayed from the river (the mainstream).

One might say that cinema has not been an effective proponent of backwoods tourism. Other hillbilly horror movies such as *Scum of the Earth, Moonshine Mountain,* and *God's Bloody Acre* reinforce the message that it's a BAD idea to wander too far off the beaten path. Typical of this genre is the *San Francisco Chronicle* description of a film in which "two prom-night couples get lost out on the highway where a creepy redneck named W.E. roams around in a satanic wrecker, collecting bodies and quoting literature and trapping teenage girls in gunny sacks." The script to *Pulp Fiction* provides for a scene at the Mason-Dixie [*sic*] Pawnshop, where "hillbilly psychopaths" rectally invade a black man behind closed doors while the audience hears sounds of "sodomy and the Judds."

The redneck villain, if he's unable to rape you, will murder you instead. Or he'll rape you and then murder you. Or murder you and then rape you. And then drive around for months with your body stuffed in his trunk. Excepting Klan movies and other such racial thrillers, rarely is there a *motive* behind redneck cinematic violence. In *Easy Rider,* when the intolerant Bubbas bludgeon Jack Nicholson to death and the evil cracker in the pickup truck blows away Dennis Hopper, the villains hardly even *say* anything. We're to assume they're just bred for violence. Just as the rapist rednecks in *Deliverance* suddenly rise from the bushes spittin' evil, no explanation (besides domicile) is given for their degeneracy. They are presumed to be creatures of instinct, swamp animals who bite if you come too close. Another breed entirely.

Could the boondocks possibly be as dangerous as they're making it appear? No. As woolly as it is, a supposed psycho hillbilly death-trap such as West Virginia has a lower violent-crime rates than the big cities where most movies are made. In fact, West Virginia has one of the lowest violent-crime rates (and highest firearms-ownership rates) in the country.[50]

But for many people predisposed to hate rednecks anyway, the threat of redneck rape and murder was taken literally, something beyond a mere cheeseball literary gimmick in which the nation examined its own anxieties. In a 1973 *Mademoiselle* article called "My Country Music Problem—And Yours," Richard Goldstein was certain he knew a villain when he saw one:

I can never encounter a white Southerner without feeling a murder-ousness pass between us. As though, whatever his personal instincts, his ethnic history predisposes him to regard castration and rape as his prerogatives.[51]

Goldstein might be troubled to learn that according to 1988 statistics from the FBI *Uniform Crime Reports,* over ninety-nine percent of interracial rape in America is black-on-white, but why let facts muddy an otherwise tidy morality play?[52] More than twenty years later, Goldstein was writing essays with titles such as "Whiny White Guys," still more hung up on white males than they were on him.

As cultural entities, rednecks have become more devalued than Confederate dollars after the Civil War. They are bargain-bin humans. Mind you, their devaluation *can't* have anything to do with money and the distribution of goods. It *can't* be related to the way in which the city always tends to rule the country. It can't *possibly* be in any way tied to the fact that the North has dominated the South since 1865. It has *nothing* to do with the fact that people—EVERYWHERE—tend to demonize outsiders. No, blame it all on the rednecks themselves. It doesn't matter if the plantation economy impoverished them—blame it on laziness. Who cares if none of them owned slaves—blame them for inventing racism. It isn't important if they suffer from poorer health care—blame it on inbreeding and bad grooming. And who told them to live up in the mountains, anyway? It's like Sam Kinison's joke during the Ethiopian famine (paraphrased): "Are you people crazy? You live in a desert! MOVE OUT!!!"

America has tended to cast all its sins into the backwoods. Blaming an innocent party for one's own indiscretions is a time-honored, divinely inspired tradition. The book of Leviticus offers handy instructions for the ancient scapegoating ritual, which traditionally came to be held on the Day of Atonement. Aaron, a swingin' biblical high priest, was commanded by Jehovah God to "lay both his hands upon the head of the live goat, and confess over him all the iniquities of the children of Israel. . . . And the goat shall bear upon him all their iniquities unto a land not inhabited; and he shall let go the goat in the wilderness." It was an odd ritual, a sort of inverse exorcism—the

99

priest didn't cast evil out of someone else's body, he cast it out of himself (and his people) and inserted that evil into the body of another living being, in this case a goat. The hillbilly, squeezed out into the thorny woods and blamed by urban ethnoimperialists for sins of a magnitude beyond his ability to engineer, serves all the functions of a modern American scapegoat. And in the hillbilly, we receive an extra added bonus—a scapegoat who also *fucks* goats.

America's hate affair with white trash is, ultimately, self-hatred. Guilt projection. A convenient way for America to demonize itself, or, rather, to exorcise the demon and place it somewhere outside of itself. In giving fangs to rednecks, Americans have defanged all the white-barbarian tendencies they fear within themselves.

To the white elite, white trash must seem like a disease in remission inside *all* whites, one that might flare up again given the right circumstances. When white blue bloods are repulsed by white trash, they are uncomfortably reminded both of what they used to be and what they may yet become. They may also quietly sense a bit of guilt for their role in the trashmaking process. Scoffing at rednecks often masks a "there but for the grace of God go I" uneasiness. It's like saying "I've come a long way, baby." While redneck-debasement is a way of claiming that one's shit don't stink, such verbal cologne hides the fear that one's shit might have stunk in the past or may yet raise a fulsome stench in the future.

Pointing an accusatory finger at the "*Deliverance* people" has become an easy way to express one's urbanity. But it also may be a way of expressing one's insecurities. Non-Southerners (and self-hating Southerners) have often alleged that the American South has a "rape complex," involving fears of a violent sexual uprising of hostile buck nigras, their ebony swords hoisted to slay lacy-white Southern belles. Oh, sure. Whatever suits your fantasies, pro or con. I think it's just as easy to argue that America, particularly in non-Southern areas, has a *Deliverance* complex. Urban America may subconsciously fear a mass invasion of stubble-chinned rural degenerates eager to settle the score.

Most of us have a redneck in the woodpile somewhere. One day the crackers may come home to roost. Howdy, Amurrika. Yoo sher dew have a purty mouth.

100

5

Workin' Hard

This morning, notwithstanding the rain, we were again at our work. We *must* work. In sunshine and rain, in warm and cold, in sickness and health, successful or not successful, early and late, it is work, *work,* WORK! *Work or perish!* All around us, above and below, on mountain side and stream, the rain falling fast upon them, are the miners at work—not for *gold,* but for *bread.* —Daniel B. Woods, *Sixteen Months at the Gold Diggings*

I thought of those who do the world's work, and are never paid enough, and never will be, and rise, and are beaten down, and always lose in the end. —Edward Abbey, *In Defense of the Redneck*

The working class doesn't write a lot of history books. The working class doesn't produce many movies or radio shows. The working class doesn't tend to hire media consultants or theatrical agents. The working class has played an itty-bitty role in fashioning its popular image.

That's because the working class was too busy working.

The working class has plenty of reasons to be angry. Unfortunately, only the working class realizes it.

Riddle me this, Candy Pants—what portion of lowbrow white rage has NOTHING to do with nigger hatred and instead bubbles up from the accumulated traumas of being a historically shit-upon laboring class? Is it thinkable that these so-called Angry White Males may be more furious with their white bosses than with their black coworkers?

What degree of their white-knuckled hatred might conceivably arise from generations of being annihilated on the front lines of war, shot down by company police, and chewed up like sausage by industrial accidents? Might redneck hostility be explicable not through bigotry, but from hundreds of years of sinking slowly into a demoralizing turd-heap of debt, overwork, and broken promises?

If someone were to devise a machine that could measure hatred—a Hatenometer®—I'd bet all my wooden nickels that more hatred exists between bosses and employees than between blacks and whites. More psychological S&M, more of man's inhumanity to man, probably occurs at the workplace than anywhere else. Wider than the chasm between vanilla and chocolate, even thicker than the wall between North and South, is the rift between boss and employee.

A kindergarten fable called the American Dream—that tooth-fairy promise of an overflowing cookie jar free to any kid who'd merely stretch hard enough to reach it—has kept most Americans in amnesiac denial of our rigid class barriers. A select few have never *needed* to dream, while the majority have been rewarded with nothing *but* dreams. The idea that America fools itself about being a classless society has been voiced so often, it's a cliché. But it's a cliché that keeps slipping our mind.

While today's young'uns are bound to know a lot about racism, they probably couldn't tell you a thing about American labor history. And it's too bad, because they're being fattened for slaughter just like their ancestors were. Ever notice that the white working class really isn't much of a cinematic theme anymore? It's all race, no class. You'll see plenty of *To Kill a Mockingbird*s, but fewer and fewer *On the Waterfront*s. We continue to flog ourselves over cowboys and Injuns, but we feel no guilt over what railroad companies did to rail workers. A second won't pass when someone doesn't reloop film reels of white cops clubbing black guys, but you'll never see footage of Pinkerton guards machine-gunning coal miners.

The hugest story in America isn't racism, it's downsizing. But the major media pip-squeaks emit nary a chirp about our widening economic apartheid. Most corpo-media bootlickers, whether flavored "establishment" or "alternative," seem vastly removed from the average white douchebag worker's experience. Their stock in trade is either status quo ass-kissing or shameless slumming—establishment reporters praise greedy yuppie sharks, while alternative writers tearfully lionize crack whores. If you aren't a white millionaire or a black derelict, no one wants to know you. It's noteworthy that both types of writer—establishment apologists and alternative excuse-makers—are typically drawn from Whiteydom's middle and upper classes. Working-class white knuckleheads can rarely afford the time and grueling rejection required to develop a writing career. So it's understandable that the preps and trust-fund brats would get the working-class story all wrong. Understandable, if unforgivable.

Of all the hating I've done in my life—and I've done my share—ninety-nine percent of it was directed at rich white people, most of them my bosses. And if it wasn't a boss, it was some media pole-stroker who'd cluck disapprovingly at me just like the boss did. GGRRR, I remember how they'd blame me. I would awake, drag my sagging hog-tush into work, shackle down for eight to ten hours of abuse, clock out, scoot home, crash in front of the TV, and flick through the channels to find each announcer cursing me—an EVIL WHITE MALE—for causing all the world's suffering. It didn't seem to matter that in my entire life, I hadn't made a single decision that had affected anyone else. Not ONE. I had been born into a class where I was on the RECEIVING end of decisions. I flippin' had no CONTROL over anyone else's life, and mastery of my *own* was compromised by the need to work a full-time job. Hell, I couldn't oppress anyone even if I WANTED to. As a friend recently put it, "If I have so much power, why the fuck do I have so much trouble making rent every month? If the black man is under my thumb, why can't I get him to do my dishes?"

Skin privilege is largely a myth peddled by those who are made uncomfortable by the idea of class privilege. It ain't about skin, it's about class. It ain't epidermal, it's hierarchical. Sociologist Max Weber once defined "class" as "chances on the market." [1] Almost everyone except politicians and rich schmucks realizes that we don't all hurtle out of the bleeding womb with an equal chance. Not everyone is born with an equal chance to avoid dehumanizing labor. Not everyone is equally likely to dodge military service. We aren't all born into neighborhoods equally free from crime. Not everyone has an equal shot at going to college. We can't all expect to face equal occupational and environmental hazards. Not everyone inherits equal amounts of land or money from his or her parents.

In the neighborhood of my tarnished younger days, I knew plenty of brilliant sunzabitches who are now homeless and/or alcoholic merely because they weren't given much leeway to fuck up. And as a worker, I was forced to bow to an endless caravan of luminously STUPID people whose only bragging right was that Mumsy and Daddikins had showered them in green.

The sheltered, pampered, weakened, atrophied, protected kids who never HAD to work hard to survive won't have the remotest clue what I'm blathering about. To them, working-class anger always seems dumb, violent, and—beyond all else—groundless. The kids who perch mosquitolike atop their parents' wealth, the "nice" kids with nice teeth from the nice side of town, have no solid explanation for white trash's existence beyond the purely behavioral. They just shake their heads until dandruff flakes flutter gently to the marble floor, wondering how anyone could ACT that way. They seem to think that if rednecks just showered, dressed nice, and kept their noses to the grindstone for a few weeks, they'd all blossom into investment bankers.

Some nincompoops think that if racism disappeared, injustice would, too. They appear to believe that the underclass would vanish if people stopped discriminating on the basis of race or gender. As with all wishful thinkers, they're tragically wrong. Getting rid of discrimination won't eliminate unemployment. It won't dismantle the class system. It won't wipe away the line between those who sweat and those who don't. Quite simply—too simple for the simpletons to get it—social equality is impossible in a world composed of bosses and workers.

People who twiddle their scrotums and labia into pretzel shapes getting upset over the mildest racial slur aren't nearly so bothered by obscenities such as "war stimulates the economy" or "the poor you shall always have with you." Those dictums are never questioned. But that sort of thinking—properly called Economic Supremacy, since it esteems money over human lives—has killed more people, black and white, than racism ever has.

It's been said that racism is America's dirtiest little secret. If so, America's a big blabbermouth who can't keep a secret very well. Sorry to bum your high, but I think someone let the Klan out of the bag a long time ago.

Classism, however, remains a largely unscratched pimple on our nation's swinish ass. If every American thought about class instead of race for only five minutes a day, some revolutionary things might happen. And by "thinking" about class, I don't mean in a detached, role-playing, Marxist Trivial Pursuit sort of way—I mean seriously pondering the degree to which inherited economic status affects actual human lives. This obsessive focus on rednecks vs. niggers—far out of proportion to any demonstrable racial unrest—successfully obscures the possibility of what might happen if everyone phrased things in terms of workers vs. bosses.

Redneck psychology is best understood by exploring labor history, not racial theory. Amid all the cream-puff rhetoric about racial equality, we've entirely lost sight of economic equality. TV talking heads keep yippie-yi-yo-ing about racial injustice, but the fact that there are rich people and poor people is accepted without question. While all the "white" and "colored" drinking fountains may have been removed, there remain thousands of restaurants and nightclubs and golf courses and gated neighborhoods where working-class chumps of *any* color wouldn't be welcome. As things stand, it's blasphemous to exclude someone from your neighborhood based on any color but green.

Today, the person who proposes economic equality is held to be as nutty as someone who believes in racial *in*equality. It's swallowed as an article of faith that we just couldn't survive without bosses and workers, without investors and the vast bloc of human capital in which they invest. We can imagine a world without Nazis, but not a world without bosses.

"Free labor" is an oxymoron, and only morons believe it can exist. It is impossible simultaneously to labor for someone else and be free. Most people are free to make only one choice in life: work or starve.

The rest is up to the boss. Look at any of the hundred million frowning faces on their way to work every morning, set free in a world where everything carries a price tag. If wage labor was actually a free contract between equals, it should be equally easy to switch between roles of boss and worker during one's lifetime, shouldn't it? And it would stand to reason that both boss and worker profit equally from the worker's labor.

Work is for slaves. As much as we'd like to pretend that wage labor is somehow slavery's opposite, it is merely an ingenious mutation. Karl Marx, that pickle-faced commie bastard, didn't seem to think that wage labor represented much of an improvement over bound slavery.[2] And Marx's ideological nemeses over at the Bank of England agreed that wage labor enriched the already wealthy. In an 1862 letter sent to his American investor chums, a Bank of England representative named Mr. Hazard hungrily rubbed his roach antennae at the prospect of an emancipated South:

> Slavery is likely to be abolished by the war power, and chattel slavery abolished. This I and my European banker friends are in favor of, for slavery is but the owning of labor, and carries with it the care of the laborers, while the European plan, led by England, is that capital shall control labor by controlling wages. . . .[3]

While New England abolitionists were popping blood vessels cater-wauling about the horrid South and its cruel slavery system, two of every five factory workers in their own backyard were white children under sixteen years old—some as young as seven—who often worked longer hours than Southern slaves.[4] Just like the hundreds of thousands of European child laborers who were seized, drugged, beaten, and worked to death throughout the 1800s, American kiddie slaves worked insane hours in dark, airless rooms, losing their limbs and lives under the cruel gaze of sadistic adults. Although the black slaves were alleg-edly freed in 1863, children of all races labored under the factory lash until the early 1900s. All of these kids, mind you, were free laborers.

Free, too, were the millions of former Southern slaves whose emancipation only returned them to the plantation as sharecroppers and tenant farmers. Cynical about the dirt which settled after Reconstruction's dust storm, the writer for one black newspaper said that the Civil War seemed a better deal for Northern investors than Southern blacks: "The slaves were made serfs and chained to the soil. . . . Such was the boasted freedom acquired by the colored man at the hands of the Yankees."[5]

The Southern crop-lien system earned high marks in the Shitwork Derby. The creeping centralization of Southern farming, financed mostly by nonfarmers who had never lived on a farm nor picked a ball of cotton, fenced off much of the public-domain land upon which countless white independent farmers had survived. Although nominally free to compete on the market, the yeoman farmer was consistently undercut by the huge landowners who hired mammoth armies of worker spuds. Like the majority of small businessmen today, the self-sustaining farmer was kicked out of the game by the Big Mules, and most small players slid down onto the dunghill of sharecropping and farm tenancy. Both ex-slaves and white ex-farmers were squashed down into this class. By the early 1900s, even Northern farmers were working longer hours than slaves had in the antebellum South.[6]

If it was true that the owner of the giant Southern sharecropping plantation didn't own his workers' bodies for life, it was also a fact that he didn't have to feed or house those bodies for life, either. He could always hire new bodies. Workers who complained were immediately cut off from credit and evicted from the farm, becoming "no-account trash" in a shattered economy where a credit account was necessary to survive. Those who wanted to remain on the farm were forced to prostrate themselves before the Big Bosses. The Southern tenant farmer (who differed from the sharecropper in that he owned some tools) was said to be a free laborer. But he had no control over the credit system, no control over bookkeeping, no control over crop sales, no control over market swings, no control over prices at the Boss Man's local store, and no control over the riding bosses who were hired to beat him if he seemed to be getting lazy. "To call these people a peasantry is to upgrade them," claims historian David E. Conrad, "for, unlike the peasants of medieval Europe, they had no guarantees to the land and no rights that the landlord or the government was bound to observe."[7]

Tenant families, mostly illiterate and unaware of the swindle to which they were being subjected, found themselves packed into matchbox shacks without electricity or running water. As late as 1935, fewer than one in twenty-five Southern farms was wired for light bulbs.[8] Of the millions of Southern tenant families, perhaps two of three were white, with the sharecropper ranks split almost evenly along the color line.[9] Sweltering through summer and shivering through winter without so much as an outhouse in which to take a private dump, tenant families dutifully heeded the morning bell that summoned them to WORK. Throughout the year they'd wrestle with fickle weather, dead soil, ravenous hordes of bugs, malnutrition, and debilitating disease. But the worst insult was usually reserved for the year's end, when it came time to settle accounts. For all his sweat, calluses, sore muscles, and withered skin, the Southern farm tenant most often received absolutely ZERO yearly income and instead found himself indebted to the Boss Man. Rather than being an aberration, a negative yearly income was the rule. Further credit would be eagerly extended, and the ditch would be deepened until it was impossible to claw upward and escape. As a white tenant woman put it, "Them that has can always fix it so the po' won't even have a chance to make anything."[10] Some bosses benevolently explained that debt-slavery actually benefited Southern farmers, for debt guaranteed that lazy niggers and poor white trash would keep working hard.

Even with the most fertile of harvests and the rosiest prices, a crop slave might be lucky to clear a couple hundred dollars TOP for a year's work. But as prices plummeted in the 1920s, he might only be able to afford a new suit in exchange for another year of soul-bludgeoning labor. By the 1930s, the nation faced the ironic specter of farmers who were starving to death. Government "aid" programs such as the Agricultural Adjustment Act of 1933 funneled funds directly to those who owned the land rather than those who worked upon it. Landowners thus consolidated their command of larger, increasingly automated farms. Aping the British enclosure movement of a few centuries prior, they cast hundreds of thousands of farmers off land that their families had worked for generations. Bulldozers easily crushed their abandoned shacks. As brutally thankless as sharecropping had been, it wasn't even an option anymore.

The farmer continues to be enclosed. In 1950, ten million Americans plowed dirt for a living. In 1980, it was fewer than four million. In 1990, around two million. And probably at least half a million of those are gone by now. I doubt any nonfarmer can appreciate the degree to which the American farmer has been fucked. As someone who's never planted so much as a grass seedling, I won't pretend I know what it's like to have a creditor come and snatch my land away because the boll weevil killed most of this year's crops. I'll just respectfully state that farmers, whether white, black, or brown, have been one of the most consistently abused and undervalued groups in our history. While comical rural bumpkins leap from your TV screen every minute, you won't see many tragic farmers in prime time. Perhaps many of the TV stations are owned by the same guys who now own the farms.

Likewise, the homicidal Hatfields and McCoys are deeply encrusted in our pop-cult legendry, while the savagery visited upon Appalachia by coal and timber companies during the same era is mostly unknown. As railroads began slithering up into the Appalachian woods in the late 1800s, capital-rich boys from the East realized that the mountains' largely untapped natural resources were a cash register waiting to be looted. As soon as they stepped off the train, they began snorting up as much land as they could. Fraudulent contract bargaining was rampant between well-trained company smoothies and unsuspecting mountaineers, only a quarter of whom knew how to sign their names. By scratching an X on the dotted line, many hillfolk unwittingly surrendered all the mineral wealth beneath their topsoil to corporate raiders. They'd wake up one morning to find earth-moving machinery digging in their front yard.

Mountain life, still smarting from anarchic post–Civil War guerrilla ransacking, was further dislocated by the outsiders' voracious land-gobbling. The West Virginia Tax Commission prophesied in 1884 that if trends continued, the state would soon "pass into the hands of persons who do not live here and care nothing for our State except to pocket the treasures which lie buried in our hills. . . ." The commission predicted that once absentee entrepreneurs had sucked the region dry of its wood and coal, the local population would become "poor, helpless, and destitute." [11] Been to West Virginia lately?

Most scalawaggy cheerleaders of the "New South" and their media Howdy Doodys did not share the tax commission's concern and instead sided with the company boys over the local yokels. Kentucky and West Virginia's upper classes stood to profit more from the conquering robber barons than from the indigenous corn-crackers. That's why the gentry-owned regional newspapers kept silent while the coal companies were killing more people than all the mountain feudists combined.

It's no coincidence that sensationalized news accounts of feuding mountain cannibals cropped up while mountaineers were being widely defrauded of their land. The golden age of family feuding lasted roughly from 1875 to 1915; during the same span, ownership of Appalachia switched almost entirely from local hands into the mitts of outsiders. And to the moneyed interests who spoke through the newspapers, the lanky, violent mountaineers were blocking the path of progress. An excuse was needed to knock them out of the way, and this was found in the time-tested Barbarian Smear. To excuse what amounted to economic rape, it had to be argued that the hillbillies had asked for it. And so the mountaineers were portrayed much as the Indians had been before them—as volatile primitives who had lost their rights to land stewardship by dint of their prehistoric laziness.

In order to feel better about robbing the hill people, it was thought necessary first to dehumanize them. On February 12, 1888, the *Louisville Courier-Journal* decried the "white savages" of the hills and their "inhuman tortures." [12] Six days later, the *New York Times* noted that "the purely savage character of the population" might necessitate the imposition of some "civilizing influences" to uplift and modernize these "simple children of nature." [13] Trying to paint a cheerier color on events, local promoter J. Stoddard Johnston explained that hillbillies were not to be blamed if they acted like screeching wildebeests—they simply suffered from a lack of wage labor. But Johnston said not to fret, because "help has come to these marooned people" in the form of industrial-strength messiahs. [14]

The newspapers didn't seem nearly so concerned that mountaineers were sprinkling each other with buckshot as they were worried that stories might leak out of Appalachia and discourage investors from sprinkling a li'l sugar their way. "Capitalists," lamented the *Wheeling Intelligencer,* "refuse to come and prospect because they say they are afraid of our outlaws. You cannot get them to go into the interior to inspect our timber and coal lands for fear that they will be ambushed." [15] While the clanging echo of mountain blunderbusses may have scared away a yellow-bellied city sapsucker or two, this was not true overall—capitalists were snappin' up land as quickly as they could draw up phony contracts. In truth, the mountaineers would have more to fear from the capitalists than vice versa.

Even though fewer than one percent of the mountain folk ever became embroiled in the feuds, the ol' Barbarian Smear pretty much stuck to all of them. And though over a hundred people died in the history of mountain feuding, more than that would be slaughtered in a single coal-mine explosion.

Boom! Three hundred sixty-one blasted to death in Monongah, West Virginia, in 1907. POW! One hundred eighty-three exploding bodies in Eccles, West Virginia, seven years later. *Crunch!* One hundred twelve West Virginia miners killed in one shot at Layland in 1915. BAM! One hundred nineteen slaughtered in Benwood, West Virginia, in 1924. Even though World War I left ten million corpses in its wake, American soldiers were statistically safer on Europe's battlefields than coal miners were in West Virginia during the same period.[16] Appalachian miners had the industrial world's steepest death rate. Bodies were being hauled out of the mines with the same casual indifference as if they were lumps of coal, only the coal was worth more.

So many dead flies along the windowsill. Shove another body under the pile driver and watch it get crushed. Mounds of dead workers. Their blood soaks through work shirts into the soil, fertilizing the economy. They enter the fun house young and healthy; they are shit out the other end hobbled, deformed, and cancer-stained. All those eviscerated coal-miner corpses were nothing unique to the world of free labor. The crude machinery of the old British workhouses had always served as accidental torture racks, shredding the fingers and limbs of adults or children so deadly tired they didn't realize they were leaning too close into the churning metal. American railroad workers dropped dead at the clip of around two thousand yearly throughout the 1890s. Another two hundred thousand rail workers were maimed and injured during that decade.[17] In the year 1914 alone, an estimated thirty-five thousand Americans lost their lives while working.[18] Throughout the 1920s, roughly a quarter-million Americans were killed on the job, and an additional million were crippled for life.[19] During the Vietnam War, there wasn't one year in which soldiers' casualties outnumbered those killed in American workplaces.[20] And that statistic only counts death by accident, not all the fatal work-related illnesses such as black lung, blood poisoning, nerve damage, and any one of countless types of cancer. Even in the brotherly 1990s, the American workplace murders around fourteen thousand bodies yearly, not counting deaths linked to work-related illnesses.[21] Long-haul truckers, those archetypal redneck workers, wind up as roadkill every year. In 1992, six hundred one trucker deaths were traced directly to falling asleep from overwork.[22]

My Uncle Arnie died of heat exhaustion while working under a Texas oil rig. There are also rumors—difficult to confirm since the raging lush abandoned the family—that my paternal grandfather died of multiple injuries sustained in a rock-quarry accident. There's reason to suspect that the cancer which snuffed out my father at age fifty-nine was related to all the toxins he breathed and bled as a plumber and oil-refinery worker. Who knows how many of my American ancestors, in the spermy string that runs from the original indentured servants and convicts all the way to me, were eaten alive by the machine?

The coal companies of eastern Kentucky and West Virginia had a traditional method of dealing with workers who had been disfigured, blinded, or crippled in mining accidents. It was called eviction. After going through the soul-cauterizing pain of becoming disabled, the miner was then sternly ordered to vacate the premises along with his family, unceremoniously cut loose from his lifeblood and unlikely ever to find work again. His house would soon be filled by another family, this one headed by a man whose able body could chip away at hard rock day and night.

But even those who escaped accidental death and dismemberment weren't likely to fulfill their dreams in an Appalachian coal town. As with the sharecropping plantations further south, company bosses controlled every square of the playing board. They handpicked the figureheads of local government and law enforcement. They owned the town's housing, schools, churches, stores, gas stations, movie theaters, and hospitals. Although the miners were paid wages, almost all of their pay went back to the company in the form of rents, utilities, tools, and groceries. Workers were often paid entirely in scrip coins, chintzy brass and aluminum tokens redeemable only at the company commissary. But because of superinflated prices at these "robbissaries," one-dollar scrip coins were only worth around sixty cents. While the bosses were making back their entire mining investment through the collection of workers' rents alone—not counting a penny of the money they made selling coal—the ordinary miner always wound up owing his soul to the company store. Although bosses and workers were theoretical equals, all money stayed on one side while all the work was reserved for the other.

When the coal industry was thrown into chaos by crises of price and production, it was doubtless the fault of the Boss Man's lousy management. The miner was too busy mining to affect corporate planning. But it was the miner, not the boss, who would be forced to suffer. Coal-industry downsizing meant that fewer miners would be working longer hours for smaller wages. There would also be fewer paid supervisors and engineers, so deaths and crippling injuries would NOT be downsized. After twelve hours of crouching in near-absolute darkness, inhaling coal dust and monotonously pecking at rocks, a miner was fortunate to afford a tiny sack of flour with which to feed his family. But more and more, even that nightmare scenario was withdrawn as a choice because available work hours were drying up throughout coal country.

Those who complained about the new conditions were handed pink slips. Those who tried to unionize and counter the bosses' power were attacked by hired armies of club-swinging company police who left miners crawling on the ground, bleeding from cracked-open skulls. Although the coal companies were downsizing, they had enough money to hire armed guards and private detectives and masked goons to smash the fledgling unions through terrorist violence. Execution-style slayings of union organizers were common. And beyond these privately owned militias, the Big Bosses had enough political sway to call in the state militia or National Guard when it appeared that the miners weren't being beaten down easily enough.

The majority of the nineteen miners killed by company police in Pennsylvania's Lattimer Massacre of 1897 had been shot in the back. So had all ten strikers murdered by police during Chicago's 1937 Republic Steel Strike. The names given to some of the era's company/union clashes—"Bloody Harlan," "Bloody Mingo," and "The Matewan Massacre"—show that it was a thunderously violent period. Typical of the antiunion hatred endemic to police was the late-1930s boast of Dadeville, Alabama, Sheriff Cliff Corprew to striking workers: "We're going to use machine guns and we're going to mow every God damn one of you down." [23]

Machine guns—specifically, Gatling guns—were what the Baldwin-Felts Detective Agency fired on striking miners during 1914's Ludlow Massacre in southern Colorado. Sixty-six people were murdered by Rockefeller-hired police. Eleven of the victims were women and children who had been burned into human toast when guards set fire to the strikers' tent camp. Megakaskrillionaire John Davison Rockefeller, concerned that his public image had been damaged, posed for several photographs of himself giving dimes to needy children.

Although labor vs. management had all the trappings of a war, the casualties were grossly lopsided. In the history of Southern labor violence, not one employer was ever killed.

Force, of course, has always been used by bosses to maintain power over workers. But force is so immediately ugly, such a clear display of the master/slave principle, that it often provokes an equally violent defensive reaction. Subtler methods of worker control have proved more effective.

Immigration has historically been one of these methods. I realize that in the premillennial case of sniffles that afflicts American society, anyone who questions our spread-eagle immigration policy is automatically tagged as a racist. The "give me your tired, your poor..."

mantra from the plaque at the Statue of Liberty's base is quickly trotted out to shame those who'd dare assail the wisdom of our open-door policy. This, however, ignores two very damning facts. First, that hokey plaque wasn't attached to Lady Liberty's toes until several years *after* massive immigration through Ellis Island had been curtailed by law. Second, a large proportion of those immigrant masses, huddled though they were, had been shipped in by company bosses to serve as strikebreakers and wage deflaters. A point that's often lost is that Ellis Island flourished concurrently with tremendous levels of labor violence. If anti-immigration sentiments were strictly racist, black leaders such as Frederick Douglass and W.E.B. Du Bois wouldn't have pleaded with capitalist management to stanch the flow of European immigrants and give the jobs to native-born blacks instead. And if all the anti-immigration forces today were merely redneck bigots, opinion polls wouldn't show native-born blacks and Hispanics consistently outscoring whites in their resistance to further immigration.[24] The working class, regardless of color, knows keenly that we aren't suffering from a labor shortage. Look at how the special-interest groups skew on the topic, and a clearer picture might emerge: Monstro-corporations are funding pro-immigration causes, while labor unions and workers' organizations oppose them.

Polls repeatedly demonstrate that three of every four Americans disapprove of further immigration.[25] Ignoring the public's wishes, George Bush in 1990 conjured an imaginary "labor shortage" and pushed through legislation that cracked open the floodgates a further forty percent. More immigrants have entered this country legally over the past ten years than in Ellis Island's heyday.[26] This doesn't count an estimated five million immigrants who slipped through the turnstiles illegally. This all happened while labor unions were being dismantled, employment benefits eliminated, wages deflated, and full-time job security vanished.

I want to make it clear that I'm objecting to corporate policies and am not placing a molecule of blame on the immigrants. Yes, Gandhi, I realize that most of them were downtrodden peasants in their countries of origin. Sure, Mother Teresa, our nation was founded on the violent theft of land, but so was every other fucking nation on earth. But with only five percent of the world's population, is there some reason beyond drippy universal brotherhood that we're still receiving more immigrants than the rest of the world combined? Is it possible that behind all these multicolored balloons and heartwarming interracial photo-op handshakes lies the desire for a surplus pool of tractable laborers? At what point does "give me your tired, your poor . . ." translate into "keep us supplied with cheap labor"? When do we start feeding the ones already at the table instead of adding more dinner plates?

In the Appalachian coal towns, mass importations of foreign-born scab workers helped pulverize the local unions' solidarity. Automation finished the job. Just as farm technology had rendered millions of sharecroppers homeless, the mechanization of coal-digging impoverished the Appalachian plateau. In the 1950s alone, the region lost a quarter-million jobs. Unemployment, poverty, and hunger levels are now among the nation's highest. The forests are gone. Most of the mines are abandoned slagheaps. Air, water, and land are poisoned by leaking sulfur. Used refrigerators, cars, and other dead machines litter the once-green hills. Kids play on junk piles, gnats zipping around their heads and little purple spikes where their teeth have rotted away. Appalachia is a White Third World, a giant chancre sore on the nation's smiling mouth. It's the planet's biggest ghost town. Although coal companies still make a profit there, they do it with machines rather than men.

All in all, it appears that the Hatfields and McCoys were better off than their descendants. I have a friend who lives in Pike County, Kentucky, home of the McCoys. Ain't much to do there these days. The only job he could find was in the Army. And so he joined.

No matter how bad the economy is, the Army always seems to have room for one more. I find it just the eentsiest bit peculiar that our country has never been invaded (except when we invaded it), yet millions of Americans have eaten bullets and shrapnel and bombs in the name of such vagaries as "vital interests" and "national security." Invariably, these vital interests tend to be things such as oil and minerals rather than the live bodies of young soldiers. Even though the war-pushers might scream from pulpits about things such as God or nation or democracy or protecting our women, there's always some filthy, doity money at stake when nations go to war. All wars are trade wars. Of that you can be sure. Ideological excuses may be foisted upon the unsuspecting to persuade them to offer their lives, but that's a cruel joke of the deadliest sort. If Saddam Hussein had been dictator of a country somewhere in central Africa where there was no oil, we wouldn't have given a fuck how much he acted like Hitler.

It may seem strange suddenly to start bellyaching about war in the midst of a chapter about bosses and workers, but give me a minute to explain, you antsy bastard. The relationship between those who *orchestrate* wars and those who *fight* in them directly parallels the model of those who *finance* the economy and those who *work* in it. Throughout history, wealthier chaps have viewed the soldier's life as nigger work. Poor farmers and ex-servants fought the Revolutionary War without being paid, while the moneyed boys avoided service with a payment of five pounds' sterling.[27]

Racial reductivists fibrillate their uvulas about how our nation's wealth was built on cotton-pickin' black slavery, but it's probably safer to allege that more blood money was made on war than anything else. It's popular wisdom that war stimulates the economy. Ships must be launched. Guns must be manufactured. Uniforms must be sewn. Coffins must be built. "War is a racket," bewailed ex-Marine General Smedley D. Butler in 1935, sick of the whole business: "It is the only one in which the profits are reckoned in dollars and the losses in lives."[28] It should be added that those who risk their dollars are rarely those who risk their lives. And those soldiers who aren't peeled to shreds on the battlefield return home to face a skyscraping tax debt and unending labor. In essence, they are forced to pay—with interest—for the "privilege" of having nearly been murdered. Men who had sloshed around in the blood-filled trenches of World War I, that "War to End All Wars," didn't have to wait long until the Great Depression hit. And if you still think that racism has harmed more people than war, chew on this—more black Americans died in Vietnam than were ever lynched in America.[29]

Four of every five soldiers sent to Vietnam had been poor or working-class kids back home.[30] The white-collar crowd, on the other hand, was underrepresented by half. White collars got deferments; blue collars got drafted. The working class learned to hate the war by wading through jungles and rice paddies; the upper classes learned to hate the war while sitting in Political Science 101. Vietnam really took an ax to white American class relations, leaving an even deeper divot than had previously scarred the body politic. The media—and I remember this as a kid—cast the domestic battle as one between pro-war, working-class "hard hats" versus peace-loving hippies. The surprising truth, if opinion polls are to be trusted, was that working-class America opposed the war more strongly than did the middle- and upper-class families whose kids were likely to be acid-dropping, free-loving hippies.[31] After all, it was the sons of the working class who were dying in Vietnam. The point lost on the upper classes was that you needed LEISURE TIME to drop acid and attend love-ins.

Both the hard hats and hippies hated the war, but for different reasons. The hard hats worried about their brothers and sons, while the hippies worried about the Vietnamese. And the hippies, protected brine shrimp that they were, had sometimes been more likely to curse the working-class stooge who couldn't avoid the draft than to blame the rich politician who drafted him. So the cultural war between hard hats and hippies was real, but it had more to do with class antipathy than with the government's war policies. The hippies were right that the hard hats were fighting an unjust and unnecessary war, but they were wrong in thinking the hard hats had much choice in the matter. And the hard hats were right that the hippies were hip-o-critical in passing judgment about a war they had the luxury to avoid.

The 58,191 Americans who died in Vietnam were "rewarded" with a shiny black wall in Washington, D.C. The hundred and fifty thousand or so who suffered nonfatal wounds and the half-million or more who would be tortured by posttraumatic stress disorder were rewarded with very little indeed. It has been estimated that more ex-soldiers killed themselves after returning from Vietnam than had been killed in Vietnam itself. But the USA gets rid of guilt the old-fashioned way: We make movies about it.

Our military safari to Vietnam ended in 1975, two years after American workers' wages reached their all-time high watermark. They haven't stopped declining since. In constant 1973 dollars, average in-

118

come has slumped more than ten percent, while per-capita productivity shot up nearly thirty percent. Workers have been producing more and getting paid less for it. To climb back to where he or she was in 1973, the average American worker would have to bust ass for six more weeks now than he or she did then.[32] But from 1980 to the present, the *Fortune* 500 more than doubled its holdings and multiplied executive salaries over six hundred percent, all while firing more than four million workers.[33]

Most of the millions and millions of working-class jobs lost in America over the past twenty years aren't coming back. Machines took some of them, foreign workers got many of the others, and a lot of jobs just disappeared. And the new jobs being created are of a staggeringly shitty quality. Full-time employment no longer guarantees you'll meet your full-time needs. A third of full-time American workers can't even pull their chins up over the poverty line.[34] With the sinister swell of part-time and temp work, Americans are increasingly juggling two or three low-paying jobs without being able to make the rent. A growing blob of workers can't find any jobs at all. And those who haven't been serrated by the downsizing chainsaw are working longer and longer hours. The only full-time workers on earth who put in more hours than Americans are the Koreans and Japanese, and they're maniacs, anyway.[35] European serfs in the 1200s had more leisure time than the average American worker in 1996.[36] Such is progress.

Wasn't technology supposed to make us free instead of unemployed? Why is the stock market exploding while wages remain static? Why are they telling us to make sacrifices while they are tripling and quadrupling their own salaries? Silly me, I thought it would get better for workers after the Cold War ended, not worse. The "peace dividend," apparently, is being spent somewhere overseas where you can buy more workers for the buck.

At some point early in the next century, multinational corporations will become more powerful than nations. Fifty of the world's hundred largest economic entities are now corporations; the other half are countries.[37] Domestic downsizing of workers occurred while the bosses were consolidating their power and upsizing their operations onto the

119

global market. Bosses know that if workers start bitching here, there's an aborigine in Borneo's upcountry who'll happily take the job for thirty cents a day. The multinationals killed the American worker. Merged, cut, snipped, and hacked him to death. The bosses just scooped up all their marbles and went elsewhere. Soon the whole planet will be run like an Appalachian coal-town fiefdom. All over the world, we'll be heeding the morning bell of the global plantation.

My wife was told she was being fired yesterday. She's been working as a temp secretary in the risk-management department of a local utilities company. Apparently, her boss did not consider worker security as a risk worthy of being thoughtfully managed. It was my wife's eleventh temp job in less than two years here in Portland. I saw the stiff sadness on her face this morning as she smeared on some makeup and squeezed into her corporate-friendly dress for one of her last days at this job. She's been working steadily since she got out of college twenty years ago. And I've seen this same look on her face eleven times in the past two years. Her expression told me she'd dutifully played by all the rules, worked hard, and things were still out of her control. I remembered all her slimy bosses. I remembered the one who years ago told her he'd hired her because she had the best tits of all the applicants. I remembered the boss who humiliated her with his little notes about how she should cut down on her trips to the bathroom. When she cried this morning, what was I supposed to tell her? That things would get better? All evidence leans in the other direction.

She always hated swallowing her individuality and being a team player. Being a "team player" really means being a blind worker ant who cleaves to the anthill. It means having no opinions, feelings, habits, or aspirations that veer from those of the Corporate Death Star. It means being a pleasant-smelling android. It means looking, dressing, and smiling exactly like the rest of the team. It means laughing (or getting offended) at the same jokes as everyone else. When the boss says jump, you do it with the grinning panache of an organ-grinder's chimp.

The office is a coffin. Everything has the soullessness of synthetic carpet fibers. Even the water tastes blander. Watch what you say. Watch how you act. Keep it in check. Smile, but not too much. Laugh, but politely. Even if your heart isn't in it, pretend. If you feel anything negative whatsoever, bite down until your lip bleeds. Keep it to yourself. Don't let them see. Don't let them suspect. MUST . . . NOT . . . THINK . . . BAD . . . THOUGHTS.

I flash back to some of my bosses. The philanderer who got manicures and burned his skin into a hideous rust color at the tanning salon. The one whose wife's parents owned a gambling casino and thus funded his little pet projects, and how I felt like strangling him with his ponytail when he fired me to cut costs. The woman who ate egg-salad sandwiches and read New Age magazines and pinched me sadistically when she was angry. The pink-cheeked mommy's boy with his Pee Wee Herman doll and condescending jabs. The one who inherited the business from his father and sat with his feet on the desk talking on the phone to his stupid drinking friends. The married couple who fucked everything that passed through their doors except each other. The fat, fifty-year-old telemarketing supervisor who flirted with sixteen-year-old teenyboppers in their phone cubicles. The psychotic, tax-evading, shoe-sales gangsters and their plastic-surgery girlfriends. The bearded buddies who left early on Fridays to play golf. The born-again Christian who barked orders at me through a stereo speaker embedded in the wall.

None of these bosses was particularly bright. Rather, they had inherited their wealth. While rarely acknowledged, inherited wealth (and inherited poverty) constitute a birthright system in much the same fashion as white supremacy.

Born to work. I remember the transmission falling right out the bottom of my cab, luckily while I was idling at a red light. I remember my cab's entire steering column falling into my lap while I was driving, and how I had to swerve to save my life. I remember driving the cab for twelve hours and going home with five bucks. I remember giving bodily fluids and being stuck with needles at the local university's medical-research center to make enough money to get by. I remember losing a large degree of innocence when I realized that my boss was billing clients ninety dollars an hour for work he was paying me twelve dollars an hour to perform. I remember snagging only ten dollars per hour—without benefits or vacation—in 1995 for doing the same work that in 1987 brought me sixteen dollars an hour with full benefits. Even though my wife and I both have college degrees and no kids, we were each working full-time and struggling. My father didn't finish high school, and he was able to support a wife and four kids by himself.

There's no hope anymore, and that's dangerous. We're left with a defanged, deballed, demoralized, degraded, devalued, disillusioned, downsized work force. A wet raisin-dick shriveling in the icy winter wind. All the factory whistles have been silenced. All quiet. Punch the card. Clock the fuck out. Go home and scrub all the crud off your skin. Try to forget. They don't need you anymore. But who's gonna clean up all the shit after the circus leaves town?

It has never been a fair fight between bosses and workers. Rather than being a free exchange between equals, it more often takes the form of an angry pimp slapping his uppity bitch.

In Spain during the time of Columbus, a mere two percent of the population owned ninety-five percent of the land.[38] In America during the Revolutionary Era, more than two-fifths of the wealth was hogged by one percent of the people.[39] The three hundred and fifty-eight billionaires currently on earth are sitting on more booty than is owned by nearly half the world's population combined.[40] And every one of those three hundred and fifty-eight human beings, I'm sure, feels equal to you and me.

An estimated twenty-five million white Americans currently live beneath the poverty line.[41] Many of them are working full-time. Many of them can't find full-time work. Many of them have given up. Many of their ancestors struggled and died through much the same bullshit. I think the workers have made enough sacrifices. It's time to start downsizing the bosses.

How will the country change when the millions who've always teetered just above the poverty line start free-falling into the pit? Utter hopelessness has a way of smacking people out of their stupor. If most of white America *becomes* white trash, redneck rage might suddenly not seem so uncool to them. When all these peacenikky, tie-dyed, dreadlocked, baggy-panted, snot-bearded, eyebrow-pierced community-college graduates realize they'll never do much better than $5.50–$7.50 an hour part-time without benefits, their equation of working-class anger with bigoted backwardness will evaporate. Their Fabergé-egg ideas of cultural etiquette won't appear nearly as pressing as immediate material needs.

The other day I went into a North Portland auto-parts store to return some pistons that didn't fit the engine in my little Jap car. Two straight-arrow Beefy Guys were working behind the counter. While one Beefy Guy quietly leafed through the yellowing pages of a giant auto-parts catalog, the other one began doing the paperwork for my piston refund. As he pecked endless serial numbers on a weather-beaten keyboard, we started talking about the sad state of work in America. "You know where we're headed?" he asked ominously, then answering before I could open my gob: "Corporate feudalism. You know what that is? The oligarchy, the elite, is going to keep squeezing us dry, giving us just enough to live and no more." I said nothing, momentarily startled that an auto-parts clerk was talking about oligarchies and feudalism. "Aww," chimed in the other guy, "we wouldn't want to say anything bad about corporations and government officials, would we?" In the span of fifteen seconds, I had witnessed more political discourse than I'd seen in years from TV or newspapers.

It's always dangerous when workers start thinking. When guys who sell pistons for a living can see things more clearly than our sycophantic media yes-men, I'd say we're in trouble.

The American working class is dead. What happens now?

6

Playin' Hard

TOO MUCH RAIN. Ever since Noah's deluge, the Lord forgot to turn off the sprinkler system over the Pacific Northwest. Except for a brief, hostile summer blast, the area is perpetually shrouded under a bleak sky the color of dirty nickels. As if there weren't enough clouds in the sky, low-lying puffs cling leechlike to the dark-green hills across the river. And often the clouds swoop right down onto the sidewalk in the form of icy, milk-thick fog. Sheets of rain keep plink-plink-plinking, methodically pockmarking roadside puddles. The soggy soil can only handle so much moisture until it liquefies, leading to mud-slides, rockslides, and house slides. No chance of a drought. This town is wet.

TOO MUCH INDUSTRY, both dead and alive. You can sometimes sniff the vaguely fartlike downwind of wet wood chips from a pulp mill twenty or so miles north on the toxic Willamette River, up near where the Trojan Nuclear Plant sits permanently closed. Much closer to home, hazardous-waste workers in white astronaut suits slosh around the lonesome stockyards of an abandoned creosote factory. Rain-eroded brick warehouses sit with shattered windows and three-foot-high weeds. Rows of rusty truck axles and piles of crushed truck cabins and hand-painted signs that scream WE BUY JUNK! Bursting with life are the poisonous-particle–spewing smokestacks and waste-water-treatment plants and petroleum refineries and steel mills. Train tracks crisscross near end-of-the-line bus terminals and dismal truck depots. This is an industrial hinterland attached to a postindustrial economy.

TOO MUCH CHOLESTEROL. Food that turns the most nimbly peristaltic colons into cold granite mausoleums. Hungover and half-awake workers hunker down for breakfast at the local greasy spoons, clogging their arteries just like the river's clogged with hazardous sludge. It's a hyperbolic diet—eggs, butter, syrup, pancakes, sausage, sour cream, and grease-dripping home fries buried alive under bacon-laden country gravy. So much fat, you might as well be scooping raw lard from a can with your hands or Dumpster-diving outside a liposuction clinic. It's fat over fiber, mammals over plants. No tofu or brown rice here. If you didn't have to shoot or stab your breakfast, it isn't food. And it tastes just as good on the way back up as it did going down. Real food is strong enough to kill a man.

TOO MUCH COFFEE. Espresso-machine steam rises as the cold rain falls. Within a two-block strip right around the corner from where I live, there are eight establishments where the morning buffalo herd can buy coffee to kick-start their ventricles. Two of these joints are devoted mainly to coffee, doling it out in algebraically multiplied combos of -ccino and -spresso suffixes, a pagan cult of obsessive bean-worship peculiar to the craggy Northwest.

TOO MANY BARS. Five of them within the same two-block strip, not counting a take-out liquor store. There's Slim's, Dad's, The Blue-bird, The Wishing Well, and Dooley's, where nude girls swing around a fire pole. All of these bars feature video poker and bathroom condom machines. Three of these watering holes are open by seven A.M., and business is always good.

The neighborhood is called St. Johns, and there's too much of everything except money. Property values in the North Portland community are among the city's lowest, lower even than in the northeast section's predominantly black ghettos. St. Johns sits at the tip of an extended peninsula. It is North Portland's glans penis. The dickie head. Depending on which way your skull's screwed on, it can look like either the beginning or the end. The alpha or omega. St. John, remember, was the hallucinating psychopath who wrote the Book of Revelation. But these days, I don't think St. John would be caught dead in a place like this. If St. John once lived here, he must've skipped town. Or maybe he was chased out by a torch mob. He ran away and took the apostrophe with him.

A hundred or so years ago, these muddy streets were roamed by waterlogged seamen and semen-laden loggers, maniacs on furlough looking for heads to crack and cherries to pop. A local reporter called these types "slime,"[1] but I'll bet he didn't say it to their faces. Early in the twentieth century, North Portland was host to such medieval-sounding workhouses as Portland Chain Co., Forrester Fertilizer Co., and St. Johns Ice & Coal Co. During World War II the area was said to have received a large infusion of ex-Okies who'd been stranded without jobs in northern California.

St. Johns is one of those rare places that's such an inherent over-statement, it's almost impossible to caricature. It's a thick-necked, broad-shouldered, foam-chugging, boilermaker, blue-collar-with-a-grimy-ring-around-it type of place. St. Johns has no symphony orches-tra, only cheapo lounge acts and country karaoke. No art museums, unless you count the black-velvet titty paintings in the bars. No rolling vineyards, but the big semi trucks haul in canned Coors daily. No crystal healing therapy, but slushy mounds of crystal meth. The resi-dents know not a whit about global diplomacy, but everyone knows how he got the black eye and why she aborted the baby.

Most outside commentators and self-made sophisticates find this area grotesque. When I tell other Portlanders I live in St. Johns, they pause and give a look of half-pity as if I said I'd been adopted. Either that, or they laugh. To many Portlanders, St. Johns is a punch line, an amusing local reminder of the Appalachian Nation they've always laughed at and feared.

I came for the attitude, which is hard enough to break a tooth. The whole place has the tastebud tang of small-town America gone rancid. Of a pretty cupcake being eaten by ants. Things are quaint, but rotting around the edges. It's like Norman Rockwell with herpes sores. Apple pie with a razor blade in it. Main Street after being vandalized. I wouldn't trade St. Johns for all the nipple-piercers in Northwest Port-land, nor the power-lunchers downtown, nor any of the acidophiluslappers who sit lotuslike in the city's southeastern plains. I'll keep my ass glued right here, the only place in town with honky soul.

Lombard Street is the main drag in St. Johns, host to all the afore-mentioned diners, bars, and coffee shops. Its wet sidewalks are runway ramps for a never-ending White Trash Fashion Show. Musty-looking broads and crinkle-faced fellers. Strung-out biker chicks and angry old longshoremen. People who have lost so many teeth, their faces slump down onto their chins à la Popeye. A teenage girl in short-shorts scratches at flea bites and glowers at passing cars. A cretinous male sneezes loudly and keeps walking as a three-inch snot string dangles from his nose. A wheelchair-bound headbanger with a steel rod in his spine says he's excited about the upcoming KISS reunion tour. Petty thieves walk from storefront to storefront, trying to sell red meat stolen from a local supermarket.

The bodies along Lombard Street come in two shapes: pumpkins or stringbeans. Circles or line segments. Blubber or bone. Morbidly obese or anorexically thin. And they're usually either gluttons or crankheads.

General Custer caters to the crankheads, and he's not too hard to find. General Custer isn't his name, but I figure he doesn't need to get busted again. I gave him the nickname because of his blond hair and nineteenth-century grooming habits. Along with a sand-colored pit bull sidekick, Custer lives in a makeshift community of broken-down vans and camper trucks parked in a glass-strewn lot behind one of the local bars. Custer's a liaison between those who make crank and those who take crank. He probably helps more St. Johns residents get started in the morning than all the coffee shops combined.

Crank is to coffee what sexual homicide is to a goodnight kiss. It's the black sheep of the speed family. Also called crystal meth, zip, or monster, crank is rocket fuel for sputtering workers. Although suppos-edly a recreational drug—a fun thing—crank's usually taken to facili-tate work performance. It treats your bloodstream as an assembly line and pushes up the production quota. When someone inhales a thick line of crystal methamphetamine, they summon an invisible angel who holds a gun to their head, commanding them to keep working. Heroin gets all the glossy press, but it's mostly for slackers who can afford to fall asleep in mid-sentence. St. Johns is a working-class neighborhood. These people need to stay awake. So it's a crank 'hood.

Crank is a homemade biohazardous brain-scalder produced by white outlaw chemists acting in the entrepreneurial tradition of their moonshining ancestors. Speed is whitey's drug, from the palefaces who cook it to the Caspers who deal it to the ofay vanilla wafers who snort or spike it. Very few *schwartzes* are crank-tweakers. The brothers, and most of the others, won't touch the shit. Why so white? Is this merely genetic preference? Some adrenal predisposition? Perhaps, but it probably has more to do with distribution patterns. Biker gangs and long-haul truckers, whose ranks have always been white-male–dominated, were America's Johnny AppleSpeeds. They disseminated illicit vitality to millions of Caucasians who couldn't afford to be tired.

But rather than appealing to all whites, crank more specifically skews downward toward white trash. While the loftier echelons powder their noses with the purest Peruvian *cocaína,* such upper-class uppers cost a lot more than trailer-park bathtub meth. Crank's a lot cheaper than its glitzier cousin, and much longer-lasting. While a toot of cocaine may buzz you through an episode of *Seinfeld,* good crank lasts at least eight hours—a full work shift. But crank wreaks more long-term physiological havoc, too. It is the poor white man's cocaine, analogous to the role crack cocaine serves for poor blacks.

I've done crank a few times, mostly during college finals, or while working multiple gigs, or while slogging at a full-time day job while editing a magazine at night. Hold my hand, and I'll tell you how it feels. Immediately after the snort comes a burning, eye-watering pain as if someone's inserted a welding torch in your nostril. The stronger the burn, the better the crank. You keep snorting in and wincing. The crystal powder mixes with nasal mucus and dribbles like cave slime down the back of your throat. The flavor is a potpourri of raw fish, steel shavings, and drain cleaner. It tastes as if you've swallowed the distilled toxic nectar of the entire Industrial Revolution. The fact that crank is frequently cut with things such as photo developer, insecticide, and paint remover merely enhances the factory-waste ethos.

Then cometh the rush. A potent batch of crank can really drive a corkscrew through your dome. All the electrolytes in your brain are fired up and hummin' like a V-8 engine. Seven hundred and fifty trillion microscopic fingers massage your scalp. Your feet feel as if they've been screwed into giant light-bulb sockets. Your peripheral field is edged with a humid mist. Your heart is ready to splosh through your ribs like a prisoner trying to squeeze through cell bars. Your beta waves are cresting at high tide. And, goddamnit, the work gets done. Your body performs while you just sit back and watch. It's effortless, as if someone else was doing the work.

Crank exaggerates and parodies the work cycle. As with all forms of redneck vice, it overstates things. Higher highs and lower lows. But just like the weekend never lasts forever, neither does the high. Crank is pleasure which knows that pain will soon follow.

All rockets have to land somewhere. This roller coaster didn't climb that high not to go down again. *CRASH!* The crank hangover feels as if someone's drained your veins of blood and filled them with wet lumps of chilly sand. With a balloon-light head and a whirlpool stomach, the only mystery is whether you'll faint or vomit first. Crystals and diamonds that had sailed through your head turn to hailstorms of white-light glass fragments lacerating your inner skull. Blazing schizo paranoia. Brain lesions sprout up like teenage acne. What if every capillary from my lungs up to my brain explodes in a shower of blood? What if I lapse into a coma, never to return? How long do I curl in the fetal position before the shock waves pass? If this is recreation, why all the ODs and heart attacks and bullet wounds and exploding laboratories and snarling dogs and unprovoked blowtorch flare-ups of ultraviolence?

Although crank abuse knows no gender, it wears worse on a woman's face. You can spot the crank girls running all day up and down Lombard Street, their spines taut like archery bows, their feet pressed down on some imaginary accelerator, their hair falling to the sidewalk in chemotherapy-sized clumps. My ex-landlord told me of one St. Johns crank skank who wouldn't settle for just enough when she could shoot for too much. A friend had cut the girl a free line of crank, and she snorted it with anteater enthusiasm. Careful not to swallow, she hurried home with the crystalline solvent clinging to her nasal membrane, as if her nose was a squirrel's mouth and the crank a friendly little acorn. Upon reaching home, she honked out the gob of crank-snot from her nose onto her hand, wiped the mess on a spoon, cooked it with a flame, and injected the methampheta-mucus into her arm. She's a real trouper who went the extra mile down the self-destruction highway. There's another St. Johns girl—well, she looks fifty, but she's probably in her twenties—whose beef-jerky facial skin is so withered from constant crank abuse, she looks like a burn victim. She's always tweaking, twitching, and fluttering like a dried leaf up and down Lombard. With yellowish skin pulled tightly over frail canary bones, clad in an array of filthy rags, and wearing a headband to rein in her scraggly longish hair, she looks like Aerosmith's Steven Tyler if the singer had years ago decided to pursue a path toward abject homelessness rather than international pop superstardom. She has the Gypsy Hag look down pat. She's the emaciated incarnation of recreational excess. A walking exaggeration. TOO MUCH on two legs.

Working-class amusement is always too much. It operates from an Overdose Aesthetic. It's nominally leisure, but it often seems more like an endurance test. You don't make love, you fuck your brains out. You don't laugh, you piss yourself laughing. You don't listen to music, you pump up the volume until your ears bleed. You don't just drink, you drink yourself blind. You don't want to get high. You want to get FUCKED UP. BLASTED. OBLITERATED. You don't punch someone, you beat the shit out of him, kick the snot out of him, and thrash him until he pisses blood. If it can't kill or permanently maim you, it's not a sport. If nothing gets blowed up real good, it isn't a movie. And you don't want to see just one murder, you want mass murder, preferably thermonuclear annihilation.

It's overstatement for the overworked. High drama for low attention spans. A school of art that owes more to the *Guinness Book* than to the Left Bank. The imagery is Brobdingnagian. Paul Bunyanesque. Drenched in hyperbole. Superlatives. Big is never as good as bigger, and that's tiny compared to biggest. But then comes ultrajumbo. . . .

White-trash fun is desperate fun. Painful fun. Risky, bleeding, murderous, frightening fun. It's fun that in any other context wouldn't seem like fun. It owes something to Russian roulette, autoerotic asphyxiation, hot-rod "chickie" races, and those suicidal Argentinian kids who "surf" atop moving subway trains in Buenos Aires. But while the nihilism may be what catches your eye, there's also an upside. Flapping around in the mud and the blood and the beer can be a cleansing experience. And unless you've personally known the joy of smashing everything in a room to pieces, judge ye not another man's moccasins.

The spectacle requires a violent decisiveness, a slashing finality. In classic white-trash sports such as ice hockey, rodeo, and drag racing, the fun hinges on the risk of severe bodily injury to the participants. Wrestling, whether real or choreographed, is one of the evergreens of redneck playtime. On the untamed colonial frontier, eye-gouging matches were common. The object was to plant your thumb deep enough in your opponent's eye socket to pluck his eyeball clear out of his skull. Innumerable hillbilly Cyclopes were thus created, and a good time was had by all. If an occasional nose, ear, or finger was bitten off in the fray, it was all part of the fun.

Better living through bloodletting. A recent mail-order wrestling-video catalog promises enjoyment from maltreatment:

> This show has matches where people get thumbtacks stuck in their head, wrestlers receive bad burns and a combined stitch count of over 500!!!
>
> Witness the daredevil flips to the concrete, the breaking of bones while smashing tables, and the bloodiest hardcore action seen in the states!
>
> NO ROPE BARBED WIRE DEATH MATCH ... TONS OF BLOOD AND GRAPHIC BARBED WIRE SPOTS ... AND REMEMBER THESE ARE WOMEN. . . .[2]

There used to be a wrestling arena in St. Johns where now stands a government-subsidized apartment complex. Portland wrestling scholar Phil "Whiskey Rebel" Irwin used to attend the matches up here. He says the more popular brawling lunkheads attracted a breed of female groupies who were all succulently gorgeous, except they'd each have one drastic flaw. She's a knockout, but what happened to the other leg? Tantalizingly globular maracas, but why does she talk through a surgical hole in her throat? She'd be a perfect "10" if it wasn't for the severe male-pattern baldness.

Steroid-pumped endomorphs still slam to the canvas every Sunday night in Vancouver, Washington, just across the Columbia River from Portland. Z-circuit fleshgrapplers threaten and flip each other in the downscale digs of a high-school auditorium. The line between Good and Evil couldn't be clearer: Righteous Rambos vs. Growling Ostrogoths, Honest Injuns vs. Villainous Afrikaners, Handsome Heartthrobs vs. Bald Butterball Ogres. In the main event I witnessed, the shaggy-haired loser was tied to the ropes with a leather strap and had his head shaven clean while feigning unconsciousness. There are no ambiguous endings here.

The real show, naturally, is in the audience, with its raised fists and throat-corroding chants of "U–S–A! . . . YEW . . . ESS . . . AYY!!!" Obese humans sit with legs spread wide to accommodate bellies the size of small planets. Gum-popping housewives wave flags in one hand while bobbling their colicky diapered progeny in the other. Heads are shaped like all manner of squash and legumes. Tragic limps. Wooden canes. Metal walkers. Facial deformities. Large purple blemishes. Nerve-damage spasticity, rocking back and forth in the bleachers. You'd think they were here to see a faith healer. They all scream bloody murder because the good guys won and the bad guys lost tonight. Wrestling always delivers a more decisively positive verdict than the personal lives of every howling disfigurement from ringside up to the peanut gallery.

Miss Manners and Mr. Blackwell are predictably appalled at all this senseless gore and sleaze. The Redneck Way of Leisure simply doesn't jibe with their vibe. But they've probably never been pinned down for a three-count in situations that beg for gut-wrenching catharsis. Culture buzzards sniff at overstatement as artistically inferior to subtlety. The winkers and nudgers on the upper floors look down on the literal, bludgeoning, high-decibel trappings of working-class revelry as base stupidity. They're wrong, as always. Crudity, like refinement, is less often a conscious choice than an instinctual response to one's surroundings. Overwrought power fantasies serve the emotional needs of white-trash Walter Mittys.

Different strokes. Some need bullwhips, others need feathers. The decision makers and check signers like it nice 'n' easy. They languidly swing at golf balls or slump their tanned bodies halfway out the Jacuzzi onto the wet bar. They want tinkly Muzak jazz, wryly phrased verbal bonbons lobbed weightlessly over candlelight dinners, and avocado facials while sunning themselves at Club Melanoma. The top brass don't need monster trucks. They have monster bucks. No lust for heavy-metal pyrotechnics when your finger's already on the power button. The boozhies don't require violent dominance fantasies, because their power is a fait accompli. No need for tidal-wave imagery when your life itself is sopping-wet with excess. No need for desperate fun when there's no desperation.

Work and play are the yin and yang of white-trash existence, only yang got the short end. Fifty work weeks for two vacation weeks? Five straight work days for a measly pair on the weekend? Can't hop off the fucking treadmill. Jane, stop this crazy thing.

When you bust your ass all week, you just don't have patience for the soft stuff. If you've been laying hot tar on a roof all day, I don't think Mozart and a goblet of cognac will take out all the kinks in your neck. After hearing a jackhammer for eight hours, Broadway show tunes would only induce migraines. Low-sodium entertainment won't cut it after the salt mines. You can't wash out bloodstains with a bubble wand. You don't use a water pistol to kill an elephant. You fight fire with fire. The punishment should fit the crime. It's the ol' robbing Peter to pay Paul, six o' one and a half-dozen of the other, same-o/same-o, bait-and-switch, you-scratch-my-back-I'll-scratch-yours principle.

Every work load has an equal and opposite play load. When you spend all day loading sixteen tons, you have to find a way to dump it. If you hammer nails all week, you want to get hammered on the weekend.

The little windup tin-soldier key in your back can't be wound any tighter. There's been a thorn in your side and a popcorn kernel stuck in your teeth all week. It's purification time. Whether actual or figurative, something has to die tonight. Some sacrifice must be made, payable in bodily fluids. Have some fun before Monday comes, even if it kills you. Monday's no treat, anyway.

Out with the bad air, in with the good. Bleed the office out of yourself. Smash it out of your mind. Blot it out. You need an epileptic-level release. Loud enough to kill all the noise. Bright enough to blind you. Strong enough to choke all the bad feelings. Shaking yourself that hard is a form of voodoo. Something DEFINITE needs to happen. This is recreation as a lashing-out process. Self-inflicted pleasure. Catharsis through excess. Self-abusive leisure. Maybe it involves accidentally blowing half your face off while trying to impress friends with your latest nifty gun trick. Or forgetting the condom and getting infected. Or inhaling some bad crank and becoming a vegetable. Windows have to be shattered, rocks hurled, news boxes overturned, tires slashed, and garbage cans set ablaze. This is what happens, as our parents always warned us, when horseplay gets out of hand. You'll break a neck and poke your eye out if you're not careful.

Pleasure sliding into pain. The whiskey bottle contains such possibilities. The drunk driver epitomizes this pleasure-becomes-pain principle. Total drunkenness is pleasure which can't see pain on the horizon. Lookit all them happy drinkers being torn to goo in car wrecks, suffocating on their own vomit, or falling blissfully asleep in an alley only to be murdered. They were so ecstatic, they couldn't see it coming. Maybe tonight some unhinged goofball will feel loose enough, just drunk enough, to smash head-on into a Freightliner truck and scatter his own entrails for two hundred yards down the asphalt. Or maybe, as is more often the case, he'll pulverize the poor saps in another car and walk away unscratched. Throughout the era in which liquor and automobiles have coexisted on earth, there has probably never been a drunk driver who didn't tell himself he was just having a little fun. Roll that tote board—seventeen thousand[3] squashed corpses yearly directly attributable to overimbibing drivers!!! Hate-crime fatalities don't come close to the bodies racked up by such crimes of pleasure.

The object is to wipe out brain cells as if they were cancer cells. You aren't seeking scented-candle enlightenment, you're trying to see how many sticks of lit dynamite you can toss down your mouth without exploding. It's balls-to-the-wall, boogie-'til-you-puke, last-man-left-standing-wins. With all that beer sloshing around inside you, you'll need to snort a little line of crystal meth to stay awake. Then another splash of malt 'n' hops to blunt the crank's edge. Then some crank on top of the beer on top of the crank on top of the beer. Then, naturally, some pot or Xanax or Klonopin to ease the bitter afterglow of all that crank and beer. And maybe a few cups of coffee or some cigarettes. Diet pills, prescription sedatives, acid, coke, 'shrooms, dust, whippets, amyl nitrite, tar heroin, and anything else you can shove up your nose or in your mouth or in a vein or up your ass. And maybe three or four gumball-sized crack rocks dissolved in a prune-juice enema as a nightcap. Are we having fun yet? When should we cry uncle?

I'm a dropout from the University of Overkill. My paternal grand-pappy, the town drunk of Windsor, Vermont, terrorized his family by blasting his shotgun in the house when he was too drunk and too angry. My father, to his credit, didn't own a shotgun. As a child witness to alcohol's ravages, I vowed never to drink when I grew up. That all changed when I had to start working to survive. The cork came off and the trouble started. I was a primal-scream party boy who specialized in blackouts. *Where am I?* Waking up encrusted in my own orange, chunky gut-spew. Waking up on a beach amid an angry mosquito swarm. Waking up and not knowing why the car grille was crushed and my radiator leaking. Waking up in a jail cell with my brain throbbing and dried blood all over my face. Tasted my own blood. So gleefully tanked on poppers and canned Schlitz, I rolled right off the hood of my friend's car as he feverishly drove doughnut circles in the mall parking lot. Tasted my own blood again. So overjoyed to be winning the fight, I didn't see his buddy come up behind me and swing the steel keg pump at my face. Tasted my own blood again. So happily smashed, I didn't need anesthesia as they stitched up my skull under hot emergency-room lights—on FOUR separate occasions. Blinking at the flashbulbs, so blotto I didn't know they were taking mug shots. I put a cold-turkey end to all that alcoholic fun fifteen years ago, or I probably wouldn't be here to annoy you today.

What the fuck is going on? Why is all this recreation so traumatic? Why does it frequently cause more problems than it solves? Why does playtime often seem more like a nightmare? Why are loud barroom laughs frequently punctuated by shouted threats and despondent sobs? Why does the corner bar seem as likely to produce death and dismem-berment as the workplace? How hard do they have to play before they start bleeding from every pore? Why don't I just give you some an-swers instead of rephrasing the question?

I have a theory. I have a lump on my balls, too, but that's none of your business. So I'll explain things by using yet another disgusting metaphor: When you die, your sphincter muscles relax to the point where you empty your bowels. While alive, you instinctually maintain enough anal tension to hold it all in. Redneck leisure is the same way —it releases tension, but it's careful not to release too much. Most people would lose all stability in their lives if they ever jumped off the carousel. When there's no way to get off the merry-go-round, you'd better learn to enjoy being dizzy. If they learned how to mellow out, they'd never go to work again, and then they'd starve to death. Self-esteem would probably cost them their jobs. If the waters were too tranquil, they'd see the bottom too clearly. Getting rid of all their problems would mean getting rid of their job, and where would that leave them? Enlightened, if penniless. Sure, drug and alcohol abuse create more problems than they solve. But that's precisely why people abuse them.

What seems like self-sabotage may actually be a flexing of the survival instinct. It's a battle mentality. You're a weekend warrior. Traumas and hangovers and hospital stitches are there as equalizers. All this spilled blood and broken glass is not as purposelessly nihilistic as it looks. It's a subconscious way of maintaining the work vibe. By winding up in jail Saturday morning with a headache and a black eye, you're actually preparing yourself for work on Monday. Just as debt keeps you working, so does tension. You have to be crazy to take orders from a boss. It isn't natural. So staying fucked up is a way of hooking yourself on the work vibe. Keeping yourself agitated and off center. Hair o' the boss that bit you. A sour stomach. A fire under the ass. A carrot on a stick. A hungry oyster snatching up another grain of sand with which to irritate its mucus lining. A way of staying insane enough to work, to reinoculate yourself with the work virus. Anything to make you feel lousy enough about yourself to go back into work and take orders. It's pure workaholism in the sense of never being able to relax. Slow suicide to complement the workplace's slow homicide.

Doing what you don't want to do is a soul killer. After years, you're still running in place. Still back to square one. Still broke at month's end. And congratulations, you now have a month less to live. Why make your bed if you're going to sleep in it again tonight? Why shave if the hair keeps growing back? All the beer in St. Johns won't stop Monday from coming. While the grind seems forever, the escape is only temporary. Self-actualization's nice, but it doesn't pay the electric bill. Sensitivity training and yoga classes would only be a Band-Aid on top of a severed artery. So instead, they learn to like the taste of their own blood.

All this white-trash leisure, this redneckreational activity, manifests a need to FEEL something apart from a working life in which you're treated with all the warmth of a Plasticine toy robot. It doesn't have to feel *good*. It just has to be FELT. Pain isn't the first choice, but you'll take it when the only other option is the gonad-shrinking numbness of worker complaisance. The workplace is no place for human beings. Everything's so fucking clamped down, dictated, and circumscribed. So it's not too bad if I cry in my beer all weekend, goes the logic, because they didn't let me feel a thing all week.

There are only sixty-four hours from Friday five P.M. to Monday nine A.M. This scanty sliver of leisure time is when it all comes crashing down. These panting, mangy dogs crouch intently at the starting blocks in the race to find out who's gonna get fucked, who's gonna get fucked up, and who's gonna get the fuck beaten out of them. Clear the decks, ye mateys, methinks the great white whale's ready to blow. I hope you brought your napkins.

These snaggletoothed St. Johns bars start humming around seven or eight P.M. on Friday night. The hum grows louder every hour until closing time. Push open the heavy wooden door with the NO MINORS sign, and you can hear the hum for yourself. Entering one of these joints is like walking into the mouth of someone who hasn't brushed his teeth for a while. An ever-present gummy tobacco fog has left a visible, tangible nicotine resin on everything. Christmas lights and dusty tinsel are stapled up around the bar, even in midsummer. Walls are tacked with Polaroids of regular patrons hooting, hugging, and hoisting suds. Downy mildew and dart-tournament trophies and muddy work-boot tracks all over the carpet. Incest victims sit on bar stools next to war cripples. A little scrunched-face Manson character with crusty jeans hanging off his bony ass is trying to convince the bartender to cash a disability check. Grizzly-bear truck-studs stare bitterly into space. And a woman who looks like Buddy Hackett is talking about dick size:

> I don't know—they say you can tell such things by shoe size, but that's not always true. My former husband was six-two, and his shoes were 11EEE—and—*"My baloney has a first name—it's S–M–A–L–L. . . ."*

Everyone laughs. Here at the Flea Ranch, crudeness serves our needs. Refined behavior wouldn't come close to scratching our itch. The crasser, the ranker, the tawdrier, the easier it fits on a T-shirt or bumper sticker, the better. I'M 51% LADY, 49% BITCH—DON'T PUSH IT . . . I'M A MUFF DIVER . . . DON'T GIVE ME AN ATTITUDE—I HAVE MY OWN . . . YOU STOLE MY HEART, THEN TOOK A SHIT IN MY MOUTH.

Come in, will you? Have you met my friend Pathology? And did I introduce you to Trauma, Abuse, Denigration, and Frustration? They're all here on the dance floor, shaking their rumps to a schmaltzy Neil Diamond tune. Shitting out the psychic waste they've accumulated all week. Be careful not to skid on all the blood, cum, piss, and beer.

The female bartender has a black eye, which she claims came from breaking up a bar fight. People just out of prison. People ready to go back to prison because of something they'll do later tonight. The couple who were arguing a half-hour ago are now making out. Give 'em another half-hour, and they'll be dry-humping. A few video-poker zombies, drawn in by the terminals' satanic blue glow, reflexively poke at the touch-activated screen, dealing, discarding, redrawing, doubling up, losing it all, and delicately feeding more crumply dollar bills into the machine's thin, eager steel lips. When you don't have any money, you might as well spend it.

> OLD MALE WORKER: They got both husband and wife working these days, and they *still* can't keep up.
>
> YOUNG MALE WORKER: I can't keep up, and I make *good money.*
>
> OLD MALE WORKER: It's a shame. It's not like it used to be.

YOUNG MALE WORKER: Working people *built* this fucking country, and they don't give a damn about us.

Smell the rage. The bathrooms are redolent with equestrian-strength urine, constantly at battle with those gut-churning mentholated urinal cakes. As you step up to the hitching post and let the yellow water tinkle from your Pink Begonia, your eyes can't avoid the condom machine, ingeniously mounted onto the wall a foot above the urinals. Ribbed rubbers. Glow-in-the-dark ones. French ticklers. Cock rings. Corny sex-themed gag gifts. Lubricant oils. Erection-prolonging cream. Removable tattoos designed somehow to enhance foreplay. The ever-popular flavored neon body paints. Any one of these pleasure enhancers can be yours for three quarters in the slot. Plastic decals are slapped onto the chrome-plated machine, advertising each of these rest-room aphrodisiacs. A pouty-breasted, thick-eyelashed, hiphugger-wearing woman apparently photographed in the late 1960s beseeches you to tickle her swee'pea with the latest musk-scented, stegosaurus-plate–textured, rubberized contraption. Some prankster, probably using a car key, has scratched a rude-looking monster cock snaking its way into the condom-model's crotch. It was probably the same guy who etched the flock of levitating dicks that surround Miss Eyelashes' face like cum-squirting seraphim. As crude as this ad was by itself, it took some piss-drunk St. Johns dude to draw deeper meaning into it.

I figure the HIV Splash Factor is lower with a toilet bowl than a standing urinal, so I usually head for the stalls when I need to drain my vein. I've seen greasy pubic hairs on these toilet seats. I've seen blobs of what looks very much like male cum on these toilet seats. And the bowl itself is usually stuffed to overflowing with soggy toilet paper and bloody water and angry blackish turds—someone else's— that circle like barracuda when you try to flush, never going down.

Is anybody hungry? There's a cornucopia of bar snacks to satisfy the most finicky epicure. Pickled eggs in crusty mason jars. Pickled sausage. Pickled pork rinds. Pickled peppers. Pickled pickles. Popcorn so old and stale, the butter topping has congealed into yellow candle wax. Salted pretzels. Salted cashews. Dried salted shrimp. Free potluck buffets and serve-yourself ptomaine fondues. Sour-cream-and-onion-flavored potato chips. Chicken-'n'-chive breadsticks impregnated with a cheesy paste. Jalapeño corn dogs that have been sitting there a while. Hickory-smoked preserved meat snacks coated in dried ground chilis. Pepperoni-flavored imitation cheddar curls. Food that floats comfortably atop a gutful of cheap alky-hawl.

One elderly bartendress takes a break to sing a karaoke version of some love-rolled-a-tractor-over-my-heart country ballad. Her hair is a gray horse's tail, her face a dry creek bed. And she means the words so deeply, you have to turn your head away. Country music is trauma music, with more booze, drugs, and murder than all other pop formats combined. More rubbed-raw emotions. More take-this-job-and-shove-it worker rage, too. For all its alleged reactionary spirit, country-and-western lyrics address the indignities of working life far more than any other pop format. The folk-singing hippies who demonized working white stiffs never copped to the fact that they stole their whole shtick from Woody Guthrie and the coal-mining bards. While the Alternative Nation meows about personal fashion angst, the Appalachian Nation still sings about unemployment.

As the honky-tonk beat plods along like an old leather shoe, I think of Johnny Cash gulping down a bottleful of pills a day and tearing down hotel walls. The lonely heart-attack OD of Hank Williams in the back seat of that taxi. Hank Jr.'s face-mutilating car accident and how he always wears sunglasses. TV news footage of Jerry Lee Lewis being wheeled into a Memphis hospital on a stretcher, shaking like a palsy victim from an alleged allergy to "medication"; memories of The Killer marrying his thirteen-year-old cousin and demolishing out-of-tune pianos into heaps of splinters and wires. Ernest Tubb firing a .357 Magnum in a Nashville life-insurance building's lobby. Faron Young shooting out the lights of a Nashville bar (and only recently shooting out his own brains). Spade Cooley stomping his wife to death. George Jones driving a golf cart to the liquor store. Tammy Wynette stumbling down a rural road dazed and covered in bruises. Entertainers, all of them. People who brought happiness to others. Miserable.

Poke me again! Poke me, motherfucker! You're fucking *dead!*

Bar fights always start for the most inane reasons—a sideways glance, an accidental bump—but the real reason is always personal frustration. Satisfied minds don't start fights. The other guy's just a punching bag for what's been happening in your own life. And as ugly as it sounds, it feels good to punish someone else for the pain you feel inside. Fuck or fight. As closing time nears and all these horny dudeniks realize they ain't getting no hoochie-coochie tonight, the fists start swinging.

Legend is that St. Johns got its rep as a danger zone mainly thanks to its infamous brawling families, two or three major clans depending on whom you ask. These contentious kin roam from bar to bar shitfaced drunk, looking for asses to pinch and heads to bust. They are said to be the result of intermixed European and Native American bloodlines, a feisty cocktail of rednecks and redskins. I've seen one of these ass-kicking families enter a bar all wobbly-drunk and wearing their feathered Yakima Nation hats, and they really send a jolt into the air. There was something undeniably heroic in their sense of family values. The family that drinks together throws chairs and smashes bottles together.

The pool table is currently ruled by "Ma," a sixtyish woman with a gnarled puggish face. Her long hair is combed straight back and seemingly held in place by dirt and oil. Ma is a pool hustler. She takes on a string of malt-swilling trailer studs and beats them all. Her first victim is an amiably chubby black guy with a shaved head. (Ironically, all the redneck bars I've seen are more racially integrated than any culturally sensitive upscale lounge you'd care to name.) Ma next dispatches a stocky longshoreman type with a mop-bristle beard. Then a lanky mountain man with harsh, haunted features. Every mullethead and keg-gut who dares step into Ma's lair is quickly humiliated by her cue-ball wizardry.

Cheering on Ma is a much younger-looking woman with her hair dyed a don't-stare-into-the-sun shade of blonde. Her jeans are blood-circulation-threateningly tight, straining against logic to keep her ample ass cheeks from gushing loose like symmetrical watermelons. Flabby cantaloupe boobs jut out from within an equally tight denim vest, her bumper-crop mammaries muzzled only by a leopard-patterned strapped blouse. Her mascara is raccoon-thick, as if it had been applied

with a black felt-tipped pen. Her left hand and wrist are wrapped in an
Ace bandage. One of Ma's husky male victims, still licking his
wounds, asks Raccoon Girl about her wrapped-up wrist.

> RACCOON GIRL: My ex-boyfriend sprained my wrist. [She holds
> it up for inspection and flashes an inappropriate brown-toothed
> smile.]
>
> MR. HUSKY: Oh, so that's why he's your *ex*-boyfriend?
>
> RACCOON GIRL: Yes.
>
> [Mr. Husky becomes suddenly more interested, grinding his hips
> into the bar stool.]
>
> RACCOON GIRL: Actually, it was much more than a sprain. The
> doctors wanted to put it in a cast running from my elbow to my
> fingertips. I said, "No way, just wrap it up and let me out of here."
> Shit, I *laughed* when he fucked up my arm. But my sixteen-year-old
> stepdaughter said, "You'd better get that taken care of."

Laughing at tragedy. Crying during playtime. Raccoon Girl tells Mr.
Husky that Ma is her cousin. She says Ma's pool game, as good as it
is, hasn't been the same since Ma's son broke her wrist during an
argument. Here are two women, both with fucked-up wrists. As Ma
studiously circles the pool table looking for the best shot, I wonder
how many two-ton wrecking balls she's had to dodge in her life merely
for being poor white trash. Don't misunderstand me. Ma seemed entirely happy—happier than me, I'm sure—and the last thing she needs
is another patronizing missionary journalist. But the lines in her face
are hieroglyphics. As she effortlessly slams balls in side pockets, I
wonder how many people in her family she's sent off to war never to
see them again, how many cousins are in jail, how many were killed
or maimed in industrial accidents, how many male family members
slugged their wives, and how many mothers smacked their kids in
ugly displays of powerless frustration. Ma is an archetypal white-trash
Mother Hen. Like the stereotypical strong black mother, her life has
been a struggle to impose order on chaos.

Time has not been kind to the white-trash woman. Lips as red as
rubies, bruises as purple as grapes. Dental algae on crocodilian teeth.

Ashtray voice and vacant stare. Armpit hairs jutting out like weeds from a sidewalk crack. Translucent, microwaved crater skin, every vein visible. Track marks, beepers, and see-through fishnet blouses. Perfectly shaped body with a ninety-year-old's face. These girls show much more wear-and-tear than their cartoon bimbo ancestors. They come off like Elly Mae Clampett if Uncle Jed had molested her from infancy until age eighteen. Or like Daisy Duke with scabby knees, rushing in high heels to flag down a taxi for her date at the methadone clinic.

Some of the gals make an effort to splash on perfume and change their panties, but there's really no need. Any woman, no matter how severely disfigured, who'd dare stray into this bar with an operational vagina and pair of milk-teats is guaranteed of being able to grab at least one desperate stud by the hose and drag him out the back door as if he were a pull toy. Even if a disembodied hairy vagina—a solitary organ without arms, legs, head, ass, or torso—were somehow to nuzzle atop a bar stool, that amputated muff would have two free drinks and three marriage proposals in under a minute. So why squeeze on high heels and shovel on makeup if they're all coming off, anyway? Any mustachioed fishwife willing to drop her sweatpants behind the restaurant Dumpster is considered a goddess here. So relax, ladies—they'll fuck you just the way you are.

White-trash woman. Her hygienic habits may be those of a cockroach, but *cucarachas* can live through a nuclear war. She has seen too much brutality to retain any vestigial wisps of daintiness. But what she's lost in frilly femininity, she's gained in a scrappy, cynical spirit that comes from having survived. Hard knocks make for hard women. In the sense of being able to take care of themselves, they're better hard-line feminists than many of the sheltered gals who so loudly espouse vagino-supremacy. I've always thought that working-class women—stuck in the suffocating sort of conditions that most often spark violence—needed feminism more than the blue-blooded lassies who commonly practice it. But I was wrong. You don't need *any* sort of indoctrination if you already know how to survive. You don't need theory when you have practice. And white-trash girls can usually cut down a rude male quicker than most college feminists, either with words or a knee to the balls.

I'm a survivor, baby. I've been in a car accident, I've fallen asleep
with a needle stuck in my ass, and I'm still standing.

She's still standing, although she walks with a severe limp. Barely five
feet tall, with a perky gymnast's body and the mouth of a sailor. She's
telling a friend about the afternoon she went over some dude's house
and how the rude bastard shot up some brown heroin and passed out
blue-faced on his bed. Rather than try to revive him, she just picked his
wallet clean and left. She switches the topic to pit bulls, how it's all over
when they smell blood, how they'll just clamp down and never let go.

Could she be the infamous Pit Bull Girl of St. Johns? A rumor has
been circulating about General Custer, his pit bull, and a girl who
couldn't wait for love. I've heard the story through two different
sources. It seems that the crank-dealing Custer was waxing amorous
with a local girl in his van. It may have been love, it may have been a
pussy-for-crank swap. Prior to penetration, Custer excused himself and
went into one of the local bars to get a slot-machine rubber. When he
returned to the van, he noticed it was rocking, with loud moans coming
from the inside. Custer opened the van's back door to reveal the bestial
specter of his pet pit bull humping his crank girlfriend, her legs akimbo
and howling like a bitch in heat. The girl had apparently been the
aggressor and had manually inserted the doggie dingus inside her sugar
walls. For Custer, it sort of took the romance out of the moment. "Most
guys use their dogs to get chicks," the owner of a local coffee shop
later kidded him. "Looks like this time, your dog used you."

The party never stops. "Kerosene Eyes" is looking a little haggard
lately and has taken to smoking her crystal meth in a glass pipe.
She has your run-of-the-mill chemical-burn peroxide engineer-boot
biker-chick look. She's been known to stay awake for days working on
car and motorcycle engines, laboring to squeeze the last drops of
crank juice from her dried, rubbery veins. She usually works alongside
her husband, but it doesn't look that way anymore. Not after all the
rumors of her stabbing him repeatedly in the calf with an ice pick. Not
after a few months in jail because she ignored the restraining order. It
looks like she'll stay away for good after hubby finally struck back,
hurling an asphalt meteor through her car window and nailing her

head. She drove away bleeding from her fake-blonde scalp into both eyes. She has another boyfriend, anyway. Sixteen years old. He's younger than her son. And the Young Stud is also fucking Donna Summer when he isn't sticking it to Kerosene Eyes. Not Donna Summer the disco singer—just a black-male transvestite coke dealer who looks identical to Summer circa the hot pants, roller skates, *Bad Girls* era. And the Young Stud, dumb donkey that he is, doesn't even know he's fucking a guy.

Only a block removed from Lombard Street's gloppy sleaze, a group of bitter old church ladies is eating breakfast at a wholesome Christian restaurant. Good food here. No intestinal parasites in the home fries. No alcohol. No condoms in the bathroom. No crank deals going down on the pay phone. Clean, if dull. And these quilting-bee ladies sit around in judgment of the world's immorality like a group of Supreme Court justices. Their thinning hair is teased skyward and tinted light blue like a swirl of cotton candy. They wear false teeth and Orlon leisure suits. They never smile, never approve. Shaking their heads with pious censure at antispanking ordinances and breast implants and teenage pregnancies. They don't like all the coloreds and Spanish moving into the neighborhood, either. They never had such things in their day. These old guernseys are wrenching the last moments from their daydream of eternal middle-class sunshine. They seem to have a little nest egg in the bank. And nice lawns. And they're mortified that the rest of St. Johns isn't as fucking morally irreproachable as they are. The world is no longer like it was on V–J Day. Whatever happened to Edward R. Murrow or Ed Sullivan or Tex Ritter or Garry Moore? I'll bet John Wayne never snorted drugs or let his dog make whoopee with his girlfriend. Forget about the New World. Nice luxury cars with soft stereo music and cruise control. Roll up the windows, turn on the Mantovani, and hold out against all the filth.

Fifty years ago, it must have been much easier and simpler to be a St. Johns girl. Things seem much worse, the future much grimmer, for the young ones now. And that, of course, is why the young ones are out there having too much fun.

7

Prayin' Hard

Let me get this straight—your religion preaches that two thousand years ago, a Middle Eastern virgin was impregnated by a ghost. And the spawn of this ethereal sperm grew up to walk on water and multiply bread loaves and heal the sick and raise the dead and cast out literal demons. And this Love Child wasn't just any ordinary spud, it was God incarnate who willingly submitted to a bloody S&M crucifixion to pay for OUR sins, when it would have been much easier (and less messy) if He'd merely made us sin-proof in the first place. And this Miracle Baby, son of a (cough) virgin, rose from the dead after three days and now gets very upset when heavy-metal musicians slander His name. And Moses parted the Red Sea, Noah had an ark, God rained frogs on Egypt, and Joshua made the sun stand still. And even though Adam and Eve only gave birth to two boys (one of whom killed the other), the human race somehow fruitfully multiplied while avoiding the sin of incest. And remote Polynesian islanders will boil in molten lava eternally if they don't embrace the gospel, even if they've never had a chance to hear the gospel. And the God who gave you a weenie will also zap you with a lightning bolt if thou darest toucheth the weenie which he didst create.

Is that it? Did I miss anything? Is this the horseshit you're trying to peddle me? That's not the Greatest Story Ever Told, it's the craziest. And you tell me perhaps a third of the people on earth believe this fairy tale? Many of them are willing to kill or die for it? That's frightening. You're sure this isn't some sort of sci-fi novel or supermarket-tabloid conspiracy theory?

No. It's business as usual. All the holy scriptures of all the world's major religions are nonsense. Lies. Fabrications. Dangerous mythmaking. All religions are wrong. All of them. And the more they insist on being right, the wronger they are. There is no such thing as a religion that makes sense. All religious leaders are liars and con men. DON'T trust them. Above all, DON'T give them your money. If anyone tells you they know God personally, punch them in the nose. Jesus Schmeezus. Jew Schmoo. Nazi Schmazi. Moslem Schmoslem. Cool it, kids. None of you is right. I realize I'm stepping on most of the world's toes here, but c'mon. You actually *believe* that shit? Resurrection? Chosen people? Vengeful Allah? Do you pray to a God who loves Christians (and no one else) or Jews (and no one else) or Moslems (and no one else)? It's ridiculous. Jesus is dead. Moses is dead. Mohammed is dead. Buddha, deceased. Every one of these know-it-alls has turned to dust. That should be commentary enough on whether they were the final word on anything.

The phrase "nutty religion" is a redundancy. So is "false prophet." And "cult" is a loaded word used by high-moneyed religiosos to describe any group that threatens their power base. It's a smear term used by ex-cults who've gone professional. Yet there remains a tendency among small-brained nimrods to distinguish between "legitimate" and "fringe" religions. This shows a basic misapprehension of the certifiably cuckoo-nut premises upon which all major world religions are built. They're ALL goofy ontological conspiracy theories, no more or less plausible than the Wizard of Oz. In honest moments, like, say, when a gun is held to their head, most spiritual leaders would admit they don't have the remotest clue why we're here on earth. When push comes to shove, what's their authority? NOTHING beyond some hallucinatory, desert-baked literary blatherings from thousands of years ago. How much blood has been spilled over the imbecile myth of Christ's resurrection? How much Arab-Israeli tension would be eased if both sides just admitted they'd never spoken directly to God?

God. The Big Kahuna. Head Cheese. *Il Capo di Tutti Capi*. The Host with the Most. The Original Gangster. What a retarded concept, even for a movie. Yet our planet teems with twerps who'd murder someone because they think God's so friggin' insecure, He can't stand to be slandered. Their mental image of God, as always, is a refracted semblance of themselves—Someone so emotionally vulnerable He'd need to surround Himself with sycophantic toadies who kiss His ass and cower in His presence. You'd think that God would be a little more self-actualized than to need constant back-patting. It's God as played by Frank Sinatra. What sort of sick, immature, ultimatum-delivering Creator is that?

Why am I so hot under the priest's collar? Because organized religion doesn't get blamed nearly enough. For EVERYTHING. Our hands-off sense of religious tolerance shouldn't overlook organized religion's many sins. For a thousand years, the brutalization of European serfs was excused as God's will. The original pitchmen of black slavery and Native American genocide were more likely to do it in the name of Jesus Christ than in the cause of white supremacy. Christopher Columbus, who of late has been painted as the original bogeyman of white imperialism, was more properly a Christian imperialist: "Let us in the name of the Holy Trinity go on sending all the slaves that can be sold," he wrote to a business partner.[1] Virginia aristocrat William Byrd didn't call his black slaves niggers, he called them "descendants of Ham."[2] The atrocities of Manifest Destiny weren't explained with eugenic theories of biological supremacy, they were excused with the scriptural admonition to smite the heathen and grab their land.

Mainstream religions aren't *less* absurd because more people follow them, they're all the nuttier for it. Stuffed with cashews, filberts, pecans, and macadamias. If a billion people believe in a resurrected virgin's son, instead of only one lunatic apostle, that's a billion times more delusion goin' on. All ideas that promote social cohesion are crudely constructed fibs which soften what otherwise might be seen as just another bleak form of control. But the bigger religions aren't dismissed as insane cults because the social architects realize how effectively religion can absorb and divert unrest. Pie in the sky keeps your mind off pie before you die.

This isn't to say that mythological systems can't serve a positive purpose for the believer, merely that you shouldn't mistake a postcard for actually going on vacation. As crazy as religion is, many people still seem to need it. Christianity, Judaism, and Islam will all die before the human need for religion does. The God Quest lasts forever. Religions are lucky if they get ten minutes.

I look at religion as any other tinhorn existentialist does. The need to *believe* is stronger than the need to believe in something *true*. In *Man's Search for Meaning,* Nazi concentration-camp survivor Viktor Frankl observed that it wasn't the strongest bodies that survived the camps, it was the inmates who had the strongest *ideas* to live for—whether the belief was philosophical or religious or the promise of a reunion with relatives. The idea didn't have to be factual—many prisoners' family members were already dead—but hope was what kept them going. Ideas, even if false, can be more powerful in keeping a person alive than a hearty metabolism or healthy appetite.

Since I don't know a thing, I figure I'm as qualified as anyone else to talk about religion. I have no inkling why I'm here on this dirtball planet, and I'm even less sure about you. I'd call myself an agnostic, but that sounds as if I'm nasally congested. I'm a simple boy. My life has never been French-kissed with supernatural phenomena. Never had a personal chat with God. Can't say I've had a tumor disappear through the power of prayer. Haven't seen any suspicious flying objects. No Sasquatches rooting around in my garbage can. I've sometimes been relaxed enough to feel what you might call "one with the universe," but that's as profound as it gets. Sometimes you want to feel connected to the universe, sometimes you don't. I get more religion taking my dog for a walk than I'd get in any church on earth. I've taken shits that have provided me with more exquisite spiritual satisfaction than twelve years of Catholic school.

If there's a God, one of His best skills is concealing Himself. I ascribe to the Cosmic Joke theory, that God puts us through the motions for no reason beyond His own sadistic delight. But I just can't trust a God so cruel He'd force me to live forever. I don't believe in an afterlife apart from the literal fact of biological recycling. After croaking, you decompose into mulch and thus aid the growth of plant life, which feeds the cows, who are eaten by humans. You turn to food when you die. Surviving *Homo sapiens* feast on your recycled protoplasm. What a treat. Makes it worth getting up in the morning.

The best thing about personal spirituality, as opposed to organized religion, is that you can make things up as you go along. You're able to tailor your beliefs to your specific needs. Religion is like masturbation, one of those things that's best practiced alone. What scorches my bikini briefs is when metaphysics are used as a social tool rather than a personal palliative. Institutionalized religion takes a simple, perfect principle and proceeds to demolish it. It injects an unnecessary and destructive social element into something better left in the personal sphere. Like organized government, organized religion demands your soul so it can give it back to you.

Whenever two or more are gathered in His name, there's usually trouble. Individual spiritual curiosity GOOD, organized religion BAD. Vote YES on inquisitiveness, NO on inquisitions. To the extent that religion encourages ecstatic dissociative experiences and transcendental ideological epiphanies, I say go for it, Rocky Balboa. Religions are like assholes—everyone has one. If you want to worship your seven-hundred-watt hair dryer, that's peachy-weachy with me. Whatever cools your jets. Swats your fly. Trims your fingernails. Waxes your fender. Lubes your axle. Greases your wheel. Floats your boat. Pulls your trigger. Massages your muscle. Hoists your flagpole. Whatever soothes your weary, horny soul. It doesn't have to be true, it just has to get the job done.

Most persons' lives are so crammed with meaningless indignities and fuzzy gray patches of nothingness that an intense, body-slamming, nose-diving, kamikaze sense of religion can mean all the difference. Religion is false hope for the truly hopeless. The religious impulse arises most fiercely among unhappy campers. All religions express dissatisfaction with the world as it is. Religious yearnings are an attempt to cure depression or alienation. When you're already living in the Garden of Eden, you don't need abstract dogma to assure you things will eventually be different. A religion, stripped of all the shellac, is any belief system that tends to get an individual—even if it's only one lonely bastard—through the night.

Religion gets louder as the paycheck gets smaller. Cinder-block storefront churches invariably make more noise than granite cathedrals. Lower-class religion tends to view the world as irredeemable, and they're mad as hell about it. The howlers, shakers, shouters, and screamers have always come from the lower ranks. The less your prayers seem answered, the louder you apparently have to scream.

And, *mais certainement,* it's the screamers and tremblers and nut-jobs for whom I have fondness. In a cultural sandbox saturated with postmodern smugness and hollow irony, I give high grades to anything that is literal-minded and heartfelt. I'm not worried so much about the veracity or falsehood of the beliefs in question; I'm just impressed that they MEAN it, mannnn. Being unafraid to make an ass of yourself is the first baby-step toward enlightenment. I enjoy religion that arises more from compulsion than obligation. More from a need for answers than a desire to conform. A religion of extreme emotion and desperate escapism. Religion unashamed of sweat and melodrama. Religion as it should be.

Innovation, religious or otherwise, has never come from the mainstream. Since the larger denominations have had time to consolidate and sacramentize and codify everything to death, high-nitro spirituality is usually confined to the heresies.

The frontier, not the city, has always been the land of heresy. The further you stray from established religious meccas, the more likely you'll find schisms and splinter groups and truly odd pockets of intense belief. Appalachia's hillfolk, often portrayed as the lowest-common-denominator buffoons of mainstream Christianity, have historically boasted the nation's *lowest* rates of organized church affiliation. If hillbillies attended services at all, it was often to disrupt them with pistol shots and rebel yells. Abandoned in the wilderness, more dependent on their own wiles than on societal networks, mountaineers developed religious formats with a distinctly personal slant.

Non-Christian hillbilly spirituality was a witch's gumbo of European peasant superstitions mixed with African and Native American folklore. As with most forms of preindustrial animism, spirits were thought to be everywhere. Angels were given credit for good things. The Devil was blamed for sickness, misfortune, or crappy weather. Omens. Rubbing an X on your forehead in blood to conjure a vision. Folk remedies involving spiders' webs and the cold hands of human corpses. *Jack and the Beanstalk* and ninety-foot tapeworms. Broken mirrors. Black cats. Seventh son of the seventh son.

And then there's Jesus with a Southern accent. The poor white Southern interpretation of Christianity has always seemed to embarrass the rest of the nation. Tacky toupeed faith healers lapping their tongues in glossolalian gibberish. Red-faced Ozarks preachers screaming blood clots out of their lungs. JESUS SAVES plastered on barns. Jimmy Swaggart prematurely ejaculating with a motel hooker. Oral Roberts and his vision of a nine-hundred-foot Jesus.

To the mainstream mind, no manifestation of Southern-white Christianity seems so nauseatingly psychotic, such incontrovertible evidence of redneck degeneracy, than the snake-handling cults of Appalachia. Founded in 1909 by illiterate Pentecostal preacher George Went Hensley in Sale Creek, Tennessee, snake-handling arises from a literal interpretation of quotations attributed to Jesus in the sixteenth chapter of the Gospel according to Mark:

> And these signs shall follow them that believe; In my name shall they cast out devils; they shall speak with new tongues; They shall take up serpents; and if they drink any deadly thing, it shall not hurt them; they shall lay hands on the sick, and they shall recover.

Now, what could Jesus have meant if He wasn't speaking literally? How could you possibly interpret that passage figuratively? This was a man alleged to have performed literal miracles, and He's saying that true believers should be able to do as much. According to Christ's own instructions, snake-handlers and poison-drinkers and faith healers are the only true Christians. Serpent-lifters take Christ at His word. No pussyfooters here.

If Jesus was willing to be crucified, why shouldn't His followers be equally suicidal? The early Christians didn't mind being fed to the lions. Today's snake-handlers are the only Christian sect willing to walk that extra mile. It's about as far as a Christian can go without crucifying himself. Snake-handling is Christianity that puts some meat behind the motion.

The snake, my dear, is a sexual metaphor. Handling a legless reptile signifies mastery over the flesh. It was a snake that tempted Eve. Although St. Patrick is depicted as driving the snakes out of Ireland with a flute, the truth is that his missionary Christianity allowed no room for native Celtic serpent cults. In several artistic renderings of *La Madonna,* the Virgin Mother is shown crushing a snake beneath her feet. Christianity has never been herpetologically correct. What's initially disturbing about the specter of Christians handling snakes is that it somehow seems *pre*-Christian, a vague reminder of sex-and-blood pagan temple religions that Christianity was supposed to have permanently eradicated.

Caucasian snake-handlers aren't much different from Puerto Rican Santeria chicken-stabbers or Haitian voodoo hex-throwers or Hindu yogi fire-walkers. But most white Americans aren't likely to see it that way. Slobberingly emotional worship services are somehow seen as a vibrant sign of uplift and hope if practiced by "people of color," but of insufferable backwardness if whites are involved. Only when white people start barking and foaming is it viewed as cause for alarm. But this is almost its own form of racism, showing an acceptance of primitivism in all species but whites. It's like saying it's "natural" for any other race but Caucasians to act primitively.

> Snake-handling emerged in eastern Kentucky during the early 1930s in response to the social anomie that resulted from industrialization. . . . Attacks by the media and authorities have reinforced the [snake-handlers'] idea that "the world" is hostile to them. . . . [R]efusing medical attention and putting their fate in the "hands of God" is a symbolic rejection of the world. (David L. Kimbrough, *Taking Up Serpents*)

> Snake-handling occurred most frequently not in the most isolated regions of Appalachia, but in peripheral areas undergoing change from subsistence agriculture to industry. The cult helped its members cope with the humiliation attendant to being poor and a hillbilly. (J. Wayne Flynt, *Dixie's Forgotten People*)

A nice cup of strychnine, a blowtorch in the face, and a cottonmouth curled around your neck. Believers say there's no high like it, and I believe them. They say it's almost impossible to remain a spectator, to avoid being sucked into the maelstrom. It probably comes close the excitement of religious ceremonies from ten thousand years ago. I've only seen snake-handling ceremonies on videotape, and I always get the uncomfortable feeling that I've stumbled upon a nude couple fucking in the woods. There's something so intensely emotional about it that you feel like an interloper if you aren't part of the ceremony.

Frenetic hillbilly space gospel. Jagged-edge feather-plucking electric gee-tar. Rattlesnake tails and tambourines. Yelping, flapping, hooting, shouting believers. The congregation starts buzzing like a locust swarm. Sweaty men guzzling fruit jars filled with strychnine or battery acid. Live exorcisms. Faith healings of humans and livestock. People being "slain in the Spirit" and falling to the floor in wiggly ecstasy. Rumored levitation. Speaking in tongues. And the practice of fire-handling, in which true believers hold flames to their faces for flesh-melting stretches of time. The most impressive thing about fire-handling is that Jesus didn't even require it as a sign of faith. One supposes it's done merely for brownie points.

A belief strong enough to die for is usually one that keeps you living. Usually. Sometimes you die for it. Swollen cheeks and thighs and wrists. Gangrenous chunks of dead, blackened flesh. Vomited blood all over the chapel floor. Shirts and towels soaked in blood. Cups filled with the red stuff. If their arms bloat up with purple, football-sized sacs requiring amputation, it just shows how much they love the Lord.

> I have been bit fifty-four times and they never put nothing on me. I drink strychnine like cold pop and have handled a bunch of fire. (Pastor Dewey Chafin, Jolo, West Virginia)[3]

> [I've] been bit four hundred times 'til I'm speckled all over like a guinea-hen. (Pastor George Went Hensley, founder of the modern snake-handling movement)[4]

A poisonous snake once bit Hensley so hard in the nose, a fang snapped off and lodged there. He received a fatal snakebite in the Florida summer of 1955. At least seventy-four other believers have died by the fang since Hensley started preaching his hyperliteral gospel in 1909. This doesn't include a minimum of five strychnine-related deaths.

I figure the best way to avoid snakebite is to NOT HANDLE THE SNAKE. I wouldn't rassle a rattler. If that's what it takes to prove my love for God, I don't love Him. Imagine being on a date and having your companion ask you to prove your love by fondling a hissing water moccasin. You'd think they wuz bonkers. So what's up with God? I wonder how a Christian who's dying from snakebite feels when he realizes that the problem wasn't a lack of faith, but TOO MUCH faith?

That's the problem with religion. The more you take it literally, the more disasters you invite. Jesus Christ increasingly represents a time and place no longer relevant to your average trailer-park redneck. Christ is getting a little long in the tooth. He can't cut the mustard anymore. Probably hasn't had an erection since the Middle Ages. Jesus had a fantastic run—longer than either *Cats* or *A Chorus Line*—but His day is over. Jesus was a well-meaning, suicidal schmo. That's it. No more. If He even existed in the first place. Time for new cartoon superheroes.

The *Weekly World News* calls itself "America's most exciting newspaper." As I write this, the cover of the supermarket tabloid's current issue features twin headlines in the *WWN*'s inimitable screeching block type:

CAPTURED ALIEN WARNS OF INVASION FROM SPACE!
. . . and . . .
FEMALE BIGFOOT SAVES HUMAN BABY'S LIFE!

For verification, the *News* shows an "actual Polaroid photo" of the heroic female Bigfoot and an "official CIA photo" of a handcuffed alien "being hustled into a car by U.S. agents." Space aliens and Sasquatches are familiar guest stars to *Weekly World News* readers, a group to which I proudly claim fealty. The smudgy, all-B&W newspaper's weekly crossword puzzle is called BIGFOOT®, and one of the publication's most popular covers was of a generic hairless nude Martian shaking hands with the president next to the headline ALIEN BACKS CLINTON!

The *News* received perhaps its greatest publicity when it "broke" the story of Elvis Presley being sighted in a Kalamazoo, Michigan, Burger King. Knowing who butters their bread, the editors have since treated us to a string of other Elvis sightings. My favorite was the photo of a paunchy Presley being secretly escorted from a hospital on crutches.

This week's issue of the *News* included a self-congratulatory puff piece in which they asked four presumed experts these hard-hitting questions:

> What makes the *Weekly World News* the most compelling newspaper on earth? Why do over five million readers in 45 countries await each new issue with such wild anticipation?

An Australian psychiatrist answered the questions best:

> *Weekly World News* reassures us of what we know in our hearts to be true: That there's more to the world than the narrow-minded mainstream press lets on. Deep down we all know that space aliens, Bigfoot, ghosts, ESP and near death experiences are real. By covering these phenomena, the *News* acknowledges their reality and supports the reader's own truth.

The *Weekly World News* is a form of modern white-trash religious scripture, and I don't mean to sound glib or facetious or cheeky or cute when I say that. In its throbbing-vein paranoiac certitude that Armageddon's only a whisper away, the *WWN* most resembles the biblical Book of Revelation. Nuclear accidents and deadly viruses and alien invasions. Lizards that crawl in your mouth and eat through your intestines. A new breed of worms that feed on human brain matter.

There's the occasional Christian theme, but it almost always focuses on Satan rather than Christ. In recent issues, Ol' Scratch has been blamed for making his face appear in clouds only moments before the TWA plane crash over Long Island; for winning a man's soul in a card game; and for manipulating Germany, Russia, and China into a war that will become global. A reader writes to Serena Sabak, *WWN*'s resident crystal-ball psychic, with a problem worthy of Kafka's *Metamorphosis:*

> Dear Serena:
> My problem is extremely serious. I woke up this morning with a tattoo of the Devil's face on my chest.

The *Weekly World News* is a mail-order shopping mall for wannabe trailer mystics. It gives you more choices than Christianity does. The advertisements for debt-consolidation lawyers and get-rich-quick schemes signal that this is not an affluent readership. But the ads for lucky talismans and pricey phone psychics show the readers are looking for answers. The Fortune Key. The Four-Leaf and 33 Wishes Clover. The Mystical Ring of Ré. The Extra Strong "Lucky Gamblers" Necklace. Miracle Magic Dolls. Wrinkle cures. Zodiac perfume. "Please RUSH me the Miraculous, World-Famous Cross of God ... for only $17.95 plus $2.05 shipping and handling." Ads for haze-beshrouded telephone psychics who all claim to be the world's best and warn you that all other telepsychics are charlatans. And they have the nerve to say "Only $3.49 a minute." But the fact that there are so many of them charging so much money is telling. If the priests and ministers were doing the job, this sort of telecommunicated mysticism wouldn't be raking in the dough.

Careful perusal of the *WWN* reveals that the editors are in on the joke, even if the scoffers aren't. The editors and their advertisers are merely filling the gaps in the craving for quasi-spiritual arcana. The question is: Why do their readers need Elvis and Bigfoot and Martians?

Elvis Aron Presley is probably the most famous white country boy in history, and that alone is enough to qualify him as front-runner for Redneck Messiah. Yet amid the hipster set, he's more likely a musical Antichrist, a laughable emblem of white-trash fashion gaucherie. One cultural critic called him "vulgar, uneducated, tacky, a drug addict, a sexual pervert, a redneck ... America's favorite cultural joke, the epitome of everything low class, white trash, trailer-parky, hillbilly, and kitschy."[5] However, most of the geeky rock-crit types who use Presley's cellulite-ridden ass as joke fodder lead personal lives more pathetic and insignificant than Elvis's in every way imaginable. We need more jokes about rock critics and fewer about Elvis. Elvis splurted a bigger cum stain on the world's maw than you or I ever will. So the joke is on us.

Elvis is frequently blamed for single-handedly stealing rock 'n' roll from black people. "Whites stole rock 'n' roll from blacks," chant the sensitive music butterflies again and again. Sure, white-owned record companies shamelessly defrauded countless black musicians, but the hillbillies were robbed, too. Rock 'n' roll was essentially Southern music, with interwoven black and white influences. After all, even the darkest-skinned Delta bluesman sang his songs in English. More on the mark, Northern and British record companies stole rock 'n' roll from the South.

If Elvis was trying to sound black, he didn't do a very good job. I hear more jittery hillbilly/western swing—WHITE influences—in his music than I hear black jazz or blues. The thumbprint of black music seems much deeper on the Beatles and Rolling Stones, but those limey ratfinks don't get blamed nearly as often as Elvis. Why? I'll venture that the Beatles and Stones get off easy not because they're more authentically "black" than Elvis, but because they're less actual hillbilly than he was. Elvis-bashing doesn't show sensitivity for blacks, it shows hatred of hillbillies. Ironically, the Beatles and Stones got away with performing Southern music because they weren't Southerners.

Elvis-bashing and Elvis-worship sprang forth independently of each other, but they also tended to fuel each other. The more his image was maligned, the more his supporters sought to repair it. And the more feverishly Elvis was defended, the easier it was to jeer him. As he grew more ridiculous to one side, he became more saintly to the other.

Elvis Presley seems an unlikely candidate for sainthood. He wasn't even a suitable teen role model. In that famous photo where he's posing with Richard Nixon as part of some antidrug campaign, he looks so high it's a wonder his sideburns aren't flapping. Elvis didn't appear to be a particularly complex soul. He loved his momma and showed no evidence of messianic delusions. Except for the rare stab at social commentary in songs such as "In the Ghetto," his music was barren of messages. Elvis seems almost a moral/spiritual blank—neither moral nor immoral. An amoral canvas. He seems substance-free, but being an open container makes it easier for people to fill him with their own meanings. He's so empty, you're able to stuff his pastry shell with whatever cannoli filling you choose.

Pop stars are the devotional fetish items of modern worship in ways identical to which saints were venerated in the Middle Ages. Dead pop stars all the more so. But unlike most resurrected idols, Elvis had already started to rot before he died. If he had ever played the shaman's role, of someone who channeled spiritual energy to a rapturous audience, it was in his early days as the Hillbilly Cat. He allowed the ritual to possess him, which is all you can ever ask of a priest.

But by the seventies he had become entirely ossified, a mockery of his earlier performances. He had become an Elvis cutout figurine, beyond self-parody. A heterosexual Elton John. A sequined, karate-chopping drug pig. A nunchaku-swinging, pill-gobbling, muttonchop-sideburned, comic-book Godzilla Elvis. Eating doughnuts and forgetting song lyrics. That whole Hawaiian Vegas Werewolf thing he had going on is inexplicable to me. A cultural mystery. Perhaps it's some cabalistic cryptic symbolism that is flying right over my head. If he had lived, it wouldn't have been pretty. Elvis with a grape cluster of hemorrhoids and a hearing aid. The Lord snatched him up not a moment too soon. Elvis wasn't *so* dissipated or old at the time of his death that it's impossible to imagine him in heaven achieving an erection. Up at the right hand of God, Elvis can stay hard forever.

Interestingly, it's the latter-day, drug-addled, World Wrestling Federation Elvis upon which most spiritual devotion is focused. Almost all Elvis impersonators depict him not as the Hillbilly Cat, but as he appeared in the mid-1970s, shortly before he fell dead off his toilet while reading *The Scientific Search for the Face of Jesus,* his body stuffed with a miniature pharmacy's worth of pills. Likewise, most Elvis-fan iconography—the cocktail coasters and collectors' plates and statues and whiskey decanters and music boxes and table lamps—concentrates on this later period.

I think there are two reasons for this. First, as already stated, the

1970s Elvis had become a hollow ritualistic shell. To capture Elvis from the 1950s, you'd need actual inspiration; to simulate Elvis from the 1970s, you merely needed to buy one of those spangled, rhinestone-and-mirror-studded jumpsuits. Elvis had provided his followers with an easily duplicated format. An Elvis-impersonator concert is like *Beatlemania!* or the Catholic Mass—the bland liturgification of something that long ago was inspired.

The second reason is more important—the 1970s Elvis was the one who most needed redemption. Elvis had been an object of great pride for many oft-insulted Southern whites. He conquered an entertainment industry controlled by non-Southerners who only made fun of him after his death. By denying the blubbery dope-blimp excesses of Elvis's last years and instead rendering him as a godlike figure, Elvis's fans are performing their own act of redemption. By redeeming Elvis, they play God. They are reconstructing this much-maligned Son of the South and shifting the blame onto a cutthroat entertainment industry that poisoned his hillbilly purity. There's something cautionary about the Elvis saga, that perhaps po' white trash should stay on their own side of the tracks.

Denial of Devil Elvis, and his transformation into Angel Elvis, is evidence of his fans' need to make him into something he obviously wasn't. It shows a wish to make pop stars into something beyond what they are, a desire to set things back in place even after they've shattered. A need for some perfect eternal template. It shows that the representative icon is more important than the real McCoy.

> Elvis—he's the greatest entertainer of all time, and he is the King of Rock and Roll, now and forever. (Elvis Impersonator Number One)
>
> Elvis was the most charismatic person ever on earth except for Jesus. (Elvis Impersonator Number Two)
>
> His name will be around until the end of the world. (Elvis Impersonator Number Three)
>
> To me there will only be one Elvis and no one else will ever follow or entertain in his footsteps. (Elvis Impersonator Number Four)

Elvis, by far, is the greatest person that has ever walked the face of the earth. No one, and I mean no one, will ever replace him. (Elvis Impersonator Number Five)

If he had lived, Elvis would have brought peace to the world. (Elvis Impersonator Number Six)

His fans chant "Elvis is King" and talk constantly about keeping his memory alive with a prayerlike determination, as if Elvis would vanish the moment they ceased with their mantra. And they're right—he would. So that's why they keep chanting. Keep thinking about him, and he'll never go away. An immortal Elvis would mean that they are in some way immortal, too. If Elvis lives forever, so does white trash. THE KING LIVES . . . ELVIS DIDN'T DIE, HE JUST MOVED TO A BIGGER MANSION . . . AND ON THE EIGHTH DAY, GOD CREATED ELVIS. It's a way of codifying, of vindicating and ritualizing, a very specific white American experience. It's more *pertinent* for a white Southerner to pray to Elvis, born in Mississippi in 1935, than to Jesus, born in Nazareth in the year 0.

Like Jesus, Elvis has been kept alive by a memory, and a largely embellished one at that. Those who spiritualize Elvis show a blind-faith unwillingness to believe that this water-retaining, colonically impacted, peanut-butter-and-banana-sandwich–eating hillbilly boy is dead. To them, Elvis lives on through conspiracy theories and numerology. His stillborn brother Jesse. The mysterious misspelling of Elvis's middle name on the Graceland tombstone. And how the date of his death, 8/16/1977, "adds up" to 2001, and it's no coincidence that his mid-seventies concerts always started with the theme from *2001: A Space Odyssey*. Elvis lives in the visions, dreams, and prophecies he sends through his more rabid adherents. He lives on in relics such as the alleged vials of "Elvis' Sweat!" and bags of Graceland's topsoil sold in souvenir shops. He lives on by revealing his face in the clouds or on an ice-covered windowpane. He lives on in the candlelit remembrances of his birthday, his death day, and every holy day in between. He lives on in whispered reports of faith healing through the invocation of his name. He lives on through the people who claim to be his children or who change their surname to Presley or who get plastic surgery to look more like him. A friend of mine named his kid Elvis. There's even an Elvis Goad living in Illinois.

And from many accounts, the religion works. Look at these personal testimonials:

> In a roundabout way, he did save my life. I was feeling extremely depressed, almost suicidal. (Elvis Impersonator Number Seven)[6]

> Here was somebody [Elvis] who took up ninety-nine percent of my time, and my money, and yet the thought of killing myself never, ever crossed my mind. *Never.* And I don't understand that. (Frankie "Buttons" Horrocks, a middle-aged, chain-smoking, female Elvis fanatic with peroxided gold hair and a rusty-Brillo Jersey accent. Frankie moved to Memphis immediately upon learning of Elvis's death. She says if she were ever to meet Elvis, she'd rather fuck him than have him sing to her. When her daughter was murdered by a sexual predator, Frankie buried the girl with a copy of the "Burning Love" 45 RPM single in her casket.)[7]

> And like I'm saying, [if] it wasn't for this Elvis collection, I figgered I'd be dead—or locked away in a crazy house 'til the day I died. . . . I was actually a [sic] animal. I mean, a beast, no-good animal that would feel like killin' anybody just for a drink of water. For the pleasure of it. I had those kind of feelings. But this Elvis collection took that away from me. I don't have to feel that way no more. 'Cause just like I said, just like, there's a burden lifted from me. (Jesco White, a Boone County, West Virginia, gasoline-sniffer, mountain dancer, reformed burglar, and Elvis impersonator. Jesco once held a blade to his wife's throat because she cooked him a plate of runny eggs. His performances as The King are largely confined to his trailer home's "Elvis Room," which is filled with Presley-related knickknacks and tchotchkes.)[8]

Elvis himself seemed highly self-destructive—Elvicidal—so his qualifications as a suicide counselor are unclear. Obviously, it isn't Elvis himself who gives hope (he's dead), it's the believer's mental image of a redeemed Elvis. The *idea* of Elvis has saved lives, probably at least as many lives as snake-handling has killed. That fact alone qualifies Elvis-worship as a religion.

Along the time continuum of white-trash belief, Elvis signifies the present. He's gone, but still relatively contemporary; there are first-generation apostles who touched the hem of his garment while The King was still alive. Looking backward in time for inspirational imagery are the Bigfoot Fetishists. Their idol, also known as Sasquatch, Yeti, Momo, Yowie, and the Abominable Snowman, represents an idealized past.

Suddenly the entire forest smells as if it were swept with unbearable halitosis. A dry-heaving malodorous mix of stagnant pond slime and musky gorilla feces. He bastes in his own funkiness. He wears no deodorant. He's Bigfootloose and fancy-free. Moss between his toes, dried mud and blood encrusted in his shaggy ass hairs. Hygienically, Bigfoot is a mess. *Très gauche.* Oscar Madison. But once you get past the smell, you've got him licked.

And he's a large fella. Nine feet tall and a thousand pounds. Can cross a two-lane road in two strides. Hair from creamy white to carrot red to coal black. Endowed with log-throwing, boulder-hurling, fuel-drum-heaving strength. You can hear his high-pitched, Rodan-like squeal for miles.

There were giants on the earth in those days. . . . (Genesis 6:4)

Many world cultures have some variant on the Big Hairy Apeman myth. And there may be some literal basis to it. Archeologists digging in China have uncovered the bones of an extinct *Gigantopithecus,* a hairy headbanger who ranged from eight to twelve feet. Most Native American tribal myths allowed for some mountain-devil character. The word "Sasquatch" is derived from the Salish Indian word *saskehavas,* for "wild men." One Pacific Northwestern tribe called him "Free Man," the one who couldn't be tamed.

Although Bigfoot has been allegedly sighted in all fifty states, his myth has largely been propagated in the tall timber of the Pacific Northwest. There's a lot of room for him to hide up here. True believers allege there could be up to two thousand Bigfeet hiding in these mighty north woods.

The Western Bigfoot Society is headquartered in a used-book store located smack-dab in the heart of fun-loving St. Johns, Portland, Oregon. The WBS boasts a membership of around one hundred fifty believers, nearly fifty of whom claim to have seen Bigfoot in the flesh. The Western Bigfoot Society networks (footworks?) with other 'foot-seeking groups such as the Kansas Bigfoot Center, The New England Bigfoot Info Research Center, New Mexico's Southern Sasquatch Society, and The Western Bigfoot Research Project.

Ray Crowe owns the used-book store that houses the Western Bigfoot Society Museum in its basement. Ray is also the society's founder and president. He's a chubbier, slightly more distracted version of Floyd the Barber from *The Andy Griffith Show*. A local paper described him as "rumpled," and I can't really improve on that word. Ray is cognizant of the "chuckle barrier" that prevents people from believing in Bigfoot, and he doesn't seem to care. Ray, whose eyeglasses always seem slightly crooked, even advises those who purchase WBS literature to "Wear your SKEPTICALS when reading."

One of Ray's store display windows is a shrine to Sasquatch. A hand-drawn poster of Bigfoot makes him look like NBA superstar Karl Malone. There are Bigfoot dolls. A BIGFOOT—ALIVE AND WELL T-shirt. A Western Bigfoot Society baseball cap. A 45 single of "The Legend of Big Foot" by Kim Olson on Big Foot Recordings. Several plaster-cast impressions of giant footprints that remind me of Cynthia Plaster Caster and her collection of rock stars' cocks in the 1960s. A spice shaker–sized vial filled with alleged Bigfoot poop, available for ten dollars within the store.

The door to the basement museum/meeting room is marked PRIVATE and is only open to the public on the third Thursday of every month, when the society convenes at seven P.M. Wooden stairs lead down to a cold, damp basement in which seemingly every inch of the walls is covered with Bigfoot memorabilia: numerous yellowing newspaper articles, maps of sightings, photos of muddy WBS field trips, alleged Bigfoot hair and bones, more plaster foot casts, more drawings, more alleged poop. Roughly fifty fold-out chairs face a podium, behind which lies a wooden coffin occupied by a life-sized gorilla costume. Bigfoot is everywhere down here. This is the chapel. The ritual chamber. The catacombs.

I've been privileged enough to attend a few WBS meetings. At one, grown men performed ear-piercing elk calls and explained how the sounds differed from Sasquatch's wail. The premise of another monthly meeting was something like "What Would Happen If Bigfoot Were Bitten by a Poisonous Snake?" but that seemed like an excuse for Ray's herpetologist friend to pass a series of de-venomed serpents around the willing audience as if it were a snake-handling ceremony. These are believers. A murmur arises from the group whenever a new sighting is announced. Some members allege that Bigfoot has been spotted in the hills of Forest Park, visible from my front porch. Another guy thinks Bigfoot keeps evading capture because he's a master of time travel.

As much as I admit being on the giggling side of the "chuckle barrier," I was impressed with the group's amiable sincerity. None of them seemed insane; they just appeared to be on a quest. It was all as harmless as if they were looking for a set of lost car keys. Bigfoot provided them with something to believe in beyond what they knew to be true.

Apart from the ritual of monthly meetings, the Western Bigfoot Society has something akin to an annual holy season: a three-day summer festival called Bigfoot Daze out in Carson, Washington. The town of Carson is in Skamania County, which has an actual law on the books penalizing any Sasquatch-killers with a $10,000 fine and one year in jail. The Bigfoot Daze festivities include a Bigfoot Dance and the crowning of the Bigfoot Queen. Food served includes Yeti Spaghetti and Abominable Potato Salad.

The closest thing the Western Bigfoot Society has to mythological scriptures are two fiction books self-published by WBS members: *Children of a Lost Spirit*, by Nancy R. Logan, and *The Bigfoot Bar & Grill*, by Ray Crowe himself. Logan's epic novel seems like about a thousand pages set in tiny, medicine-bottle type. Ray's opus is more properly a novella, only thirty-two typewritten, spiral-bound pages. But both books sketch out remarkably similar stories.

Both novels feature Sasquatch clans whose members have kooky names. In *Children of a Lost Spirit,* the Bigfeet call themselves Baa, Geh, Walat, and Haelwa. In *The Bigfoot Bar & Grill,* we get to meet Poooz, Plaaax, Skaaaz, and Sraaar. Both Bigfoot families are Sasquatch Separatists who warn their members that only trouble could result from interacting with humans. Both books mention lingering karma over the white man's thievery of the land from Native Americans.

A wandering, dissatisfied Caucasian housewife is the protagonist in both books: *Children of a Lost Spirit* tells the story of Camille, a battered woman who strays too far from a camping trip with friends. *The Bigfoot Bar & Grill* focuses on Goldie, a bartender who lives in the Sasquatch R.V. Park and can't get her logger ex-husband to cough up his alimony checks. While hiking the Wind River wilderness area, Goldie encounters more nature than she expected.

In both novels, Bigfoot is quite the ladies' man. An indefatigable lover. Musky, hairy, and buffed-out. An eight-foot Priapus. He seems like he'd deliver in the bedroom. He's the sort of grocery boy who knows where to dump his package. Big feet. Big hands. Big body. I mean, do you need cue cards to fill in the rest?

> She looked closer at the sitting Creature and saw that it was indeed a male. . . . Geh was by far the largest, and she could not help but see that his manhood matched his body in size. (*Children of a Lost Spirit*)
>
> [B]ut his cock . . . a large normal man sized at first, but then it swelled up until I hurt inside . . . I can't imagine anything like it. (*The Bigfoot Bar & Grill*)

Both books feature graphic scenes of male Sasquatches raping the white female heroines. *The Bigfoot Bar & Grill* crams four rapes within its slim thirty-two pages—three of protagonist Goldie (you'd think she'd stay out of the woods), and a fourth of her friend.

> Poooz . . . jammed his organ into her from the rear end. She coughed and choked, then continued screaming, and wiggling to

get away. The motion excited him all the more, and he hugged her closer, sinking even deeper into her . . . bigger and bigger . . . this evil monster that was raping her. . . . Forty-five minutes later . . . a whitish puddle [lay] near her crotch. . . . Her crotch hurt so much that it was a chore to get dressed. (*The Bigfoot Bar & Grill*)

The rapist villain Poooz squirts his thick genetic material as if it were Silly String. He even accidentally discovers how to get a blow job. And when he isn't raping human women, he's beating his Sasquatch wife and withholding sex from her.

In *Children of a Lost Spirit,* Camille is raped by the evil Otta:

He dropped to his knees as he thrust himself deep into her body, and she screamed from the pain. . . . [H]e hit her and dropped to the snow on top of her as he rammed himself into her violently, again and again, and finally spurted his life essence inside her and cried out with perverse pleasure. (*Children of a Lost Spirit*)

Camille is eventually saved from Otta's further sexual predation by a valiant, sensitive, Alan Alda/Phil Donahue–style Sasquatch named Geh. He massages her back and playfully engages in snowball fights with her. He eventually impregnates her (consensually, of course), and Camille is certain that the baby will be much more like a nature-loving Bigfoot than a monstrous human. She embraces the teachings of Sasquatch religion, a matriarchal brand of animism that proposes that humans and Bigfeet had once belonged to the same tribe but suffered a tragic split in which the humans were left physically weaker and morally empty. The title's *Children of a Lost Spirit* are the Sasquatches, who eventually found their souls deep in the mountains. Camille learns Sasquatch prayers, such as this one for the dead:

> Great Mother Spirit of All Things
> Let the chipmunk lead his way
> Until he reaches the great mountain.

At the risk of offending feminists (like I'm worried), one could read rape fantasies as a symbolic longing for complete spiritual possession.

Ultimately, what's the difference between praying, "Fill my body with your love, sweet Jesus," and begging, "Take me right here on the carpet, big boy?" Bigfoot represents nature as Avenging Rapist. Just as the white man defiled Bigfoot's landscape, he in turn defiled their women. Bigfoot rape fantasies show a guilt complex in the process of unfolding.

Both *Children of a Lost Spirit* and *The Bigfoot Bar & Grill* end with the female protagonists emboldened and their white-male ex-lovers humiliated. How much of this is anxious hallucination? An estimated ninety-five percent of Bigfoot sightings are of male Sasquatches. To what degree does Bigfoot represent unspoken anxiety about the black male? How much of this is foot envy? Bigfoot is the logical extension of tall, dark, and handsome. He's a seventies blaxploitation super-badass pimp with a stable of long-legged hoes. Bigfoot is a muskily potent sexual athlete. He may not be Wilt Chamberlain, but he comes close. If Bigfoot rape fantasies aren't a distinct yearning for a black dude, they show a desire for a stronger man who hasn't been weakened by civilization.

If a Sasquatch were ever captured, what would his message to the world be? Probably, "Don't shoot!" Bigfoot doesn't bring a message, he keeps running away from us. That's his message—get out of Babylon before it's too late. The forest is a symbol for preindustrial Edenic conditions. The search for Bigfoot is actually a wild-goose chase for the Garden of Eden. It's a quest for Sasquatch nirvana, where everything is pure, even if it stinks to high heaven. Bigfoot is a way of examining one's anxieties about losing primitive zest in the swap for modern convenience. There's a bit of the Mud Ritual in all this Bigfoot Fetishism, of connecting with a preindustrial past.

The cover to *Children of a Lost Spirit* is a full-color painting of a gigantic Sasquatch with his arm around a white woman who barely reaches his hairy navel. She's in a typically tattered cavewoman's dress and wears a smile of radiant satisfaction. The Sasquatch has a lascivious leer on his face, a "Will ya look at the babe I snagged?" sort of mischievous grin. My copy is signed by the author, who added an inscription that sounds like religion to me:

For those who want to know.

Space Contactees also want to know, although they look to a hairless alien future rather than a hairy Bigfoot past. Unlike Bigfoot, space aliens are frequently desexed—whiter than the whitest white person, almost as white as the Japanese. A blazing white light appears, and a small, dickless man emerges from the hovercraft. Or was that the latest Michael Jackson tour?

Whether gray-skinned humanoids actually crashed in Roswell, New Mexico . . . or whether the U.S. government is warehousing Martian remains in Area 51 . . . or whether the Nazis perfected antigravity devices that will one day usher in the Fourth Reich . . . isn't a matter of concern here. That's for science and journalism to decide.

What's relevant are the religious implications of the UFO contact experience. Interplanetary invaders usually play either the role of Good Alien or Bad Alien; rarely are they both. When they come as benign angelic figures, it is usually as intergalactic missionaries who choose lonely earthlings to spread a message of universal brotherhood. The Good Aliens depict earth people as primitive and violent, a herd of slowpokes on the progress meter. If earthlings submit to a New Age of evanescently wise alien-imposed brotherhood, they will be spared from calamity; otherwise, the peace-loving, beneficent Martians will kill 'em all and let God sort 'em out.

Love for space aliens is multiculturalism taken to its logical extreme. Space-brethren theology is probably an unconscious gesture toward racial unity. UFO-longing is perhaps one of the primary religious longings, for it seeks oneness with the universe.

Then there are the Bad Aliens. The more sinister side of the abduction experience often involves forced genital mutilation and reconstructive sexual surgery. In these testimonials, space aliens are usually cruising for only one thing: human genitals to mutilate. They want to chop, slice, dice, and make julienne fries out of those earthling genitals. Aliens usually aim straight for the crotch. BAD alien. DIRTY alien. A buncha sek-shul pree-verts, those aliens are. If I was an alien, I'd go for somebody's wallet, not their genitals. Then again, when you've been traveling through space for millions of light-years, it's understandable that you'd be hornier than a sailor on furlough.

Close your eyes to the searing white lights and submit to sexual humiliation before the omniscient, bubble-skulled Martians. Not that there's anything wrong with surgical genital manipulation of the unwilling, but a little foreplay would be nice. Maybe it isn't the testicular scarring that hurts so much, but the fact that they never call in the morning. It's the feeling of having been used by a horny space creature. *Wham-bam, I sliced your penis, now it's time to fly back to Venus.* Who knew that space critters would be such hornbags? What kind of parties are they throwing out in far space? They travel eight billion light-years only to probe your anus? How anticlimactic. How ordinary.

The UFO abduction experience is analogous to trance spirit possession. It would probably be classified as a mental illness by contemporary clinicians, but so would all the experiences of so-called religious visionaries throughout history. Do people actually think Moses saw a burning bush that spoke to him? Or did he merely forget to take his medicine? St. Anthony being tempted by demons in the Egyptian desert isn't all that different from an alcoholic taxi dispatcher being anally probed by aliens somewhere in Tucson. The trailer-park lady who sees a UFO in 1997 is probably the same psychological type who'd receive visions of the Virgin Mary if she'd lived in medieval Europe. Certain forms of what is classified as schizophrenia can produce hyperclarity and deep insight rather than scattered, dissociative experiences. The trick is in telling the difference.

I tend to believe that most sincere UFO sightings are probably observations of top-secret high-tech government-aircraft test-fly sessions. A little green man told me that.

Elvis is that which is. Bigfoot is that which was. Space aliens are that which will be. The Holy Trinity of white-trash religion. And an honorable mention goes to snake-handling, which is miraculously able to breathe some life back into Christianity's corpse. All of these belief systems seem eminently more reasonable for a white working-class American than any major religion. These creeds haven't had the life sucked out of them by overorganization. They're still somewhat open to personal interpretation and direct emotional experience. Just you and the snake. Just you and Elvis. Just you and Bigfoot. Just you and that team of aliens operating on your genitals. Maybe there'll come a day when Elvis's anal secretions will cure world hunger. When Bigfoot's bedroom hijinks could cure frigidity. When our space brethren could help us with our homework. For all I know, Elvis and Bigfoot may be copilots of a rattlesnake-filled flying saucer as we speak. These are all things that are hyperimplausible. Pure religion. To an open mind, nothing's impossible, although most things are highly unlikely. Bigfoot lives. So do Elvis, space aliens, and the God who shields you from snakebite. It's all in your head. And you better get your head checked out.

Religion has always been a sponge mop to absorb class tensions. It's a safety valve. Without it, class matters would come much more sharply into focus. Those who belittle pork-faced stupid rednecks and their primitive caveman religions should be HAPPY that the trash has been placated with false creeds and phony promises. For if these hardcore believers were ever to focus their gaze earthward, they might realize how badly they've been screwed and would turn from reactionary religion to radical politics.

8

What's So Bad About Hatemongers, Gun Nuts, and Paranoid, Tax–Resisting Extremists?

Intro: Invasion of the Militia–Chasers

Boy, there sure are a whole lotta them neo-Nazi UFO silver-currency posse comitatus tax-hating militia gun nuts stockpiling weapons out there in the boondocks, talkin' 'bout killin' Jew bankers, lynchin' nigras, and makin' gub'mint buildin's get blowed up real good. Sure is *scary*. I wonder when the gub'mint's gonna ride in on a white horse like a bare-chested stud on the cover of a Harlequin Romance novel, sweeping us off our feet and protecting us from danger? Probably sometime soon.

They tell us that the danger's right around the corner. When a bomb explodes or a plane crashes in America these days, people have taken to blaming hillbillies rather than Arabs. And they're sure that the violent doofus rednecks, instead of having any legitimate political complaints, are throwing bombs due to groundless hate and paranoia. How do people know these things about the hateful, paranoid, bomb-chucking rednecks? The experts told them.

In the Cold War's wake, hunting domestic terrorism has emerged as a lucrative cottage industry. A class of neophyte "extremism experts" has sprung up, many of them former Satan-chasers and Nazi-hunters. Rick Ross, who's been all over your TV dial recently as an "extremism group expert," had a career in the late eighties as a satanic-cult deprogrammer. It was an easy career switch. Like the old Satan-slayers, the new hate-hunters are naively snooping around for PURE EVIL when they should be looking for human alienation. Since they're trying to catch something that isn't always there, I call these people MILITIA-CHASERS.

These "sensible," polyethylene, TelePrompTed, Barbie-and-Ken, TV/radio/newspaper cyborgs dismiss militias with a raised eyebrow and a hearty chuckle, tossing out vague, unquantifiable words such as "extremist," "bizarre," and "paranoid," slaloming around the facts as if they were ski flagpoles. With all the militia-dissin' going on, you see very little of what might be considered REFUTATION of militia rhetoric fact-by-fact, point-by-point. Instead, the experts throw a sucker punch, take the cheap shot, tell the fart joke, and pile on the "tooth-less," "inbred," and "nut-case" swipes. If you pay attention, you'll notice they hardly ever address the issues directly. What exactly are these antigovernment groups saying, and why is it wrong? I'd like to know, so I can decide for myself. The "experts" will say it's "un-usual" or "twisted" or "extremist," but that's all the explanation you get. It's almost as if the existence of these allegations is such a crude affront to their well-honed expertise, they *deserve* no factual retort.

The "experts" on militias or "hate groups" are invariably antago-nistic toward their subjects. In short, they HATE the hate groups. That's why it's misleading to call them "experts." They're hostile *advocates* rather than objective reporters. Although they feign objectivity, it's not very convincing. The only workers they seem to care about are federal workers, and the only taxes that seem wasteful to them are those spent prosecuting tax protesters. And they always seem to live in big cities —hundreds, and sometimes thousands, of miles removed from where these sociopolitical phenomena are concentrated. Wouldn't it make sense for at least a few of the leading "experts" on these groups to actually COME from the groups themselves?

Because the militia-chasers prefer taking sides to actually knowing the truth, contradictions abound in their rhetoric like ticks frolicking on a bloodhound's ass. They'll paint the so-called "hate groups" as child-

173

ishly superstitious for fearing an abusive, evil, dangerous government. That's *wunderbar.* But then the militia-chasers reveal their own nursery-school anxieties about the abusive, evil, dangerous militias. They accuse antigovernment agitants of paranoia, yet they spin around and claim that militias speak in coded phrases, have underground bunkers, and are secretly conspiring to take over the world and enslave minorities. They say it's lunacy to allege that men at the Pentagon can conspire, yet they're certain that farmers out on the plain are plotting as we speak.

They depict the United Nations as weak and ineffectual, yet they portray raggedy-ass backwoodsmen as the world's biggest organized military threat. The militia-chasers insist that the KKK is STILL politically powerful throughout the country, yet they'll jeer at the notion that the World Bank or CIA are influential. They tippy-toe around the sleeping-ogre fact that militias aren't the "well-armed bullies" who consistently extort nearly fifty percent of every American's productive energies under threat of imprisonment. They don't like to mention that the militias, for all their alleged racism, aren't the ones sending Americans to foreign lands to kill foreigners.

As generally self-identified sympathizers with "the left," many militia-chasers are predictably (and justly) outraged that the government spied on communists in the 1950s. But then they'll do a pirouette and beg the feds to increase surveillance of those on "the right" in the 1990s. They accuse the militias of conducting McCarthyite witch-hunts, yet they praise groups that actively maintain thousands of database files on THEIR ideological enemies. They aren't nearly as alarmed by well-funded private spy agencies such as the ADL, which was recently convicted of illegally procuring private citizens' records through bribes to a San Francisco cop.[1] The militia-chasers will scoff at the NRA for being Capitol Hill fat-cat lobbyists, yet the groups they point to as "grassroots" are inordinately well-funded, too. For example, the Southern Poverty Law Center is America's second-*wealthiest* nonprofit organization,[2] even though its puppy-dog-eyed leader Morris Dees flies around the country like Superman, protecting America's poor from hate.

The militia-chasers think it's horrible hate speech that NRA executive Wayne LaPierre called ATF officials "jack-booted thugs," but they'll compare even self-proclaimed NONracist militia members to Nazi storm troopers. They'll curse radio "hate speaker" G. Gordon Liddy for recommending that federal agents who knock down your door be shot in the head, but they don't mind the fact that federal agents are trained to shoot CITIZENS in the head. And they never seem to wonder why those federal agents were knocking down your door in the first place.

These are the sort of discrepancies that inevitably arise with ideological bias, no matter on which "side" of the imaginary seesaw you plant your splintery *tuchis*. Whenever you "take sides" in an argument, you wind up denying at least half of reality.

I started to notice that while all the antimilitia "experts" had a tendency to portray themselves as Common Joes just helping to shield the weak against a racist mainstream, these suit-wearing jokers were ALL wealthier and better-connected than the hicks who were cranking out antigovernment "hate literature" in their moldy basements. When I was repeatedly left with the instinctual aftertaste that most of the high-profile antimilitia "hate experts" you see on TV are well-paid, biased, scare-inducing muckrakers, I decided to research the topic for myself. I wanted to hear what the "extremists" were saying without having a highly subsidized spin doctor condescendingly act as a tour guide.

Am I being paranoid? Why shouldn't I trust the mainstream media to give me the full militia story? Could it be that a hefty quotient of what's being labeled "hate" literature, instead of coon-huntin' or Jew-bakin', actually attacks CORPORATE culture? Is the media possibly gun-shy about the real issues because they're financially beholden to huge corporations and their advertisers? Could it be that as the media become concentrated in fewer and fewer hands, reporters are afraid of losing their jobs if they rock the boat too much?

If our media aren't biased, tell me why we were shown EXTEN-SIVE DRIPPING KIDDIE GORE from the Oklahoma City bombing, but not so much as one drop of Iraqi blood during the Gulf War. In Iraq and Kuwait, our armed forces—paid for with your tax dollars—recently killed roughly ONE THOUSAND TIMES as many humans as the Oklahoma City bomb blast did, but our "objective" media didn't show ANY dead Iraqi babies. That's all you need to do to rest my mind—just 'splain this inconsistency to me. If I'm forced to pay taxes to have all these innocent people murdered, I should at least be entitled to watch.

By constantly poking you in the eyes with antiterrorism scaremongering, the major media practice their own brand of psychological terrorism. If you've been scared by any of these images, you've been terrorized. In the new climate of iron-fisted "tolerance," it's no longer acceptable to phrase upper-class fears of lower-class revenge in terms of a Nigger Invasion. But it's quite alright to terrify people about a Hillbilly Takeover. The coverage has been so vague and one-sided that most Americans are probably convinced that the militias want to murder niggers, and they leave it at that.

High percentages of adult Americans are functionally illiterate and can't find the U.S. on a world map. So it's not too hard to divert their attention and sell them on dumb ideas. To a generation fixated on TV, the media spin-meisters have sold the impression that if you can't SEE the killing and robbing, it must not be happening. That's why Charles Manson seems like a more prolific murderer than Norman Schwarzkopf, and why the storefront-looting L.A. rioters appear to be bigger thieves than investment bankers.

Semantics are deadly. Any government's definition of crime must by necessity exclude its own actions. Officially sanctioned killing is never counted as murder. Taxation isn't called robbery. Even if the government murders a quarter-million foreigners in the name of cheap oil, this somehow isn't "terrorism." It seems as if the mainstream defines terrorism as any politically motivated murder that isn't excused with a lawbook. If one were to start actually COUNTING stolen money and murdered bodies, things would look much worse for the establishment than for the so-called extremists.

Hate Explains Everything

So what's the truth? Are the militias malicious? The experts will tell you that they are. But despite their millions of dollars of top-flight research, they can't come up with better explanations for WHY they're malicious than these: HATE and PARANOIA.

That would be sufficient, *if* there were nothing to hate and no reasons to be paranoid.

HATE SPEECH is the most Orwellian concept to emerge from the twentieth-century twilight. It is especially deceptive because it hides behind a Happy Face mask. Most people want to be on the side of love, right? Like all dangerous ideas, the notion of hate speech sounds good until dismantled piece by piece. The first problem is with the term's vagueness. Hate speech, apparently, has become anything *they* hate. Through relentless exposure to well-meaning, soft-suds imagery, otherwise intelligent people have been brainwashed to believe that "hate" is a satisfactory explanation for any human action. Reducing complex sociopolitical struggles to a matter of "hate" is as simplistic as blaming it on "sin," but they fall for it.

A Manhattan lawyer who describes himself as "America's leading expert on the militia movement" writes that he hugged his three-year-old kid the night of the Oklahoma City bombing. He told Junior that it happened "because they hated too much." [3]

For now, let's accept the premise that one hundred sixty-eight humans died in Oklahoma City because people "hated too much." I think it's a silly and reductive proposition, but let's accept it. Now answer these questions, if you'd be so kind: Did a federal sniper shoot Vicki Weaver in the face because he hated too much? Did our government conduct the Tuskegee Experiment with syphilis on black soldiers because it hated too much? Does our justice system ignore a quarter-million jailhouse rapes a year because it hates too much? [4]

Did LBJ lie about the Gulf of Tonkin incident, causing the deaths of sixty thousand Americans and nearly a half-million Vietnamese, because he hated too much? Did our tax dollars recently finance over two hundred thousand corpses in El Salvador because our government hated too much? Did 116,708 Americans die in World War I because our government hated too much? Did 54,246 Americans die in the Korean "conflict" because our government hated too much? Did "our" government never come clean and admit that these wars were all useless wastes of human life that only benefited the wealthy because it hated too much?

Did the U.S. government intern Japanese citizens in concentration camps during World War II because it hated too much? Did the British police drag IRA members from their beds, drop them from helicopters, apply electrodes to their genitals, drug them, and insert blunt objects in their anuses until they fainted because they hated too much? Do Israeli police shove ballpoint pens inside the urethras of Arab political prisoners because they hate too much? Did Stalin and Mao each kill more people than Hitler did because they hated too much?

I'll expect your answers next Monday morning.

America's first hate-speech law was 1798's Sedition Act. Barely twenty years after the Declaration of Independence advocated over-throwing the British government by force, the United States made it a crime to advocate overthrowing the government by force. Meet the new boss, same as the old boss. It became a punishable offense to say or publish things that could "excite popular hatreds" against govern-ment officials. So maybe all this chest-thumping about "hate speech" has less to do with racism than it has to do with criticism of govern-ment. That's the hate-speech uproar deconstructed.

So now hatred is the enemy that the experts fear. Like all objects of fear, it's something they don't understand. The problem with most "experts" on hate is that they seem truly bewildered as to what *causes* people to hate. They're aware that hate surrounds them, but they don't know *why*. They don't appear to be people who've ever had much legitimate cause to feel burning, frustrated hatred in their lives. People in Northern Ireland know what it's like to hate. Blacks in America know the feeling. But the experts scratch their heads and ask for more federal grant money to solve the problem.

Some of them actually want us to spend millions of dollars to research what causes human hate. They implore you to fight the hate. They want you to kill it, squash it, suffocate it, exterminate it. Blind as bats, they entirely miss the point that the problem isn't hate, it's human nature. Especially when human nature rubs elbows with wealth and power.

Why do people hate? It's a natural human emotion, not some sinister aberration. Just as love comes from satisfaction, hate comes from frustra-tion. Hate is as useful as love, and it often works a hell of a lot quicker. Hatespeak is usually more honest than lovespeak, and it's always better than doublespeak. Some things seem worthy of hate. People hate being told lies, especially when they might die because of those lies. People hate when others are indifferent to their situation. People hate when they realize they're being robbed and can do nothing to stop it.

HATRED comes from powerlessness, whereas DISDAIN—the sort that highfalutin media yogis show for the redneck rabble-rousers' ethno-geo-ideological world—is more often reserved to the cushier classes. Poor people hate, while the affluent show disdain. The powerful have always regarded the powerless with a supercilious contempt that could very rightly be called hate. So they're in no position to act holy about so-called hate speech.

How can you protest your oppression (perceived or actual) and sound lovey-dovey about it? The MOST important type of speech to protect is hate speech, because it often contains desperate truths that would lose their urgency if expressed calmly. Most revolutions throughout history could hardly be called acts of love.

You know what I consider hate speech? Words or phrases that are dangerous falsehoods, such as "friendly fire." That's hateful to me. Peace with honor. Collateral damage. Pacification programs. Peacekeeping actions. National security. Vital interests. Bald-faced lies that get people killed.

When D.C. powermongers accuse Montana pitchfork-bearers of terrorism and make a garish media parade of it, they should really wipe their own dirty asses first. When government PR-puppies wag fingers and preach that "with free speech comes responsibility," they should check their own words. The government never flinched from infecting Americans with hate speech whenever "vital interests" were at stake somewhere on the other side of the planet. My brother had never met a Vietnamese person until the feds armed him with an M16 and told him to go murder them. When he came home on furlough and talked about how he wanted to "kill gooks," it wasn't the Klan who put that idea in his head, it was his Army officers. At six or seven years old, I remember seeing *The Green Berets* with John Wayne and being convinced of America's meritorious mission in Vietnam. Was I influenced by hate speech? Probably.

Maybe they're brainwashing everyone to love each other because they realize we'll all be fighting over the same loaf of bread.

The Race Smear

"Racist" has become a smear term that serves many of the same functions that "communist" did forty years ago and that "heretic" did a thousand years ago. Racism is the new social leprosy, rendering its bearer untouchable. After you've been called a racist, you're an outcast. There's no reason to trust anything else you say. Being called a racist can ruin a career just like communist blacklisting could destroy someone in the fifties. Once a person has been contaminated with the RACE SMEAR, the stain is hard to wash off, whether the allegation is true or not.

The militia-chasers know how to play the race card. AGAIN and AGAIN and AGAIN. I'll bet you didn't know that anyone who criticizes bankers is a closet anti-Semite with schizophrenic delusions. And that anyone who questions the federal government's claims to historical innocence is actually hiding his sexual inadequacy and hatred for blacks.

The militia-chasers' biggest argumentative *faux pas* is what I'll call "linkage." They'll string inherently unrelated things together so often, the undiscerning reader might come to find them indistinguishable. Say I kept listing things such as: "oranges, apples, Adolf Hitler, paranoid schizophrenia, and watermelons." Or, "peaches, bananas, the Klan, chronic psychosis, and strawberries." If I did this often enough, you'd start equating fresh fruit with racism and mental illness. The militia-bashers constantly link antigovernment protest with psychotic racial hatred. Since most of the government is composed of wealthy Caucasians, that's an odd allegation to make. The militia-chasers apparently can't conceive of an antigovernment sentiment that wasn't born of FLAMING BIGOTRY and PULSATING INSANITY. To their minds, militia ideology can't POSSIBLY have any other motivation behind it than the twisted, wormy mental pathologies of forest-dwelling, kike-blaming hillbillies. Whenever the topic drifts uneasily toward the government's possibly bloody hands, they steer it straight back toward the militias' allegedly ugly hearts.

As part of the RACE SMEAR, they'll allege that militia members are all Holocaust Deniers. Of all the "hate literature" I've read, I haven't seen much mention of the Holocaust. Maybe two or three pieces among hundreds of items. And even that piddly percentage didn't deny that the Holocaust occurred, it disputed specific facts. But even though I wasn't there, I won't deny that six million Jews died in World War II. And I'm sure that the militia-chasers wouldn't deny that nine million Germans and twenty million Russians died in that war, too. Not to mention a million American casualties. And I'm sure they're grateful that my father risked his life in that war to liberate Jews from concentration camps. And they'd probably be the last to deny that proactively NONracist Marxist governments have murdered more than ninety-five million of their own citizens this century.[5] Neither would they deny that an additional thirty million or so Russians and Chinese were purposely starved by their governments' agricultural programs this century. We wouldn't want to forget anyone. I won't be a Holocaust Denier. But some people, in the phrasing of Adam Parfrey in his book *Cult Rapture,* are Establishment-Deniers.[6]

This is the same government that peddled white supremacy as a tool of social control; now they're pushing equality for the same reasons. If you take the bigotry out of government, the government still remains. Is the blackboard too blurry for you to see the chalk scribblings, Poindexter?

Is it possible to express these sort of antigovernment/antifinance/antiglobalism sentiments without a TRACE of racism? Sure it is, and that's what the militia-chasers don't want you to know. White-haired pussy-whip Phil Donahue wanted to lambaste the militias as backwoods honky bigots, so his TV producers flew in the leader of the Ohio Militia. Donahue must have shit his adult diapers to discover the man was BLACK.

Relax and Don't Be Paranoid

In politics nothing ever just happens. When it happens, you can be sure it was *planned* that way. (Franklin D. Roosevelt)[7]

I don't know nothin', but I *suspect* a lot of things. (Junior Samples, erstwhile *Hee Haw* star)[8]

PARANOIA. PARANOIA. PARANOIA. The militia-chasers repeat this word with such feverish frequency, you begin to sense they're paranoid that you won't realize they think right-wing redneck antigovernment groups are paranoid. Like all seasoned apologists for power, they label political dissenters as mentally ill. There's an equation of skepticism with paranoia, of antigovernment protest with psychosis. Sanity, in many cases, is being measured by how closely one adheres to existing social dogmas. Sounds like Russia to me. When people start being psychoanalyzed, diagnosed, and possibly medicated or injected or JAILED because of their political views, paranoia doesn't seem so unreasonable.

When the world situation is disturbing, I see nothing wrong with being disturbed. You can manage dissent by treating us to the TRUTH, not more needles and hospitals. Paranoia is always a possibility, but so is the possibility that someone who condescendingly says "you're being paranoid" is hiding something.

In the more tender moments of my impressionable youth, my parents would tell me that I was a planned baby, that I wasn't really an accident due to some drunken Friday-night condomless slipup. Up until the point where they started repeatedly reassuring me, I hadn't even considered that a baby COULD be an accident. But they kept telling me so many times, I began getting suspicious. In the same way, I didn't start to get paranoid about the government until you kept insisting that I shouldn't.

Muhammad Ali once said something to the effect of "it ain't braggin' if it's true." By the same reasoning, you ain't paranoid if it's true. When you honestly look at history, how can you be anything BUT paranoid? When it's a choice between blind faith and paranoia, gimme, gimme paranoia.

The subject of black helicopters is a good example of the militia-chasers' tendency to avoid facts and merely call the opposition crazy. Most media luminaries and "experts" smugly dismiss black helicopters as imbecilic supermarket-tabloid phantasms. I'm surprised that someone hasn't yet suggested that the militia members are merely hallucinating Giant Negro Phalluses in the sky. One self-proclaimed know-it-all likened black helicopters to Elvis and Bigfoot and UFO sightings, adding that "reasonable people reject these myths."[9] A self-described "extremism group expert" called it "black-helicopter mythology" on a Geraldo Rivera CNBC appearance. Geraldo, objective broadcast journalist that he is, added that militia members were "fruitcakes" for believing such balderdash.

So are black helicopters quantifiable fact or insane racist fiction? They're FACT, you fruitcake. The existence of a U.S. government black-helicopter base in Fort Campbell, Kentucky, has been confirmed by both Sarah McClendon of the White House Press Corps and Harvey Perrett III, a spokesman for the U.S. Armed Forces. The cost of the black-helicopter program is three billion taxpayer dollars yearly. The ebony choppers' stated purpose is "low flying country surveillance."[10] Maybe instead of swallowing whatever the "experts" say, more Americans should be asking why the government wants to watch over us in the sky.

In 1985, I was living in a section of West Philly only twenty blocks away from where a city helicopter dropped a bomb on the black-nationalist MOVE compound. For seven years while living in Los Angeles, I was awakened in the middle of the night by the loud flutter and eye-burning white searchlights of million-dollar LAPD choppers chasing Mexican kids for selling dime bags of weed. Ask the Vietnamese peasantry whether the U.S. government is capable of terrorizing people with helicopters. Ask marijuana growers in Humboldt County, California, whether the feds would ever use helicopters against their own citizens. To call it paranoid mythology is not only deceptive, it's insulting.

Paranoia? Our government doesn't allocate thirty-five billion dollars of OUR MONEY yearly for intelligence-gathering, psychological operations, and propaganda campaigns? You mean to say that COINTEL-PRO and MKULTRA were merely figments of our imagination? The CIA didn't covertly publish over one thousand books before 1967, as disclosed by the government's own Church Committee? The CIA didn't spread bacteria in the New York subways' ventilation system in the 1960s? It didn't experiment with LSD upon unwitting human guinea pigs? It doesn't indulge in terroristic political murder, including several botched attempts on Castro's life?

Paranoia? Government law-enforcement agencies don't make lists of citizens merely for having beliefs considered politically undesirable? My journalism professor was WRONG when he said the FBI keeps files on half of all Americans? The government didn't infiltrate groups such as the Weathermen (left-wing) and the Minutemen (right-wing) in the sixties? It didn't conduct smear campaigns against both the Black Panthers (left-wing) and the KKK (right-wing)?

Paranoia? There was nothing shady about the fact that George Bush became president after being a former CIA director? Nothing weird about the fact that Bush's son was entangled in the S&L scandal? There's absolutely no evidence that the CIA is involved in drug-running, and may have been since the early 1960s? Our troops didn't invade Panama and capture Manuel Noriega because he was about to spill the beans about U.S. connections to the international drug trade? Was the *San Jose Mercury-News* hallucinating when it recently printed a series of investigative pieces substantiating the long-rumored contention that the CIA supplied black L.A. gangs with crack cocaine? Is it paranoid to note that this CIA dope-dealing occurred while our politicians sonorously bleated about the Drug War, spending billions of our dollars and ruining millions of lives to "fight" it?

There was nothing strange about the assassinations of JFK and MLK? Watergate? Whitewater? The Rosenbergs? The McCarthy hearings? The Pentagon Papers? The Bay of Pigs? Kent State? Iran-contra? Wall Street junk-bond trading? Absolutely NONE of this sounds fishy to you?

Maybe we wouldn't be so FUCKING PARANOID if they hadn't FUCKING LIED to us so many times. Just a thought.

Put on the blindfold and pop in the earplugs. Otherwise, they'll think you're paranoid. You may say it's nutty to give credence to ANY conspiracy theory; I say it's nuttier to have unwavering faith that those nice men in the government with their lollipops and free hot cocoa are acting in our best interests and not their own. If you have blind faith that public officials love and respect you, I'd say that's more of a superstitious leap than if you believed in UFOs, Bigfoot, or a Living Elvis. If you think that ever'thin's fine 'n' dandy, you aren't mentally healthy, you're stupid. If you believe that those who make decisions concerning your life allow you to know everything, I'd say you have to be a little MORE paranoid. Like medicine, paranoia is something best applied moderately, for too much or too little of it can kill you.

But if the militia-chasers can trot out a few full-blown yo-yos from within this nebulous "movement," they're satisfied they've debunked the entire ideological platform. If Timothy McVeigh believed there was a biochip implanted in his ass, I suppose that means the government never harmed anyone. This tactic seems founded on the belief that if you show the public enough zany conspiracy theories—and there are plenty of 'em—you're supposed to assume they're ALL zany. The very word "conspiracy" has been discredited as if impossible.

Of COURSE it's a conspiracy. But it isn't the Mau Mau or the Klan. Not the Nazis nor the Jews. It isn't the extreme left or far right, nor any of the noncommittal nobodies who cower in the middle. It isn't even the Italians. It's POWER, stupid. It's the tendency of human nature, left to itself, to try to get away with anything it can. The government is the biggest liar because it has the biggest REASON to lie. It's perfectly understandable. Those with money and influence want to protect it. That's not insane, it's common sense. It's just the way that money flows. "Conspiracy" is a loaded term—how about calling it "the apparently ineradicable tendency of those with power to attempt to influence events toward their maximum benefit and prolonged entrenchment"? Does that sound more sensible? I'm not talking about evil psycho UFO Kosher Bolshevik Satanic World Wide Spider Webs, OK? I'm yammering about the historically demonstrable habit of those in power to spend more time trying to STAY in power than in actually helping anyone. Those who DON'T conspire don't hold on to power for very long, because there's always someone else willing to be more ruthless. That's not militia, it's Machiavelli.

I'm old enough to remember all that psychotic, paranoiac, eschatological, H-bomb FEAR the government drilled into our heads throughout the Cold War. It was as scary as anything the Catholics taught me about hell and Satan. I was force-fed HEAVY anticommie propaganda while in grade school. I remember a cartoon slide show that depicted a superevil Soviet type riding a wild white horse and spilling red commie blood all over a white globe. Our government's propagandists terrified us enough to build fallout shelters. They ran schoolchildren through insane "duck-and-cover" nuclear fire drills, as if hiding under your school desk would be an effective defense against a twenty-megaton blast. Did the commies come and rape our grandmothers? No. So who's spreading paranoiac rumors? It's hypocritical for the government to create all these magnum-level false scares and then blame Americans for developing a paranoid mind-set.

Who's to say that a lot of this "paranoia" isn't the government's own fear of its implicit obsolescence? Government officials and private investors—and all the lackeys and suckups who do their bidding in tightly structured beehives beneath them—spend much more money on high-tech psy-war propaganda to discredit militia types than the militia types spend at Kinko's trying to shame the government. Did the government FIRE its extensive spy network and bury all its bombs after the Cold War ended? What the fuck happened to all those nukes we were pointing at Moscow? The feds aren't offering to heat our homes with all that leftover plutonium, are they? They're painting peace signs on all those nuclear warheads, right? I'm sure the FBI and CIA do nothing but help old ladies rescue kitty-cats out of trees, right? And they possess smart bombs and space satellites and micro-wave/biochip/sonic technology because, dag nabbit, those Bosnians or Iraqis or Somalians or Grenadians or Panamanians or Vietnamese or Koreans are likely to paddle their canoes onto our shores any minute . . . right?

Who would have more logical reasons to be sniffing around for internal threats—cabin-dwellers in Idaho or the world's hugest murder machine that no longer has any foreigners to shoot?

Listen, dummies: The ones bringing you the Terrorism Scare of the nineties are the same ones who brought you the Red Scare of the fifties. They're portraying these homegrown "terrorist" groups to be as ever-threateningly evil and two-dimensional as they portrayed the commies. The Big Boys haven't had a change of heart, just a switch of strategy. The government must continually reinvent reasons to justify its existence, or it's out of business.

It would seem that all you'd need to do to quell this rampaging, baseless, pseudoreligious paranoia, all it'd take to settle the militias' tummies, is to refute their allegations with FACTS rather than ad hominem slander. When you call them racist lunatics, it'll only get them angry that you're avoiding the facts. But you'd call that anger HATE, wouldn't you? All you need do to help us sleep at night is mass-mail every American a DETAILED accounting of how the CIA spends the thirty-five billion dollars we pay it every year to spy on us. I don't think this is an unreasonable request, as we're paying the tab for this unsolicited surveillance. Just do that, and we won't be paranoid anymore.

Stockpiling

When the militia-chasers can't scare you with allegations of hateful racist paranoia, they'll scare you with guns. The militia-chasers HATE guns. They insist that the Founding Fathers NEVER intended for private citizens to own arms as a defense against governmental intrusion. Eez dot rite, meester? Are the militias Second Amendment revisionists? Why don't we ask the Fabulous Furry Freakin' Founding Fathers themselves? [capitalization added]:

> Americans have the right and advantage of being armed, UNLIKE THE CITIZENS OF OTHER COUNTRIES, WHOSE GOVERN-MENTS ARE AFRAID TO TRUST THE PEOPLE WITH ARMS.
> ... A well regulated militia, composed of the people, trained to arms, is the best and most natural defense of a free country. (James Madison)

> Firearms stand next in importance to the Constitution itself. ...
> [T]o ensure peace, security and happiness, the rifle and pistol are equally indispensable. The very atmosphere of firearms everywhere restrains evil interference—they deserve a place of honor with all that's good. (George Washington)

> The great object is that every man be armed. . . . Everyone who is able may have a gun. (Patrick Henry)

> The Constitution shall NEVER be construed to prevent the people of the United States who are peaceable citizens from keeping their own arms. (Samuel Adams)

The best we can hope for concerning the people at large is that they be properly armed. (Alexander Hamilton)

To disarm the people is the most effectual way to enslave them. . . . I ask you sir, WHO ARE THE MILITIA? THEY CONSIST NOW OF THE WHOLE PEOPLE. (George Mason)

No free man shall ever be debarred the use of arms. . . . Laws that forbid the carrying of arms . . . disarm only those who are neither inclined nor determined to commit crimes. . . . THE STRONGEST REASON FOR THE PEOPLE TO RETAIN THE RIGHT TO KEEP AND BEAR ARMS IS, AS A LAST RESORT, TO PRO-TECT THEMSELVES AGAINST TYRANNY IN GOVERN-MENT. (Thomas Jefferson)[11]

Always hiding from these above quotes, the militia-chasers will nervously say that the Constitution was meant for different times, that Jefferson couldn't have imagined private citizens owning nukes. That's true. But Jefferson couldn't have imagined the GOVERN-MENT owning nukes, either. The gun-controllers will stutter and say that handguns are only meant to kill people. I'll play along. So will you please explain why government agents possess weapons, if not to kill people?

Getting desperate, the gun-controllers will drag out the phallic-compensation explanation, that pro-gun people are merely hiding impotence or penile underendowment. No doubt that stereotype applies in many tragicomic cases. But the penis can point both ways. Why is the government, which owns many more dick-shaped weapons than the militias, rarely accused of having a wiener hangup, too? Isn't it feasible that Pentagon officers are practicing phallic compensation on a grand scale? I've noticed that the same gun-control fanatics who lob these pistols-are-penises accusations often appear uneasy when the government appears weak or seems like it's being bullied. Whenever some toothless rural rowdy criticizes the government, there's always some stuffed-shirt neo-Tory who can't wait until the feds "get tough" and "crack down" on such impudent upstarts. Those who identify with the government as a father figure are perpetually anxious that daddy will get castrated. The militia-chasers talk a lot about white males' anxiety of losing their race privileges, but not too much about the government's fear of losing its grip. Nixon worried about America becoming a "helpless giant." You want to talk about someone with a twisted sexual pathology who foisted his petty hatreds on large masses? How about J. Edgar Hoover?

Inevitably, predictably, when all else fails, as a last resort, the militia-chasers will say that pro-gun sentiments are merely a cover for racist bloodlust. They'll try to make you think the only reason a poor person in a poor neighborhood could possibly want to own a gun would be to KILL NIGGERS 'N' JEWS. They ignore the fact that King Henry IV of Germany disarmed the Jews in 1096, which led to their brutal persecution. They ignore the fact that black slaves weren't allowed to own guns in the South. They ignore that Hitler wasn't too keen on private gun ownership, either. It's strange that the Hate Hunters, these wacky Keystone Kops Nazi-knockers, don't use *der Führer* as an argument against vegetarianism. They never say that Hitler proves that no one should own dogs as pets. Or that the one-testicled painter with the funny mustache represents a good argument against strong, centralized government, or against censorship, or even against public-works projects. No, it's just racism, racism, racism. Race, race, race. That's racist to me.

Fanning the fear, the militia-chasers charge that the gun nuts are "stockpiling" weapons in giant "arsenals." The plain truth is that military power is SEVERELY slanted in the government's favor. The gun nuts don't have smart bombs. The gun nuts don't have neutron bombs. The gun nuts don't have H-bombs. The gun nuts don't have Stealth fighters. The gun nuts don't have battleships or aircraft carriers. The gun nuts don't have police helicopters. The gun nuts don't have tanks. The gun nuts don't have submarines, nuclear or otherwise. The gun nuts don't have sophisticated radar networks and well-financed global intelligence organizations.

Government cheerleaders are very upset that Randy Weaver sold two sawed-off shotguns to an undercover federal official. Why, that's enough artillery to start a race war, innit? Meanwhile, federal officials have funneled weapons—sometimes nuclear ones—to most of the WORLD, and not always legally. You think Ollie North was delivering saltwater taffy to the Iranians? So who's precipitating violent armed conflicts?

When people get weepy about one hundred sixty-eight dead bodies in OK City—not that they shouldn't—it might be wise to put things in perspective. Government-sponsored death, whether through war or the murder of its own citizens, is estimated to have killed one hundred sixty-nine million people this century alone.[12] That's almost exactly a MILLION times the casualties of Oklahoma City.

What are the Unabomber's dozen or so mail bombs compared to Hiroshima, Nagasaki, Baghdad, and Dresden? What are Timothy McVeigh's alleged one thousand pounds of fertilizer compared to the shit we've dropped all over the world? In Vietnam alone, we dropped more tonnage than was dropped by all sides in World War II. And who did you say was the terrorist? It's a dirty business, comparing body counts as if they were football scores. But the news media's distorted perspective has begged all of these questions.

Amid all this scare talk about militias, what you don't hear is that your tax dollars have financed illegal militias all over the world when our government didn't like who was in power.

Dollars, Taxes

People who yap about all the "good" the government does tend to skirt the issue of WHERE the government gets the cash to wreak all this gilded benevolence. At one time, I thought it was kinda nice that the government was helping all these people, and I couldn't understand why any Scrooges would want to violently "cut" social programs as if they were stabbing at human flesh. Then as I looked at the deductions on my paycheck, I realized it wasn't the government who was paying a PENNY for these things, it was me. In essence, the government is not much better than a ticket scalper. If you gave me ten dollars to get groceries and I returned with two dollars' worth of items, you'd feel robbed, not like I'd given you "aid." In almost all cases, the ten bucks would be better left in your hands. The government acts like a charity agency that absorbs most donations into "operating expenses." It's like being forced at gunpoint to contribute to the Jerry Lewis telethon.

Taxes are much higher now than the taxes that caused a revolution in 1776. They're higher than the "tribute" that feudal lords demanded of their serfs, which was usually a third of their crops. Once you count federal, state, county, municipal, sales, sin, and hidden taxes, it probably averages around forty percent of every American's income. Imagine having forty percent of your words censored. Or forty percent of your time stolen. Or forty percent of everything you own taken away at once. Because it happens gradually—and because they slip it out of your paycheck before you ever get your claws on it—it doesn't seem so much like extortion.

Picture a city at night from an aerial view. All those millions of lights. All those people. And every one of them is having nearly half of their productive earnings drained away by taxes. Everyone you'll see tomorrow—on the street, in cars and buses, on TV—is likewise obligated to pay "tribute" to the government, too. Imagine how powerless the government would be if everyone just refused.

Even though tax protest is portrayed as extremism, most Americans probably cheat on their tax reports. That's a form of tax protest, and it's as mainstream as milkshakes. Henry David Thoreau was a tax protester who was jailed because he refused to render unto Caesar what Caesar claimed was his. Thoreau said he couldn't in good conscience pay taxes that supported both black slavery and the U.S. invasion of Mexico. Thoreau, as we all know, was a real extremist racist militia redneck hillbilly firecracker lunatic. Even those wimpy, peace-loving Beatles had a song about the evil taxman.

Is it racist to ask why the debt is continually swelling? Are they going to try to argue that all these taxes are being spent to fight racism? Bullshit. WHALE shit. More taxes go to bankers' interest than to minority aid. And even of the thin budgetary slice targeted toward minority aid, most is absorbed by administrative costs. Taxation has nothing to do with ethnicity, and it's a cynical low blow to make it a racial issue.

It's a financial issue. Since the government requires everyone to pay taxes with Federal Reserve notes (AKA dollars), tax-protesting "hate literature" often targets the banking system. The militia-chasers, racial reductivists that they are, link ALL antibanking rhetoric with anti-Semitism. While this is true in some of the more occult-type anti-Jew conspiracy theories, I find it hard to believe that WHENEVER someone criticizes the banking system, they're secretly criticizing Jews. It almost seems like an unconsciously defensive implication that a disproportionate percentage of bankers are Jewish, which is an allegation I'd never be foolish enough to make.

If someone's goal was to engender hatred for Jews rather than suspicion of the International Monetary Fund, wouldn't it waste fewer breaths just to say "Jews"? If they really hated blacks rather than the government, wouldn't they bomb the ghetto instead of the Federal Building? Maybe, just maybe, is it the squeakiest bit possible that at least SOME of these guys avoid racist epithets because racism isn't their motivation?

The militia-chasers allege that militias propose "funny money" currency schemes that would take the currency-issuing power out of the government's hands. This is 180° wrong. All the antibanking "hate speech" I've read consistently argues that the government SHOULD print its own currency, and that taxpayers would thereby save around three hundred billion dollars in bankers' interest yearly. That three hundred billion dollars would be enough to build five million homes or provide ten million jobs, or house more than forty million people in apartments.[13] It seems to me that racial minorities would BENEFIT instead of suffer from this sort of savings.

The fact is, the Federal Reserve is NOT a federal agency—it's an organization of private bankers, many of whom don't even live in America. As one "extremist" ranter put it, "The Federal Reserve, contrary to popular belief, is no more federal than Federal Express."[14] The Federal Reserve itself will tell you that it's a private entity. This is from an advertisement from the Federal Reserve Bank of San Francisco:

Some people still think we're a branch of Government. We're not.[15]

Surprisingly to many, United States dollars are not issued by the United States government. The antibanking rhetoricians consistently argue that the main problem with our currency is that the government DOESN'T print it, that it borrows paper notes—with interest—from private bankers. If the government printed its own money, they claim, there would be no need to charge interest on it.

Here are some quotations that don't come from the mouths of heinous evil rural Joe-Bob weapons-stockpiling Jew-hating short-wave TV-dinner mutants, but from the fathers of international banking themselves. Tell me they don't sound arrogant and power-drunk:

> Let me control the issuance of the money in a country and I care not who makes its laws. (Mayer Amschel Rothschild)

> The few who can understand the [checkbook-money and credits] system will either be so interested in its profits, or so dependent upon its favors, that there will be no opposition from that class, while on the other hand, the great body of the people mentally incapable of comprehending the tremendous advantages that capital derives from the system, will bear its burdens without complaint, and perhaps without even suspecting that capitalism is inimical to their interests. (Letter from Rothschild Bros. of London to a group of New York bankers, June 25, 1863)

> Banking was conceived in inequity and born in sin. The Bankers own the earth. Take it away from them, but leave them the power to create deposits, and with a flick of a pen they will create enough deposits to buy it back again. . . . But as long as the public and governments will legalize such things, a man is foolish not to be a banker. (Josiah Stamp, President of Bank of England during the 1920s)[16]

Another core problem with the militia-chasers is that the "rhetoric" they label as "extremist" has often been spouted by people MORE mainstream and historically famous than the "experts." I present yet more morsels of that psychotic redneck antibanker hate speech encoded with cryptic anti-Semitism spewed out by sick racists who've since been thoroughly refuted by more sensible minds:

Banking establishments are more dangerous than standing armies.
. . . The issuing power [of money] should be taken from the banks
and restored to the government and to the people to whom it be-
longs. If the American people ever allow banks to control the
issuance of their currency . . . the corporation that will grow up
around them will deprive the people of all their property, until their
children will wake up homeless on the land their fathers conquered.
(Thomas Jefferson)

All of the perplexities, confusion and distress in America arises,
not from the defects of the Constitution or Confederation, nor from
want of honor or virtue, so much as from downright ignorance of
the nature of coin, credit and circulation. (John Adams)

You bankers are a bunch of vipers and I will rout you out. If the
American people ever find out how you operate, there will be a
revolution before morning. (Andrew Jackson)

People who will not turn a shovel full of dirt on the project [Muscle
Shoals Dam] nor contribute a pound of material, will collect more
money from the United States than will the people who supply all
the material and do all the work. . . . It is absurd to say our country
can issue bonds and cannot issue currency. Both are promises to
pay, but one fattens the usurer and the other helps the people.
(Thomas Edison) [17]

So I'm sitting up late at night under a light bulb invented by Mr.
Edison, and all this mind-bending antibanker hate speech has me worried about the national debt for the first time in my life. I always felt
in the depths of my tripe-stinking intestines that there was something
fundamentally wrong with our monetary and credit system, but I had
trusted the "experts" when they told me not to worry.

But there are REASONS to worry. Several respected economists
predict an imminent currency meltdown. Interest accrued on the national debt now means that Americans are BORN owing. I find this
eerily similar to the concept of original sin. I've always gone to work,
paid my taxes, and yet some cabal of faceless bastards keeps plunging
me deeper into debt because they mismanaged those taxes. Is it
BLOODY BIGOTED HATE merely to ask for an accounting of the

194

money they siphoned from my paychecks? I don't care whether they're Semites or skateboarders or goddamned Martians—spike me with truth serum if you don't believe it—but I AM concerned whether they're stealing from me.

Is it delusional hate-inspired psychosis merely to ASK who fucked up so badly that we turned from the world's biggest lender nation to the world's biggest debtor nation? Is it somehow Hitlerian just to WONDER why the overall inflation rate from 1792 to 1913 was only ONE percent,[18] but that it's gone up more than ONE THOU-SAND percent since the Federal Reserve was instituted? Is it a foul act of immigrant-bashing to QUESTION why the national debt was less than one billion dollars before the Federal Reserve was estab-lished[19] and now stands at over six TRILLION dollars? Is it hateful cryptic racism to ask why the national debt is now more than THIRTY-SIX TIMES the TOTAL amount of cash existing in the United States?[20] Is it kike-kicking kookiness to question why private bankers, who scream, "worthless paper money!" when someone talks about the government issuing its own currency, are themselves only required to have around three cents in hard assets for every dollar they loan?

Is someone a mouth-foaming hate-soaked daydreamer if they simply ASK why the IRS, which terrorizes U.S. citizens for nonpayment of taxes, has never itself been audited?[21] Is it cross-burning lunacy to ask why most Americans work from January 1 until around May 26 merely to pay for taxes?[22] Is it slaphappy segregationist palaver just to ask why the federal income-tax rate was only two percent as recently as 1950?[23] Is it daffy racist dementia to ask why the working and middle classes pay taxes, while the mondo-rich avoid them through private trusts and tax-free foundations? Is it screwball xenophobic Euro-rage that drives me to ask why I'm required to pay two-fifths of my income for programs and policies which I never approved?

Beware those who call you dirty names merely for asking questions.

The militia-chasers want you to believe that the direct historical antecedent to militias was the KKK. So predictable. From the little I know about the Klan, I don't recall them EVER mentioning taxes.

I'd suggest different ancestors to today's musket-toting, tax-resisting yahoos: the Whiskey Rebels of 1794, and every outlaw moonshiner who has since followed in their bloody path.

The American Revolution of 1776, if you'll remember, was supposedly an armed protest against heavy British taxation of things such as stamps and tea. When Washington called for troops, some of the first men to enlist were poor farmers from western Pennsylvania, which stood as the American "West" of the day. Many of these shabbily clad volunteers were recent Scotch-Irish immigrants with no fondness for British oppression. They were said to be some of the best fighters of the Revolution, and Washington once publicly acknowledged their contribution in helping us crawl out from under the Crown's thumb.

But to pay for a war debt of $21 million, new Secretary of the Treasury Alexander Hamilton suggested an excise tax on all booze brewed within the United States. It was the fledgling nation's first internal-revenue law. This was a slap in the face to the poor farmers returning to western Pennsylvania after whipping the British. Much of their economy was whiskey-based. Alcohol often substituted for cash. In an area isolated from the Eastern markets, whiskey brought a much greater profit than corn. The new tax would wipe out their entire profit. They had just risked their lives to avoid taxation—and they won the war—and now they had to surrender their profits to the taxman? HATE SPEECH brewed on the frontier, alongside now-illegal copper stills.

The Whiskey Rebellion broke out on July 16, 1794, when a motley group of tax-hating small-time distillers surrounded the mansion of John Neville, a federal supervisor stationed in western Pennsylvania. Shots were fired, and Rebels were wounded. A larger, more vengeful mob came back to Neville's place the next day, and after more gunfire, the Whiskey Rebels burned down his plantation. They gained momentum over the ensuing weeks. By August 1, they were heading for Pittsburgh with a force estimated at five to seven thousand drunken anarchists.

While the nobles of Pittsburgh wisely placated the Whiskey Rebels with free whiskey, George Washington summoned a militia mostly composed of poor Easterners. Ironically, some of the poor Easterners who had fought alongside poor Westerners to protest British taxation would now be fighting AGAINST them in the name of American

WHAT'S SO BAD ABOUT HATEMONGERS?

taxation. In fact, the taxing power proposed by Hamilton was LARGER than anything King George had ever asked of his colonial subjects. And the thirteen thousand troops that President George called out to crush the Whiskey Rebels was a numerically BIGGER force than the troops that Washington had used to defeat the British.

Eastern press commentators—the "experts" of their day—thought the Whiskey Rebels were paranoid wacky-sacks who shouldn't try to rise above their station. One writer called them "narrow-minded men whose views, like those of the pismire, are limited to the hillock where they lived." A pseudonymous scribe known as "Order" said it was "really amusing to hear little obscure spots of people" challenge the mighty new government.

The Whiskey Rebellion was snuffed by superior firepower, not popular consent. During the fracas, George "I Cannot Tell a Lie" Washington had told his brother Charles to keep quiet about the fact that George owned massive acreage in western Pennsylvania. After the Rebellion was squashed, with many Whiskey Rebels dispossessed and impoverished, the value of Washington's frontier holdings shot up fifty percent. He eventually came to own 63,000 acres throughout trans-Appalachia. And the fucking hypocrite was brewing his own rye liquor all along.

The Whiskey Rebellion had sympathizers throughout the South and America's frontier areas. The more hardened do-it-yourself whiskey brewers moved their operations deeper into the hills. Their descendants became some of America's most legendary outlaws—moonshiners, who plied their generations-old trade under cover of darkness. To hillfolk, it wasn't about the right to get drunk, it was about the government's unjust claim over your crops—if you grew it on your own land, they had no business taking part of it away. If you could eat corn on the cob, you should be able to drink corn in a jar.

Corn Squeezin's. White Lightnin'. Mountain Dew. Panther's Breath. Bust Head. Forty-Rod Whiskey. Moonshine. Illegal only because some politician near the coast wanted an unfair payoff that would put the moonshiner out of business. Many moonshiners were the descendants of indentured servants, pushed out onto some of the shittiest farmland in America, rock-laden hills 'n' hollers where it was impossible to eke out a living with plain crops. Making home whiskey, a tradition with deep cultural roots in the hills of Scotland and Ireland, was the only way for many mountaineers to avoid starvation.

By 1884, the whiskey tax accounted for nearly two-thirds of all federal revenue. In many areas of the South after the Civil War, moonshine itself was selling for less than the taxes the revenuers demanded. And to double the pain, moonshiners were being taxed to pay the debt on a war that they had lost. But the feds didn't phrase it that way. They came with dogs and guns. A lot of men—on both sides—died while playing revenuers and moonshiners. Many federal agents were lost in the hills or boiled in stills. Defiant "blockaders" who weren't killed or jailed became local heroes by outrunning the law, even though they've always been outgunned, outnumbered, and outfinanced. And they say there are caves in eastern Kentucky yet undiscovered by the feds, places where primo moonshine is still being made after hundreds of years' avoiding the taxman. The last outposts of freedom, as some people define it.

Many moonshiners' descendants in eastern Kentucky have lately turned to a more profitable illegal harvest—marijuana. It's been estimated that at current street prices, The Weed With Roots in Hell is America's largest cash crop, bigger than corn and wheat and all the other duller things you can plant in the ground. And Uncle Sam doesn't get a penny of tax money from its sale, although he probably compensates with all those funds allocated to put dope-smokers in jail.

Red-eyed weed-tokers number in the megamillions. Apart from those who cheat on their tax returns, reefer maniacs may be America's largest group of tax protesters. Imagine the peacenik potheads and the redneck militias having something in common. It's a real mind-blowin' scene, man.

Shut Up and Vote

The only idea they have ever manifested as to what is a government of consent, is this—that it is one to which everybody must consent, or be shot. (Lysander Spooner, *No Treason,* 1868)

Governmental apologists tell us that the political process works, and that we should channel our anger "within the system." Is this true? Voting can make a difference? Our wishes are really REPRESENTED by politicians? We actually SAVE money by letting them take it away from us? Wow. That's the same thing my grade-school teacher told me. And I believed him.

Well, here's my voting history, which is mainly confined to presidential elections: In 1980, I sidestepped the savagely ineffectual incumbent Jimmy Carter and his Dracula-coiffed challenger Ronald Reagan, opting for a silver-maned renegade named John Anderson. In '84 and '88, I yanked the lever for a dodo named Mondale and an albatross called Dukakis. In '92, I voted for the Libertarian guy, even though he had a French surname. Everyone I voted for lost. In 1996, I didn't even bother. Maybe I would have voted for Ralph Nader, but he's just too nerdy to be president.

The only thing I've ever voted for that passed was California's Proposition 103 in 1988, which mandated a twenty-percent car-insurance-rate rollback and included some retroactive refunds. When Prop. 103 passed, I finally felt like a part of the political process. ALRIGHT! The system works! Shortly after the election, the Golden State's drivers were promised we'd receive our refund checks soon. The checks never came. And within a few months, California's outgoing insurance commissioner kissed us all ta-ta by allowing insurance companies to raise their rates—astronomically. I had been dumping $575 a year into a giant black insurance pit. Only months after Prop. 103's passage, my rates had blown up to $1,050 a year, and I still had no tickets and no accidents.

Let's review—the only thing I ever voted for that hit a BINGO!— that passed—was supposed to reduce my car-insurance rates by twenty percent. Within six months, my rates had almost doubled. Instead of DOWN twenty percent, it was UP nearly two hundred percent.

So don't foist your bull-poopy on me about how the political process works. I've never had ANY say, direct or otherwise, in how the government spends even ONE DOLLAR of the money it bleeds from me— and everyone else—yearly. For the "privilege" of never electing anyone, of never having any influence on the decision-making process,

I've paid thousands and thousands of dollars without any discernible return on my investment. And this, you tell me, is freedom? Bite my schween. Fuck the Big Lie about a participatory democracy.

American politics have become a game of who can solicit enough money to blast enough TV propaganda to make enough viewers identify with enough vague, simple, feel-good images to get off their chewed-up couches and vote for them—"enough" is usually defined as at least fifty percent of the few who actually DO vote, but a plurality will work, too. Candidates are scrutinized for their haircut, their suit, their mediagenic squeezability, the way they handle babies and crowds, how they feel about the struggle of good vs. evil—in short, anything but their IDEAS. It's summed up in a buzzword, a vaguely inspirational appeal, everything but pure redneck honesty. Political ads are thirty-second slabs of heart-tugging, quick-edit sanctimony, with solemnly uttered appeals to "values," "justice," and "change." The change, inevitably, comes out of our pockets.

Our political system is a schizophrenic, dualistic, one-or-the-other, "loyal opposition," stinky plop o' donkey-'n'-elephant doody. Political campaigns are little more than two millionaires arguing over who loves the common people most. I'm surprised more than five or six voters turned out for that last election. Bob Dole, who didn't seem to mind that his hand was grotesquely mangled in a *real* battle, was worried about violence in Hollywood movies. Bill Clinton, who didn't inhale, favored stiffer penalties for drug violations.

Replundercans and Doomocrats are people who've made such a habit of compromising, they don't even have faces anymore, just soft pink blurs atop gray business suits. Am I trying to dehumanize them? No. I don't *have* to try. They've dehumanized themselves. I'm somehow supposed to feel privileged because the party politburos handpick candidates for me? A choice between Lamb Chop and Señor Wences should make me feel grateful enough to be forking over all that dough? Nuh-uh. I don't think so.

Whomever you vote for, the government still gets elected. So if I don't vote for things, I shouldn't have to pay for things. If I don't BENEFIT from things, I ESPECIALLY shouldn't have to pay for things. Is that so radical? I don't want to pay to support anyone else's baby, no matter what the color. I don't want to swell any banker's portfolio, no matter what the color. I don't want to pay bureaucrats to spy on me and curtail my natural rights, no matter what the color. I don't want to support the CIA or the United Nations or foreign "aid" or nuclear bombs. It's not that I don't want my money to go to minorities—I don't want my money to go *anywhere*.

Every four years, we're given a "choice" between a piece of burnt toast and a stale biscuit. In Russia, they used to have one political party. Here, we have two. That, my friends, is what all the fighting was for—that one extra party.

Good Government

> Government is not reason; it is not eloquence; it is force, and like fire, it is a dangerous servant and a fearful master. (George Washington)

"Government," of course, is an ancient word meaning "the biggest gang in town." How do governments arise? How do they maintain power? While politicians make insincere pitches to the "common good," they rule by one thing alone—FEAR. Once the fear is eradicated, so's the government.

It's GOOD government when the politicians are scared of the people, and not vice versa. What in tarnation ever happened to the notion of a "public servant"? The real newspeak, the real "coded speech," is the idea of government agents as public servants. IS the government a public servant? It proudly claims to be. Let's see—does a servant have the power to jail its master for disobedience? Does a servant siphon off forty to fifty percent of his master's output? Does a servant send a master off to die for the servant's vital interests? Does a servant tell a master what he can and cannot say and believe? I'd like to see the government humiliated, challenged, resisted, weakened, and truly lowered to an entity that cowers at my every whim—after all, I'm paying it, right? If it's the servant, I must be the boss. I should be able to sit at my kitchen table in a bathrobe and shout at the government to brew me some coffee. Otherwise, cut the bullshit semantics and call yourself what you really are—the public's master.

Morality ceases to be morality when it's imposed on others. It often resembles something closer to immorality. When you're FORCED to accept protection, the paternalistic sheen is considerably dulled. Freedom, it would seem, would mean the freedom to refuse participation in someone else's idea of "society." But they don't allow us that freedom. Whatever you "freely" believe, you still have to pass through their gate and pay the highwayman's toll. What, then, defines our freedom? That we're "allowed" to watch TV? We have theoretical freedom in America, and that's about it. We definitely aren't free economically. The government's soft, magnanimous hand on your shoulder always has a price. Claiming that the money's going to a "good" cause doesn't alter the involuntary nature of the transaction.

We're supposed to feel good that other countries boast even fewer rights and extort money from their citizens at even higher rates? Where have I heard this logic before? Oh, yeah—when Southern slavemasters told their slaves that workers have it worse elsewhere. It's like a state trooper during your driving test telling you that driving's a privilege, not a right.

I used to resent those who didn't pay taxes, because I sure as hell paid mine. Now I'm starting to resent the tax collectors. Why am I born owing money to the government? Why must I pay not only for a debt I didn't incur, but with interest on top of it like a thick glob of Cool Whip? Pay my fair share of WHAT? And what do these questions have to do with racism? I resent paying for someone else's fuckups. You're on your own, boys, just like I've been my whole life. Pull yourself up by the bootstraps, like you've been counseling us all these years. You've failed to prove why I owe anyone anything. And if you're going to FORCE me to pay, the legal burden of proof would seem to rest with you. If you want to label my resentment as "hate," that's groovy. Just don't charge me for the favor.

You know, I never used to be this hateful.

I never wanted to think about these things, because they were just too troublesome to ponder. I think one reason I avoided so-called conspiracy theories is because I was afraid some of them might be true. Same reason I avoided thinking about taxes, because I realized if I started, I'd just get upset. I had always said that the IRS frightened me more than the CIA, FBI, Congress, the president, the Mafia, and street gangs. I'd guess that most Americans probably feel this way. I used to pay my taxes because I wanted to be left alone; now I'm starting to wonder where the money goes and why I've been so unquestioningly compliant. I never buckled under to someone who wanted to panhandle money from me on the street; why should I tolerate it from the biggest thief of them all? Death is unavoidable; I'm not so sure about taxes anymore.

When will the government know enough about me, and when will I be permitted to know more about them? I don't trust a government that "represents" me while monitoring me—those are contradictory activities. I'm immediately suspicious when someone tells me they're doing something for my own good. Let ME determine my own good.

Every year, the government feels less responsive to my needs and more interested in my private life. I'm three thousand miles from Washington, D.C., but I feel a million miles away. If you *feel* cut off from the power structure, you probably are. I suspect that most people realize something's deeply wrong, but they're way too busy and feel wayyyyyy too powerless ever to change things. And there's such a flood of information, it's fatiguing to wade through the speed-freak factual minutiae of conspiracy literature, to sift out the crazy allegations from the frightening facts. So people don't like to think about it very much. They just pay and obey.

I have some sad news for you—the Big Boys will have contempt for you whether you rebel or submit. Better, then, to rebel.

I say it's TIME the rabble were roused. TV and false promises have kept them asleep for far too long. I don't fear people getting "stirred up" as much as I dread them slipping into docility. Civil disobedience scares the fuck out of the Big Boys, because their whole system depends on your obedience. I don't want to obey any longer. What would happen if people didn't throw any bombs, but they just stopped obeying? It might be a frighteningly peaceful coup. Maybe rather than stockpiling guns, they should ruthlessly stockpile QUESTIONS. Enough well-aimed questions would destroy this government without a shot having to be fired. If that's hate speech, then LET'S ALL HATE TOGETHER, AMERICA! Let's SHARE the hate!

It ain't got a thing to do with racism. I have no problem with the idea of one world. It's ALREADY one world, genius. It's one-world *government* that poses problems. Get rid of the government, and it'd still be one world.

I'm sick of blind trust. You'd better come up with some good reasons why I need to be governed at all. I don't NEED leadership. I don't NEED to feel part of any nation. FUCK a new morning in America. I don't WANT a thousand points of light. I'd rather NOT build a bridge to the twenty-first century. Go away. Now.

We've been fooled into believing that political matters are best handled by politicians. Just as clergymen claim to know God without ever having met Him, politicians make a big noise about justice without ever having practiced it. Most of these motherfuckers have never been in jail, yet they dictate prison policy. Never been in a war, yet they send others off to die. Most of them suffer no want of money, so they presume that everyone else is willing to part with nearly half of their income. When you see politicians sanctimoniously snort about obscenity, gun control, or welfare fraud, it's obvious that *they* feel above it all, that they've kept their morality in check while the natives are out there running wild. I'd say that the citizens, regardless of color, have behaved more responsibly than the government has. Give us our money back. Now.

When Joe Sixpack enters the political arena in a grimy T-shirt, a bloated roll of pink flab peeking out above crusty work pants, his hair matted and his beard scraggly, people suffer a prejudice that this is NOT how a political thinker is supposed to look. There's an elitist assumption that rednecks should be slung beneath an old GTO changing the oil, not thinking about politics. It's equivalent to "a woman's place is in the home." But the truth is that the government needs Joe Sixpack more than he needs it. And the government's main task has always been to prevent Joe Sixpack from realizing it.

Ask not what your country can do for you. Don't ask what you can do for your country, either. Start asking what your country is doing TO you.

9

Me and the Blacks

I've tried adjusting my TV antenna, but the problem won't stop. Every time I flick on the tube, someone mentions racism within five minutes. Ubiquitous ethnic ugliness glazed over with a thick lard-glop of self-righteous eyelash-fluttering. Another pair of white cops on trial for choking another black kid to death. The "N" word. A steamy night-time race riot somewhere in Florida. Nazi ninjas amassing nukes in remote farmland grain silos. Mark Fuhrman moves to Idaho. James Earl Ray shoots MLK a hundred thousand times. Rodney King's puffed-up, bloodied face spills onto your carpet. Rosa Parks fights for your seat on the couch. A lynch mob rings the doorbell. George Wallace blocks the entrance. Birmingham firehoses and Bull Connor's barking dogs smash through your windows. And those are only the commercials. Then Jerry Springer goes Jet Skiing with Holocaust survivors. Rolonda interviews White Aryan Pedophiles. Ricki Lake on interracial dating among dwarves. There's a cross-burning, a neo-Nazi, and a Klansman on TV at LEAST once every day. Try channel-surfing for a full hour, any hour of the day or night, and see if you can avoid racism. I doubt that it's possible anywhere in these here United States.

As spectators, Americans seem to have an insatiable appetite for racial atrocity. The fact that they hold their noses and pretend it stinks doesn't mean they aren't fascinated with it to a degree that borders on the perverse. Dripping with holiness, some people tell us we have to face the past. If we keep looking back, we're going to drive straight into a wall. You repeatedly hear that Americans need to address racism. Listen, Mr. Postman, we haven't only addressed it, we've added a zip code. They say we need to start dealing with these issues. Maybe they've been in a coma for the past thirty years. America has Race Fever. It's not an actual race war, but a sort of racial Cold War. A grinding war of nerves. And it's impossible to escape. A race war would be anticlimactic at this point. Enough. Let's put the baby to bed. And let's cool down just a tad. We don't need MORE sensitivity. If we got any more sensitive, we'd all break out in a rash.

I remember a teacher in high school saying that if someone told you not to think about a banana tree over the next ten seconds, banana trees would be stuck to your brain. The vast legions of media floodlights and high-power telescopes and ear-splitting megaphones probably make it harder than ever for Americans to imagine a world without racism. When every TV and radio station sounds a flatulent rusty tuba for yet another show on the horrors of prejudice, it almost seems like a cumulative attempt to keep everyone FIXATED on race. The solution would seem simple: If you want to get over racism, QUIT TALKING ABOUT IT. If you wish to transcend black and white, stop phrasing everything in those terms. Bombarding everyone with endless racial images is itself a form of racism. It effects a sort of mental segregation. Silence doesn't make a problem go away, but loudness isn't working, either. NO RACISM! NO RACISM! NO RACISM! Anything else on your mind?

America is still wearing racial diapers. Its ethnosocial debate hovers at a nursery-school level. Sunday-school warnings about demonic possession have more intellectual depth. Geez, we're all just a big crayon box, aren't we? Just a giant bag of M&M's. A brown-to-pink rainbow of relative melanin endowment. A colostomy bag bursting with love.

Please wake me when the race war's over. It ain't exactly brave anymore to say you're against racism. It's become a self-serving way to show what a good person you are. At one point it was courageous. Now it's almost cowardly. It's the ultimate conformist gesture. The last refuge of scoundrels. The trail has been blazed, and now the path seems worn. Saying you aren't a racist is about the safest comment you could make these days. People have become prejudiced against racists. In many circles, it's considered more heinous to hold unpopular racial viewpoints than actually to murder someone. "Racist" is perhaps a notch above "child molester," but not far. As much as the major-league antiracist shadow-boxers like to pretend they're fighting the establishment, it's clear that they ARE the establishment.

Don't believe the hype. There's a lot more racial HYSTERIA in this fair land than demonstrable racism. The whole country has a case of racial PMS. It's a national excuse for feeling uptight. An unhealthy obsession. Just because something's a good idea doesn't mean you can't brainwash someone with it. I'm aware that our society considers serial murder to be a bad thing, but I don't need to be reminded about it every fucking day. After a while, I'd want to kill the messenger.

I'm tired of racism, although the media apparently isn't. Race, race, all over the place. Stick it in your ear. Shove it in your face. The coverage is constant. Constant. Blecch. I WANTED to get along until you made it sound so sickening and treacly. If I see another holier-than-thou TV racial parable, I'll spew a rainbow of vomit. I've watched enough Norman Lear sitcoms over the years to learn that judging a person by their skin color is NOT A GOOD THING, OK? Yeah, it only took about SEVEN BILLION B-movie Simon Legrees before I realized that it's not nice to whip people on their bare backs until they bleed. If people *still* need to be clubbed in the *cabeza* with this "racism is evil" message, I don't think it's ever going to sink in. If they've yet to grasp the point that black slavery was a bad, bad, bad, bad, BAD thing, I don't think they ever will.

I really don't need any more sniffly images of black and white hands clasped together; no more magazine ads with Afros 'n' Euros laughing in unison around a piano; no more syrupy violins and slow-motion, wisdom-drenched gazes from wizened mulatto matriarchs; no more images of black and white kids squeaking gleefully together in play-grounds; no white, goggles-wearing assembly-line workers grinning amid showers of sparks at their black coworker, patting his back for a job well done; and no more sweaty, interracial, city-block basketball-game sodey-pop commercials where the white guys are somehow able to keep up. I thought we were going to get enlightenment, and all we got was more vaudeville. A social breakthrough would have been pleasant, but instead we get Al Jolson singing an encore of "Mammy."

Societies organize themselves around taboos as if they were religious shrines, and racism is currently no-no *numero uno*. People, especially my Caucasian kith 'n' kin, are flush-faced and shamed about race like they used to be about sex. Racism is the new porno, rated Triple Malcolm XXX. But even though people hate to think about it, they can't seem to stop. The flashing marquee is just too alluring. When you make something supremely untouchable, you lend it a power it wouldn't ordinarily have. It almost tempts the more malevolent souls among us to shout out dirty words as if we had Tourette's syndrome.

How can I tell if I'm a racist? Is there something I can buy at the local drug store, like a take-home pregnancy test? If the litmus strip turns white, does that mean I'm a bigot? Like some people see Satan everywhere or obscenity everywhere, some people see racism everywhere. "Are you a racist?" is about as quantifiable a question as "Are you a witch?" By whose definition? It's hard to pin down. By some definitions, I'm a racist no matter what I do—I was BORN that way, white boy. By other definitions, I'm a racist because I've somehow fed at the swine-trough of white supremacy. To some people, my mere refusal to feel guilty for my skin color qualifies me as a racist. To others, I'm a racist because I don't effusively apologize whenever I see a black person. Please help—it's so hard to keep up on what's racist and what's not. After a while, it all seems so dumb and unreal. It's like, "I'm not a racist, but I play one on TV."

Sensitivity often rises in inverse proportion to logic. Here's the point that the lunacy has reached. If a black person or a Jew says that white Europeans were involved in the slave trade (which is true), no one's upset. But if a black or white person says Jews were involved in the slave trade (which is also true), he's an oven-building anti-Semite. And if a white European male says African warrior kings were involved in the slave trade (which is also true), he's a bloated racist warthog. Woo-woo, dat's sensible. Maybe we'll have equality when we learn to spread the blame around.

Black pride good. Hispanic pride good. Asian pride good. Samoan pride good. Madagascan pride good. White pride BAD. How long before this starts causing problems? When is it enough? When do we mark our calendars for payback time? Is there a statute of limitations on intergenerational guilt? I mean, when did everyone stop hating the Vikings for pillaging Scotland?

The current tidal wave of black identity crashes onto a dry, blank, white shore. Euro-Americans are more or less FORBIDDEN to mention being white unless it's in an apologetic, shuffling, "Yes, Massa" tone. While blacks sing hymns about Mother Africa, whites are barely allowed to admit they're related to each other. Whitey floats in an identity-free limbo. He is commanded to walk the streets devoid of cultural bravado. Our ethnic fashion show welcomes the Nation of Islam, Native Nations, Aztlan Nation, and Queer Nation, but Aryan Nations are sent packing. Why are ALL blacks allowed to view themselves as a mystical brotherhood if NO whites are? I didn't even WANT to be white until you told me I couldn't. I've heard several black people mention the "white community," but no white person that I know considers themself to be a member. Where is the White Community? Is that a village somewhere in Nebraska?

Silent whitey. Scared and quiet. Smile and act nervous. Shit-eating albino chimpanzee. Take the blame. Swallow the pill. Apologize for the past. Sweat through the present. Surrender the future. Sackcloth and ashes for as long as you live. White people don't make a peep. They just peck at their birdseed and huddle within their cages. I can't see how a mental diet of guilt and self-flagellation would be healthy for ANY ethnic group. Being apologetic and meek is as unbecoming in white people as it is in anyone.

This country's racial-pride policy has always been separate and un-equal. Ethnic pride used to be only for whites. Now it's only for nonwhites. Black pride, like all hues of pride, isn't inherently good or bad; it's how it's used. What's sociologically curious is that it's flour-ishing in a climate where ethnic self-esteem is prohibited for whites. Society seems unequipped to deal with UNILATERAL pride. The mo-ment that white supremacy crashed to the ground, black supremacy seemed to rise from the flames. What is this social mechanism that allows for pride in one group only at the expense of pride in another? Ultimately, I think that ethnic pride is dumb. I take credit only for what

I've done, not what "my people" have done. Ethnic pride reminds me of flabby sports-fan couch potatoes who feel responsible when their team wins. If I were king, I'd get rid of pride altogether.

And slap me white, but there sure is a lot of extreme pro-black radical racist nationalist fascist apocalyptically bellicose rhetoric clogging our public forums these days. To my blue devil eyes, much of black America exists in a state of seeming hyperidentity. Black women in Laundromats with AFRICAN QUEEN T-shirts. Black guys at bus stops who start sentences, "As a black man, I . . ." Some black people are SO racially conscious, it's as if they're wearing blackface. After a point, I wonder whether they're applying their blackness with a putty knife.

By becoming bigots, many black people have finally proven their equality. Some say that blacks can't be racist because they don't have the decision-making power to enforce institutional racism. Well, most backwoods Bubbas don't have that sort of power, either, although they've been cast as the primary instigators of global intolerance. Make up your mind.

Be as black as you goddamned wanna be. Be so black, you cause a solar eclipse. I don't care. Just quit staring at me. And give me back my wristwatch. That was a joke. Really. Look, just give me back the watch, or I'll call the cops.

Maybe it's the hate that hate created. Maybe it's self-starting entrepreneurial hate. The bleak fact is that new tolerances often resemble the old intolerances. A lot of black people aren't talking justice, they're talking revenge. Or they're equating the two.

In many instances, bitterness over having been "the oppressed" seems to be little more than jealousy over not having been the oppressor. Many pro-black mouthpieces seem like they'd be raging dictators if only given the chance. A group calling itself the Black Israelites claims to be the True Jews and preaches that all white men are "faggots" who face certain enslavement by vengeful, effulgently hetero blacks. Cricket-faced Shahrazad Ali says that O.J. should go free whether he's guilty or not. Sister Souljah suggests that black Americans should set aside a week to kill white people. San Francisco's Zebra Killers thought they were winning points with Allah by murdering white devils. Dr. Frances Cress Welsing says whites suffer from melanin envy. Dr. Leonard Jeffries, Jr., talks about how the "African Holy Ghost" speaks through him and how "dirty Europeans" and "these damn Jews" conspired to destroy the beautiful, one-hundred-percent innocent black race. I enjoy all of these Black Racist Superstars for their defiant showmanship. Bravo! But to appreciate them as anything beyond bigoted Smurf dolls is dangerous. And to see them as fundamentally different from white supremacists is dishonest.

I've heard that Louis Farrakhan was a good calypso singer, and for all I know, he could be an excellent dancer. And he's absolutely right when he asserts that blacks should act in collective economic self-interest. He's also right when he says the federal government still systematically antagonizes blacks. It's the stuff about blue-eyed white devils being created six thousand years ago by an evil scientist named Yakub that concerns me. And it's the doctrine about a huge Negro-operated flying saucer named the Mother Wheel which is poised to annihilate all whites that makes me a little skittish. Farrakhan's a nut about some things, and he's right about others. But he's no more a messenger of God than Rochester the Butler was.

Given history, this molasses flood of black neoracism is understandable. When you tutor people in self-hatred, they eventually respond with a virulent strain of self-esteem. Tell them they're nothing, and they'll eventually bounce back claiming to be everything. My main objection to most fast-food black nationalism is its lack of specificity. They're talking about killing white people, and they aren't being very specific. When certain frisky black spokespeeples talk about "white people," it's as if we all move in tandem like a school of minnows. The problem when someone such as Farrakhan talks about the CIA destroying black ghettos with crack cocaine isn't the allegation, because it's probably true. The problem is that he seems to imply that every white person was a coconspirator. Some blacks have a tendency to lump all whites together. It's a modern form of "they all look the same to me." Do they honestly think all white people sit at a table and plot this shit? Well, if there *is* a conspiracy against black people, I was never invited to the meetings.

When whites become an American minority over the next half-century, will things such as Black Entertainment Television come to be seen as ethnocentrically racist? When will black people have achieved so much cultural identity that they're no longer allowed to act like bigoted heinie-holes themselves? People think it's important for blacks to have cultural identity, but few seem to have pondered at what point such ethnocentrism becomes something very much like white supremacy. When does "black nationalism" become indistinguishable from National Socialism? After a while, what's the difference between a Black Power fist and a *sieg heil* salute? When will everyone grow up and drop the tribal-consciousness nonsense? No one has tried to "set boundaries," as pop psychologists like to say. Although some insist that blacks need special conditions in order to "get it together," they don't ever define exactly what getting it together *is* and when certain blacks will be forced to retire their own bigotry. They're insistent about the overall principle, but extremely vague about particulars. And those who claim that double standards must be enforced until blacks achieve economic parity can't reconcile the fact that American blacks already enjoy a higher per-capita income than any native black population on earth.

Portland, Oregon, is demographically one of America's whitest cities. And ever since the highly publicized baseball-bat murder of an Ethiopian man by skinheads nearly ten years ago, Portland has had a rep as somewhat of a Nazi haven. If that's the case, all the Nazis must be sleeping when I'm out on the streets. I see nothing but peace punks, lesbian loggers, and aggressively ethnocentric "people of color." You'd think that Portland's public-access cable TV would feature at least one Nazi-flavored program, if only for comic relief. Instead, it's wall-to-wall black-nationalist yabba-dabba doo-doo. The local public-access provider is Paragon Cable, but I call it Farrakhan Cable. Paragon carries four local cable-access stations, and some unwritten rule seems to dictate that at least one Black Power show be on the air at all times.

Flick on the remote control and zap into some postmodern reverse racism. Filmed under sweat-inducing spotlights at the local cable studio, a Portland rap group called Da Rida & O.D. are threatening to murder Caucasians:

> To hell with you crackers, I'm down to burn like alcohol....
> I'ms about to kill me one, and that's for real.

Why kill just one? Now, imagine if a white heavy-metal band . . . oh, forget it. I feel that once a black fella has referred to white folks as "honky paleface devil white-trash cracker redneck Caspers," he's abdicated the right to get upset about the "N" word. But that's just me.

Flip over to another public-access station, and a group of students from a local black college are sharing their thoughts on race relations:

> Soon the black man will become extinct because he keeps messin' with the white woman.
>
> The white girls . . . they'll rub up against you and stuff. . . . It's not like I go for it or whatever, but they throw theyselves at you.
>
> The black men go for the white girls because the white girls have less respect for themselves and they be givin' it up to everybody else.
>
> As black men and women, I hope you can always see that blood is thicker than water. . . . 'Cause I don't care how many white boys or white girls you go out with, you still black.
>
> Be black, stay black, and we can all come up together.
>
> Black it was in the beginning, and black it will be in the end.

"Black it will be in the end?" Does that mean they're going to kill all the white people? 'Cause if they aren't, maybe white people should wear costumes so blacks will know which ones to kill. I'm glad they can share their feelings. And I'm tickled Nubian that after successfully petitioning white people to stop calling them "boys" and "girls," many blacks make a habit of calling white people "boys" and "girls." Honestly, none of what they said bothers me. What DOES irk my hackles is that these same crazy kids seem as if they'd howl "RACISM!" if a white person said the same things but merely switched colors.

On yet another Portland cable channel, a black man invokes Marcus Garvey's vaguely Hitlerian "Up, up, you mighty race." Another black man outlines the Negro-rific roots of Egypt. A black woman urges African-Americans mentally to transport themselves back in time and imagine they're on slave ships. Isn't that holding a bit of a grudge?

What's to be gained by conjuring pain you never experienced, especially if it isn't relevant to improving your current situation? Aye begorrah, I don't sit around and meditate about the Irish Potato Famine.

When I see a black guy wearing a dashiki, I wonder how he'd feel if he saw me walking down the street in a druid costume.

Racism, by our society's default definition, means WHITE racism. But are the hate-crime statistics remotely significant enough to warrant all the hoopla? And who is actually perpetrating the majority of so-called hate crimes in America? With the boiling-mudpot hubbub about racial hatred and blazing redneck violence, people rarely cite statistics. That's because the stats reveal a much different Nativity scene from the John Grisham movies and Oprah specials. If black people—a minority—were being so lopsidedly brutalized and terrorized, the numbers would show it. Hate to sprinkle arsenic on your cole slaw, but the statistics don't swing that way. Nine of every ten victims of interracial crime are white.[1] Although they comprise less than fifteen percent of the population, blacks committed more than half of 1994's racially motivated murders.[2] Black criminals choose white victims over half of the time, while white criminals choose black prey in only three percent of their crimes.[3] More black Americans kill each other every year than were murdered throughout Southern lynching's history.[4] These are all FACTS. Can facts be racist? Most people who insist we have to "confront racism" invariably duck from statistics such as these. That's because if they fully confronted racism, they might come nose-to-nose with different conclusions from the ones they currently hold sacred.

It happened in 1995, in Guthrie, Kentucky, over the Martin Luther King Holiday weekend. Michael Westerman, nineteen, and his wife had gone out to dinner to celebrate their twin babies' recent birth. In the back of Westerman's pickup truck flapped a small Confederate flag, which later was revealed to have been his high school football team's logo. A group of black teenagers saw the flag and interpreted it as a sign of racial provocation. In a convoy of three cars, they chased Westerman and cornered his truck. Westerman was murdered with a bullet to the heart. Why didn't this story attract national attention? That's a good question. If Westerman had been a black man blasted in the dome for wearing an "X" cap, the media would have been gnawing at his carcass like piranhas. In the future, will the establishment quietly look away while rednecks get lynched?

When did it all start? When did this genocidal, intergenerational, Hatfield & McCoy–style blood feud begin? Four hundred years ago, most Europeans and Africans were unaware of each other's existence. They weren't natural enemies, they were natural ignoramuses. So who got us into this fine mess, Stanley? Who set up the black and white chess pieces and told them to march on each other?

It sho' weren't white trash, although they get most of the blame. Those who erected the pillars of American racial apartheid were NOT the ancestors of today's rickety-shack, bloodhound-owning cracker-jacks. Today's descendants of slaveowners would more likely drive Mercedes-Benzes than pickup trucks. Although the race war always seems as if it's being fought among the lower classes, it has consistently been orchestrated from above.

In the baying, sylvan wilderness of 1600s colonial America, the elite planter classes found themselves wildly outnumbered by white servants, black servants, and red natives. They were able to spare their own throats only by manipulating these three groups against one another. Black slaves were armed to fight Indians, and Indians were brought in to crush slave uprisings. Whites were given guns to patrol groups of black servants, and blacks were sometimes given guns to supervise packs of ornery whites.[5] When there were stirrings of an anti-Crown rebellion among the colonists, the British armed Indians to terrorize whites, which was a grievance listed in the Declaration of Independence. And the wholesale genocide of Plains Indians in the late 1800s was accomplished by federal troops, a substantial portion of whom were black.[6] So since the dawn of European meddling in America, the upper orders have sent white, black, and red nipping at each other's asses in a murderous rondelet.

For most of the 1600s, white and black slaves/servants had occupied a similar legal status. They worked together, played together, and treated each other as equals *when they perceived their situation to be similar.* And throughout that century, they conspired to run away from their masters together. Many, if not most, of the underclass uprisings during the 1600s were interracial. Bacon's Rebellion, which shot a brief upward flame in Virginia during 1676, was spearheaded by a potentially revolutionary combo of still-bound black slaves and white ex-slaves who'd been cheated out of their headright.

Such underclass volatility frightened the watery piss out of the blue bloods. Trembly lips spoke nervously from behind powdered wigs, warning that rowdier elements among lower-class whites would conspire with their similarly situated black counterparts. Bacon's Rebellion and several other cross-racial flareups had proven that the planter captains weren't being paranoid—the threat was for real.

So the planter dandies desperately began scribbling laws that separated the races. There were laws that provided for whipping if you slept with a black person; laws forbidding interracial marriage; laws that doled out the death penalty to any white servant who ran away with a black servant. Most significantly, these proto–Jim Crow codes created a terraced racial caste system. Blacks who committed the same crimes as whites received harsher punishment. White conspirators of Bacon's Rebellion were granted amnesty, while their black coplanners were punished. For the first time, poor whites and blacks occupied separate steps at the bottom of the Stairway to Heaven. Blacks were pushed down into doglike slavery, and all whites were encouraged to take pride in skin color, even if they were dirt-poor and starving.

The resentment that inevitably flowed from such situations was set in motion by the upper class. Poor white trash were the tools, rather than the craftsmen, of segregation. As historian Kenneth Stampp phrased it, "The master class, for its own purposes, wrote chattel slavery, the caste system, and color prejudice into American custom and law." [7]

With forces combined, black and white servants could easily have overthrown the tiny pockets of rich planters and radically changed American history. They couldn't have done it without each other. Kept apart, they didn't. This country could have become a multiracial utopia. Or a parched wasteland covered in a dried crust of blood. We'll never know.

After white indentured servitude withered on the vine, very few crackers found their way into the Southern plantation economy. Those

ME AND THE BLACKS

who did were given the dirty work, as slave patrollers and spies and overseers and "niggerbreakers." Poor whites served as the brownshirts of white supremacy. Their role as hired thugs deflected most black rancor away from the upper classes and onto themselves. Disempowered rednecks became the shock absorbers of black resentment, a role they still serve today. Most accounts from the slave era suggest that black hostility was focused on poor white trash rather than rich white slaveowners. There's ample evidence that Massa encouraged blacks openly to mock the majority of whites who seemed too stupid to own slaves themselves. And the spite of poor whites was aimed at the slaves, whose cheap labor was cynically used to undercut and impoverish white workers. No one seemed to blame the slavemasters.

The next big opportunity for racial realignment was the Civil War. That gore-soaked conflict is one of our most precious social myths. As the story was told to me, Lincoln tried to free the slaves, and the naughty racist South tried to stop him. The North was a well-intentioned nanny, while the South was a stubborn brat who refused to take his medicine.

Dang me, they lied. It turns out that Lincoln was a gawky, bearded clown with bad breath and a crazy wife. He was also a white supremacist with no intention of ending slavery until 1863—two years into the Civil War—when he realized it would be a good way to shatter the South socially. His "freeing" of Southern slaves was a crass military calculation rather than an altruistic gesture, as evidenced by his professed war strategy of "emancipation and every other policy calculated to weaken the moral and physical forces of the rebellion." [8] You think Lincoln loved his choco-brethren? Peep out these quotes:

LINCOLN ON BLACKS:

I will say, then, that I am not, nor ever have been, in favor of bringing about in any way the social and political equality of the white and black races [applause]; that I am not, nor ever have been, in favor of making voters or jurors of Negroes, nor of qualifying them to hold office, nor to intermarry with white people; and I will say in addition to this that there is a physical difference between the white and black races which I believe will forever forbid the two races living together on terms of social and political equality. And inasmuch as they cannot so live, while they do remain together there must be the position of superior and inferior, and I as much as any other man am in favor of having the superior position assigned to the white race. (Debate with Stephen Douglas, Charleston, Illinois, September 18, 1858)

There is a natural disgust in the minds of nearly all white people to the idea of an indiscriminate amalgamation of the white and black races. . . . Judge Douglas is especially horrified at the thought of the mixing of the blood by the white and black races; agreed for once —a thousand times agreed. . . . A separation of the races is the only perfect preventive of amalgamation. . . . Such separation, if ever effected at all, must be effected by colonization. . . . I am not in favor of Negro citizenship [applause]. . . . That is all I have to say about it. (Debate with Stephen Douglas, Springfield, Illinois, June 22, 1857)

Negro equality! Fudge!! How long, in the government of a God great enough to make and maintain this universe, shall there continue knaves to vend, and fools to gulp, so low a piece of demagoguism as this? (From *Fragments: Notes for Speeches,* September 1859)

You still believe Lincoln waged the Civil War to end slavery? Think again, Charlie McCarthy:

LINCOLN ON THE WAR BETWEEN THE STATES:

I have no purpose, directly or indirectly, to interfere with the institution of slavery in the states where it exists. I believe I have no lawful right to do so, and I have no inclination to do so. (Inaugural Address, March 1861)

My paramount object in this struggle is to save the Union, and is not either to save or destroy slavery. (From a letter to Horace Greeley)

Let the South go? Let the South go? Where shall we get our revenues? (Attributed to Lincoln in the book *Memoirs of Service Afloat*)

At least Abe was honest. I'm a better friend to black people than Abe Lincoln was. And the sooner that black people realize it, the better off this country will be.

But first we'll have to get over some crucial misunderstandings. In Martin Luther King's famous "I Have a Dream" speech, he hoped that "the sons of former slaves and the sons of former slaveowners" will one day get along. So do I. But King's phraseology implies that all whites are slaveowners' descendants. This, with gracious apologies to Dr. King, is impossible. In the South in 1860—the peak of black slavery—only ONE in FIFTEEN whites was a slaveowner.[9] Ironically, the other fourteen are now being required to pay reparations.

Rich white boys, from both North and South, were able to avoid the Civil War through an easy cash payment to their respective governments. In the South, this meant that most slaveowners did not fight. An estimated NINETY PERCENT of Rebel forces weren't slaveowners.[10] Most Southern whites had been pauperized and ostracized by the slave economy, so it's nonsensical to allege they'd sacrifice their lives for a slaveowning class they deeply resented. The average Southern white trench-grunt on whose soil almost all of the Civil War was fought more likely pictured himself as defending his land from an industrial superpower that refused to let his people go. The question about whether the Union cared more for blacks or for extending its power can be answered with another question: Who's more powerful and prosperous in the South today—black people or the federal government?

But if you still want to think that the Civil War was fought over slavery, that's your prerogative, Dunkin Munchkin. If that's the case, then you must be saying that poor Northern whites and poor Southern whites slaughtered each other to free black slaves. Counting only Northern casualties, that means at least 300,000 lower-class Caucasians died to free four million black slaves. That's one dead white body for every thirteen freed blacks. In all the high-pitched, swinish squealing that goes on regarding racial reparations, there's palpable silence about the fact that so much po' white Yankee trash died in the alleged struggle to end black slavery. It would be nice to hear a "thank you."

Mr. Lincoln's War had smashed the South. Every third household had lost a family member. After being pulverized, the South naturally had to be reconstructed. The slaves had been unshackled, and Reconstruction was a chance for all mankind to stand together under sunshine and rainbows and to catch pieces of multicolored after-dinner mints as they fell mannalike from the sky. Instead, it was the closest this country has ever come to a full-blown race war.

Reconstruction is commonly portrayed as a glorious time of universal uplift, only to be interrupted by stampeding hordes of hooded Klansmen, who stole the vote from black people for no other apparent reason than, well, because the Klan were hard-hearted meanies.

Would that life were so simple and sweet. Once again, racism arose not from individual evil, but as a response to social manipulation. The conquering North was embodied by the Republican party. Still smarting from Lincoln's assassination, the Republicans were in a vengeful mood. And as a social strategy, their vengeance was phrased largely in race-baiting terms:

> We shall treat the South as a defeated enemy. . . . Hang the leaders —crush the South—arm the Negroes—confiscate the land. . . . (Pennsylvania Congressman Thaddeus Stevens)[11]

> If I had the power I would arm . . . every Negro of the South . . . and turn them loose on the Rebels of the South and exterminate every man, woman and child south of Mason and Dixon's line. I would like to see Negro troops, under the command of [U.S. General Benjamin F.] Butler, crowd every Rebel into the Gulf of Mexico and drown them as the Devil did the hogs in the Sea of Galilee. (Parson Brownlow, Tennessee's carpetbag governor)[12]

After waging literal war on the South for four years, the North fomented race war in the South for another twelve. The Reconstruction Act of 1867 disfranchised all ex-Confederates, taking away the vote from an estimated 150,000 white males.[13] It also enfranchised any adult black male who wished to register. Though blacks were a numerical minority in the South, the wholesale disfranchisement of whites made blacks an electoral majority. And the Republican party, if ya can diggit, was the black man's party. Republican legislatures and governors assumed power in all eleven ex-Confederate states. The Republicans, who hadn't received one Southern electoral vote in 1860, OWNED Dixie by 1868. The Republican governor of each state disarmed whites and established all-black militias as policing forces. Predominantly black state legislatures introduced bills intended to disarm all whites while supplying blacks with guns. There were even proposed laws of the turnabout-is-fair-play shuck-'n'-jive variety that would have required whites to tip their hats at blacks and observe other obsequious social rituals. In 1875, an aide to Mississippi's Governor Ames told a black audience that the Republicans were going to win the upcoming election even if they had "to kill every white man, woman, and child in the state." [14]

Look, if I was an ex-slave with a gun in my hand, I'd be a vengeance machine. I don't think it's racist to allege that former slaves, after being crushed and whipped and derided, would act in tyrannical revenge upon being freed. It makes sense that emancipated blacks would be a mite angry. What needs to be understood is that the conquering Northern power structure, represented by the Republican party, used poor Southern blacks as terrorist shock troops to antagonize and punish ALL Southern whites, including the ninety-four percent who had never owned slaves. It was almost identical to the way in which the vanquished Southern power structure, represented by the Bourbon Democrats, would use the KKK as a terrorist force against all Southern blacks.

Hard as it is to believe, the Democrats were the party of white supremacy and lynch-mob justice in the South. In the late 1800s, they called themselves Redeemers, saving the white race from "Negro rule." Just like the Carpetbag Republicans, the Redeemer Democrats resorted to beatings, murder, and rampant vote fraud. And their coalition of rich and poor whites, united under the quasi-religious myth of white supremacy, finally destroyed the fragile Republican coalition of white Northern carpetbaggers and Southern blacks. Ironically, white supremacy became stronger in the South AFTER the Civil War than before. The white elites who had previously taught their black slaves to scorn po' white trash suddenly found such human debris to be golden allies.

To the average white Southern shanty-dweller, the promise of white supremacy was rarely more than that—a promise. Poor whites were placated with the idea that all white men were brothers, even if some lived in shacks while others lived in mansions. The Southern underclass, both black and white, remained more degraded and impoverished than most peasant groups worldwide. The rich Boss Hogg type's winking white-power paternalism was often indistinguishable from how he had formerly treated his slaves. One hand patted the cracker on the head, while the other hand held him with a leash.

White people ruled the South in the late 1800s, but it was only a handful of white people. Power was concentrated among the bankers, landowners, and railroad men, and they weren't quick to share it with their "supreme" poor white brothers. The average nobody's status, regardless of color, sank deeper into the quicksand. It was amid such bleeding desperation that the People's Party, also known as the Populists, caught fire across rural America. The political fruition of whites-only labor union the Farmers Alliance and its brother union the Colored Alliance, the Populists called for class war in America. Unlike both the Republicans and Democrats, the Populists appealed for a cross-racial coalition of workers.

> You are kept apart that you may be separately fleeced of your earnings. You are made to hate each other because upon that hatred is rested the keystone of the arch of financial despotism which enslaves you both. You are deceived and blinded that you may not see how this race antagonism perpetuates a monetary system which beggars both. (Georgia Populist Tom Watson) [15]

For a brief flash in the 1890s, the Populists seriously threatened the Democrats' hegemonic all-whitey grip in the South. The Democrats retaliated with more courthouse-gang violence. More fraud. More KKK terror. And they erected a system of poll taxes and literacy tests that effectively disfranchised the entire Southern underclass, both black and white. In school, I'd been taught that disfranchisement only affected blacks; more properly, it affected the poor. These electoral hurdles weren't race-specific; they discriminated against those with little income or education. Populism was a class movement rather than a racial one, and the aim of late-1800s disfranchisement was to silence the poor, regardless of skin color.

And it worked. Disfranchisement destroyed Populism. White supremacy reaffirmed its chokehold. In 1904, ex-Populist Tom Watson had metamorphosed into an anti-Semite and Negro-baiter who campaigned for the Democrats. In 1907, the Atlanta race riot was started by an aristocrat named John Temple Graves who urged poor whites to lynch blacks—even innocent ones—in order to protect the tabernacle-like sanctity of Caucasian vaginas.

By 1910, poor blacks comprised a third of the Southern population. The dust-poor white-trash class made up another third. Together, they had the numbers to overthrow those who kept both classes poor and segregated. But race consciousness had entirely blinded them from developing class identity.

And so it remains today. Race is mentioned ten thousand times for every time you hear the word "class." Cultural differences drown out economic similarities.

Favoritism is often finicky. With increasing urbanization and black out-migration from the South, the trend shifted away from white-supremacist paternalism to black welfare-state paternalism. Federal bayonets helped to, eh, nudge the process along. At some point, the South's professional classes must have realized that segregation was a powder keg. Their power had always been more important to them than their whiteness. And so they began to shy away from lynch-mob justice, pretending it was the exclusive purview of white trash. Boss Hogg started pretending to be the friend of the same poor blacks he had previously ordered the KKK to murder. Today's dominant social coalition in the South is between the white professional class and the black underclass. These groups usually vote together on policies that alienate poor whites. The elites have always led the Resentment Tango; they've merely switched back and forth between dance partners. It's like a sick parent who vacillates between favoring children, to the psychological detriment of both kids.

Poor white trash has been left holding the bag. They've been framed for the sins of a race-based social system that they didn't create. For decades, blacks had been America's invisible people, and white trash only had identity by dint of their whiteness. Now white trash are invisible, and blacks have been temporarily appeased by an attitudinal climate that allows for black identity to run amok. White trash have been offered as sacrificial lambs to appease black resentment. They's dun been throwed to the wolves.

This isn't peaches 'n' cream for blacks, either. Most of the "reparations" made to blacks seem to come in the form of plaques and monuments and public water fountains. This sort of noneconomic appeasement is almost a booby prize. At best it's a symbolic brand of "empowerment." From what I've seen, there's no indication that blacks are better off financially now than they were twenty-five years ago. In fact, the ONLY place blacks have it better is on TV. Instead of anything resembling financial reparations, white people get upset about the "N" word. It's like killing someone and then sending him a sympathy card.

So now the uptown charity mavens act all innocent and pretend as if they can't understand the very predicament they've created. High society wiped their hands clean of white supremacy when it was no longer profitable. Perhaps the wealthier white classes can't understand racial strife because THEIR jobs, status, and position have always been secure. They've never felt compelled to shout "Not in my backyard!" because THEIR backyard was protected by high bushes and electronic fences. Rich people can keep black rage out of their neighborhood without having to get racist about it.

The media will pass judgment on a "segregated" working-class neighborhood such as Brooklyn's Bensonhurst, ignoring the sore-thumb fact that the tony enclaves where most communications-industry turds lay their heads on duck-down pillows are more racially segregated than any working-class 'hood in America. Apartment buildings along Central Park are more well-guarded and socially segregated than Bensonhurst, but the New York media would never demonize that area because they sleep there.

While wealthier whites piously posit integration's virtues, it's always the rednecks who are forced to do most of the integrating and to make most of the fiscal sacrifices. Corporation heads didn't get fucked by affirmative action—white workers did. Congressmen didn't take a pay cut—everyone else did. 'T'ain't the bankers who are expected to make sacrifices for slavery, it's the rednecks. In many cases, one encounters the surreal situation of white elites tut-tutting poor whites for not making reparations to blacks. Why is it that rich whites never seem to have to shoulder the white man's burden? According to civil law, a person who CAUSED the problem should be the one who pays damages. To achieve justice, affirmative action would have to discriminate against RICH whites. Don't hold your breath.

For all the showboat sympathy that the white middle and upper classes display toward black suffering, they don't spend much time living or working alongside their downtrodden jungle bruddas. The redneck truck driver and the black gas-pumper share more life experiences than either guy shares with the corduroy-jacketed college professor or perfume-stinking society matron whose tear ducts gush with self-serving weepiness over abstract notions of injustice. Rednecks—yes, those funky-toenailed, intolerant, white-trash creeps—are the group of Caucasians who have historically lived and worked CLOSEST to American blacks.

Racial struggles are never purely racial. In fact, they aren't even fundamentally racial. Most often, race is merely an excuse to mask what is actually a battle over land or the booty perched upon it. Somebody, somewhere, with a big-ass hunk of power, has found it socially strategic to cast people with similar histories and situations as warring opposites. It is in their best interest to keep black rage focused on crackers rather than bankers. On Shantytown rather than Silk Stocking Row. On trailer parks rather than country clubs. This, I believe, is why they consistently portray black rage as revolutionary and white rage as reactionary. The truth is that both the rednecks and the niggers really hate the government these days. Condemning one group for "hate speech"—while permitting another group to go WILD with it—is an effective way to reinforce the impression that these are separate groups with separate gripes. Divide and conquer, you thick-headed boobs.

Both Martin Luther King and Malcolm X were shot to the ground at a time when they seemed to be transcending narrow white/black divisions and phrasing the battle in class terms.

Am I the only guy in America who thinks that BOTH the *schwartzes* and *goyim* have a right to be angry? Am I the only one who thinks that

225

most of the anger—from both sides—is legitimate but misdirected? Is anyone out there? Hello? Could you please pick up the phone if you're there? Black anger and white anger seem like opposites; then again, maybe they're just aiming in the wrong direction.

If rednecks and blacks were ever to put aside their differences, the only remaining enemy would be the one above them. Consider "white vs. black" as a conspiracy theory that has never been proven beyond a reasonable doubt. The greasy, Jheri-Kurl–dripping, gold-chain, gym-suited, hundred-dollar-sneaker gangsta homeboy crack-smokin' mack nigger and the no-butt, thin-lipped, heavy-metal, white trash, scare-crow, glue-sniffing paleface may have more in common than you'd previously been led to believe. The redneck and black dude hate each other for a very simple reason: They've always had to compete with each other for the economy's sloppy seconds. They aren't natural ene-mies; they've just been locked in this struggle for so long, it *seems* natural. Very frequently, enemies are merely brothers fighting over the same raggedy hand-me-downs. Rednecks and blacks seem like strange bedfellows, but maybe not. "We Shall Overcome" was originally a white labor song. And Harriet Tubman was missing teeth, just like the hillbillies.

Several things, however, blunt the possibility of rednecks and blacks getting along. One is the eternally divisive game of "Who Was More Oppressed?" Some people are very possessive about their victimiza-tion and allege that white trash have no reason to complain, because they have no idea what it's like to be black. Ultimately, it's like cancer patients arguing over whose tumors are worse. A deadly serious topic has been twisted into a cafeteria food-fight over who suffered more.

A second obstacle is the illusion of universal white guilt. I think that most black people in America have every right to be angry. And I think most white people in America have every right not to feel guilty about it. I was born into a race war that I didn't start. I may have inherited this social cesspool, but I didn't create it. I'm no more responsible for slavery in America than I am for serfdom in Russia or prostitution in Thailand. If you blame me for European imperialism, I blame you for being an idiot. Anyone who thinks I'm a "white devil" is a supersti-tious retard. I never called you a "black goblin," so knock it off.

Should all black people be blamed for Idi Amin's depredations? For the atrocities in Haiti? Somalia? Ethiopia? Rwanda? Should they grimace with self-loathing over these things? No? Then why should I be blamed for what other white people did? If you don't embrace my background, I see no reason to go around hugging yours. I can't appreciate someone else's history if I'm forced to reject and feel ashamed of mine. If you don't want to hear about how my ancestors suffered, maybe I'm just a little tired of hearing about yours.

What do you MEAN my people did this to you? I don't even know where my mother lives, for Christ's sake, so saying I have any control over "my people" is stretching it a bit.

Anyone who blames ME for slavery has a TV-movie grasp of history. If you blame me, then fuck you. If you hate me for being white, fuck you again. Self-hatred is a sacrifice I'm unwilling to make. I already pay enough taxes—you aren't going to squeeze any guilt out of me. If anyone thinks I owe them something, you can get in line and keep waiting. The check's in the mail.

Otherwise, I love every one of you.

I've thought long and hard about how to recount some of my positive experiences with blacks without it sounding too much like "some of my best friends are black." I've also pondered how to state my admiration for things about black culture without appearing as if I'm saying "they're such good entertainers." And I realized that there was no way to say these things without coming off patronizing and defensive. All I'll say is that I was pro-black before it became fashionable, and I've taken a number of shots from white people over the years for not swimming with a strictly cream-colored gene pool. To this day, the wisest and most self-actualized person I've ever met was a black guy. He was the only person I've ever known in whose presence it was impossible to feel angry. And there have been countless black people who've been bountifully cool to me in situations where they had no need to be so nice. Thanks.

Los Angeles in 1994 was sick with racial tension. Like the smog, it made your eyes water and left an evil burning taste around your gums and on the insides of your nostrils. Only days before the verdict was due in the second Rodney King trial, everyone seemed primed for another round of riots. And as I sat in my car at a red light waiting to cross Sunset Boulevard, I noticed that an angry black man was running straight toward me. Tall and covered in what looked like tattered auto-shop rags, his lips flaring and eyebrows furrowed, he looked like a Saharan road warrior bearing down to kill me. Great, I thought, I get a sneak preview of the race war a few days before everyone else. He stopped in his tracks about three feet from my driver's-side window and glowered for a second. I stared back, not sure what was going to happen. Then he held up a small cardboard sign on which he had scrawled the word SMILE. He flashed a peace sign and walked away laughing. And damned if I didn't smile despite myself.

It's asshole niggers like that who give hope to honky jerkoffs like me.

Most white people who reach out to blacks come off like awkward, patronizing schlumps. So here I am—one EXTREMELY white guy—addressing all thirty-two million black Americans at once. Ahem, black people—can I have your attention? More realistically, I'd like to welcome the three or four black people who purchased this book despite its title. C'mon in. Take your shoes off. Set a spell.

I dig your groovy vibe, my cocoa-tinted coinhabitants of the planet earth. First off, terms such as "black" and "white" are divisive. I'm not literally white. My skin is a sickly sharkskin gray. And most "black" people are the rich earthen color of a ripened fig. I feel that I'm the man who can bring us all together because I'm so weird that no one wants to claim me as their own. I can heal our divisions because I can't get along with anyone. I'd like to get to know every black person in America, one by one. If I could snuggle you individually, I surely would. Door to door, down the block, across the nation. I'd like to invite every black person in America over to my house for dinner. I hope you like mayonnaise on Wonder bread and peppermint soda. Why don't we all form a large circle and give a back rub to the person on your left?

Though I may be a white man, my shit's brown just like everyone else's. As *très cliché* as it sounds, I try to take people on an individual basis. I'm neither a negrophile nor a negrophobe; I'm for negrofairness. Don't pick no pea pods from my patch, and I won't rob no rhubarbs from you. Don't take my parking space, and I won't steal your hubcaps.

I'm no fan of white supremacy—everyone knows the Jews and chinks are superior. Interracial dating doesn't bother me, but the very concept of dating does. I don't mind being called a devil so much as I'm bothered by the fact that people believe in the existence of devils. And I have no problems with anyone who has no problems with me.

For the great part of America that is one paycheck away from picking through garbage cans, it may be wise to consider the strength of organized trash. The "minorities" plus the rednecks equals the majority. It always has. And the power jockeys have always known this, so they've historically pitted these groups as adversaries. Imagine a rainbow mound of trash. The whole spectrum of societal shit. I dream of a day when people of all races can hate each other for being assholes rather than for the color of their skin. I dream of a day when a million hillbillies march on Washington, demanding equal rights. I have a dream—one day po' whites and blacks will stand together and be able to say, "It's a class thing—you wouldn't understand."

So maybe the rednecks and blacknecks, the crackers and niggers, the Abners and Sambos, Homer and Jethro standing alongside Amos and Andy, the hillbillies and junglebunnies, the trailer trash and ghetto scum, the hicks and the spooks, the honkies and darkies, the bumpkins and minstrels, the pitchforks and spades, the po'buckers and the buck nigras, the good ol' boys and the homeboys, the Archie Bunkers and Fred Sanfords, the Jim-Bobs and the jigaboos, should decide to call a truce to this centuries-old feud and try it a different way for a change. We can always get back to the race war, time and the weather permitting.

> I'm going to crusade so that someday the niggers, the polacks, kikes, gooks, whites, anybody can laugh their names off. If you've got something in the closet that stinks, take it out and air it out. (O.B. "The Chocolate Cowboy" McClinton) [16]
>
> Sisters, niggers, whitey, Jews, crackers—don't worry, if there's hell below, we're all gonna go. (Curtis Mayfield) [17]

Some well-meaning nudniks honestly seem to believe that the cure for racial tension is MORE racial tension. I think they're playing it all wrong. Oceans of racial sensitivity have only made people more tense.

Sensitivity doesn't cure tension, it magnifies it. Make people all flexed-out and uptight and frustrated, and trouble starts. What's one of the best tension-reducers? HUMOR.

Racism has become such pure evil, it's hilarious. Hopefully, all this racial hypersensitivity will one day be appreciated for its rollicking camp value. Uptight horror is the foundation of the best comedy. Fuck racial pride, let's have racial satire. There'll be peace when everyone's so tired from laughing, they're too tired to be angry. We'll all be able to get along when we can all laugh about it. I think Americans have a choice between all-out race war and all-out racial comedy. No jokes, no peace. I think TV should be chockablock full of the most horrid racism. Let's get it out of our systems. You shouldn't make racism into Satan—turn it into Bozo the Clown. Make it a laughingstock rather than a bogeyman. In the early 1970s, Mel Brooks and Richard Pryor were doing work which would bring anti-defamation lawsuits today. Therefore, I'd suggest it be mandatory that schoolteachers tell racist jokes. Bringing blackface back may be the best way to heal our racial wounds. When America can handle a sitcom about the Klan (*Ku Klux Kooks*?), I'll know we've made progress. Having everyone get in touch with their inner racism may be the best way to ensure world peace.

In olden times, the white man called himself the white man. Nowadays, the only person who doesn't call the white man "the white man" is the white man. Note the shift in its usage, from self-referential and self-congratulatory to other-referential and accusatory. In the same arena, the black man can call himself the black man, but nonblacks are not allowed to call him the black man. The white woman and the black woman, we are to presume, are doing laundry during all of this. Maybe if, I dunno, the white man, the black man, and the black and white women were to all go out together and have a nice dinner, we could solve most of the problems that face us.

"Pass the salt," the black man would say to the white man.

"Sure, here it is—could you please pass the pepper?" the white man would respond with eager solicitousness.

It would be nice.

230

10

Several Compelling
Arguments for the Enslavement
of All White Liberals

What we are trying to get at in discussing leftism is not so much a movement or an ideology as a psychological type, or rather a collection of related types. . . . Those who are most sensitive about "politically incorrect" terminology are not the average black ghetto-dweller, Asian immigrant, abused woman or disabled person, but a minority of activists, many of whom do not even belong to any "oppressed" group but come from privileged strata of society. . . . Leftists may claim that their activism is motivated by compassion or by moral principles. . . . But compassion and moral principle cannot be the main motives for leftist activism. Hostility is too prominent a component of leftist behavior; so is the drive for power. . . . If our society had no social problems at all, the leftists would have to INVENT problems in order to provide themselves with an excuse for making a fuss. —*Industrial Society & Its Future,* by "FC" (commonly referred to as "The Unabomber Manifesto")

I'll be the first to admit that I'm an asshole under almost any conventional definition of the term. I don't feel equal. I feel BETTER than almost everyone, regardless of race, gender, or sexuality. I'm a cynic. A skeptic. A partial epileptic. I'm sadistic, yet I find myself unable to enjoy it. I am a cultural mongrel and an ideological bastard. I'm a lone psychopath at the top of a bridge who refuses to jump because everyone would applaud.

I'm a fly in the ointment. A Goad in the machine. A glob of sperm at the bottom of your popcorn. Maybe I'm a free-floating cancer cell infesting the *corpus collectivus.* Perhaps I'm just a misguided cracker prawn who's flogging a dead horse. I'm not John the Baptist, I'm Jim the Accident Waiting to Happen. I'm not an evil person. I'm simply a little strange. I'm not a Nazi. My stomach's just upset. I don't want to kill any of you. I just need to get away. And I don't hate you, I just see right through you. So please clear the path.

Prodigal Yankee Trash might be what I am, but it doesn't make a good book title. I exist in somewhat of a cultural purgatory, part redneck and part brooding pariah. Maybe the proper term for me is Uppity White Lowlife. I am a train wreck of rural feistiness and urban cynicism. A nauseating stew of Roman Catholic taboo psychosis, Vermont hillbilly, and suburban Philly doggie-doo. And the fact that I suffer from Intermittently Explosive Personality Disorder in no way invalidates the facts I've enumerated for you, ladies and jellybeans of the jury. I'm proud to have a smidgen of that barbarian blood in me. So I identify with the white working class, although they probably don't identify with me. Whatever I am, it's definitely closer to white trash than white liberal. The call of the redneck was stronger. So sue me.

It's a confusing planet. I don't have a monopoly on the truth. I'm not even sure if I own Baltic and Mediterranean Avenues. I find myself unclassifiable politically. People ask me where I stand, and I say, "Anywhere you aren't standing." I'm not too keen on human nature. I think that anyone, given power, acts like an oppressor. I believe in an equality of corruptibility. I'm not pure. I'm corruptible. What did you have in mind? I have a hunch that the Grim Reaper isn't a liberal, although he is an equal-opportunity employer. I hope I'm wrong about all this. And even if I'm right, I suspect I'll be blamed.

I've often wondered how one becomes credentialed to be a social critic. Most writers have extremely poor social skills. That's why they write. It's true that most social critics have appalling social lives. I am no exception. In my case, it's social criticism from a sociopath. I'm pushing for Enlightened Sociopathy. Maybe that's my political agenda.

Part of my job is to ensure that this book gets misinterpreted the RIGHT way. So I'll predict some of the blatant ways that book reviewers will decontextualize my words to fit their framework. To save unimaginative pulp crits the task of having to slam me cleverly, I've already provided some ready-made ad copy that makes it easy to misrepresent what I'm saying:

> This book is a psychotic, self-pitying, one-sided, historically revisionist screed. What an accomplishment—making people FEEL GOOD about racism again.

> He hates the Yankee liberal-elite corporate media so much, he allowed them to publish his book. I'm sure he gave away all his advance money to unemployed Alabama truckers.

> More whining from the slobs who brought you the lynch mob and the beer gut. The last frail fart of the Angry White Male, the pathetic last gasps of a conqueror now conquered.

> Amazing. Now the BIGOTS feel persecuted. This book tries to argue that racism is caused by reverse racism. Yet more excuses for privileged white males to feel sorry for themselves.

When not accusing me of being a talentless hog-slopper, the criticism will either hinge on my "privilege" or my "bigotry" or my "fear." I'll be called an extremist, but that's not so bad, considering the middle. They'll continually try to ally me with the "right wing," although I steadfastly claim to be wingless. I'm a lone gunman here, not an army. I'll be accused of slumming. They'll say that trailer trash don't read, and even if they did, they wouldn't like this book. Zip up your pants, because your class prejudice is showing.

They'll try to act unimpressed. And next week, they'll act unimpressed again. And the week after that. They'll say I'm merely trying to offend. Why would I have to try? Most people wake up in the morning offended. They go to sleep offended. Trying to offend them would be like trying to make them breathe. I have better things to do with my time. I realize they'll get pissed off, and yet I blame their sensitivity rather than my obnoxiousness.

They'll use whatever tag that makes them feel as if I've been safely defused and pigeonholed and compartmentalized and debunked. They'll feel safer if I fit neatly into one of their grade-school lunchboxes. They'll impute all sorts of sinister, demonic motivations to me, things so clever I never would have thought of them. They'll see me as emblematic of something much more threatening than I see myself. They'll cast me as an evil Nazi psycho backsliding Angry White Male. Whatever. Just as long as I don't have to hang out with you. I don't mind that you hate me, but at least be creative. They probably hate my tone as much as I hate theirs. Fine. Looks like we won't be exchanging Christmas cards. They can hate me until there's nothing left of them but a burnt matchstick. They don't have to like me, as long as they leave me alone. Just stay away, and we should get along swell.

The only risk, as I see it, is that they'll actually like me. That could be trouble.

Liberal bastards.

Whoa, hold your horses, Nellie—I realize that the word "liberal" is often booted around in a knee-jerking, reactionary way. When I say "liberal," I'm not using coded speech because I really want to say "gay" or "Jew" or "black" or "female" instead. Your sexual preferences, religion, country of origin, and genitalia bore me to tears. If you thought I was losing sleep over any of these things, I'm sorry to disappoint. The word "liberal," as I'm using it, isn't meant to imply anything other than someone who identifies *himself* or *herself* as a liberal. Since I don't believe in the tangible existence of "left" and "right," I don't believe that liberals actually exist. The problem is that liberals believe they exist.

Liberalism, like obscenity, is in the eye of the beholder. Because I criticize liberals, some binary brains automatically register me as a conservative. If the marble doesn't fall on the left, it HAS to fall on the right. What neither liberals nor conservatives comprehend is that anyone could be anything other than a liberal or a conservative. Liber-

234

als and conservatives are two ass cheeks surrounding the same hairy bunghole. Constipervative. Liberrhea. They need each other.

Conservatism is a bedtime story believed in only by fat old grizzly bears. I don't identify at all with conservatives. They're varicose-veined mannequins. Blow-dried crash-test dummies. Middle of the roadkill. Walking around as if they forgot to remove the coat hanger from their suit jacket. You had mentioned the huckleberry-pie, fuddy-duddy, Burl Ives, Choo-Choo Charlie, psychovangelical, anal-retentive, hanging-judge-loving, sex-fearing, missile-worshipping, Satan-obsessed, xenophobic, law-abiding, abortion-clinic-bombing, flag-draping, kill-for-Christ, deport-the-Arabs, bash-the-queers, horn-swoggler type? It ain't me. People think that if you attack liberalism, you must be a straw-hat-and-seersucker-suit-clad old puff of flatulence. I don't think so. Limbaugh is Limburger to me. Reagan was a dopey thespian who nearly nuked the planet. Pat Robertson and Ralph Reed are as useless as testicle cheese. I don't like churches or book burnings or witch-hunts. I don't like crowds, period. I hate both liberals and conservatives. I have plenty of hate to go around.

Some people probably assume I was born a shit-kicker and never cleaned off my boots. They presume I've never pondered the liberal platform's glorious wisdom and that I'd see the light if I opened my eyes JUST ONCE. Funny thing, I used to identify myself as a liberal. I used to be one of THEM. I'm a recovering liberal. That's what makes me such a slippery eel. If I seem unnecessarily angry with American liberalism, it's because I feel betrayed by it. I'm mad at white liberalism like I'm mad at Christianity—because it's a lie that I once believed. These days, I hate liberalism with the ferocity of a vengeful ex-lover. I'm a STALKER of white liberalism.

After a while . . . NO, I just didn't have the same endlessly lachrymose reservoirs of compassion that they did. I had my own problems.

But just to be an asshole, I was a liberal throughout the eighties. There seemed to be no other choice during the time. Everyone was a conservative, so I veered the other way. The eighties will go down as one of the worst decades in American history. Everyone pretended. Perceived status was more important than reality. *Lifestyles of the Rich and Famous* and infomercials. Greedy and empty. Multiplexes and malls and scented potpourri and ATM machines. A cold time. Icy synthesizer dance music, jingoistic flag-waving, and the Moral Majority. Blind asset/debt cycles. Cocaine and Valium. Michael Milken. Imelda Marcos. Ivan Boesky. Prince Charles and Lady Di. Leona Helmsley. Donald Trump. That faceless pestilence known as the yuppie. I hated it all. After working a nighttime job in Manhattan, I'd pass the POVERTY SUCKS posters and smirking preppy society-brat *New York* magazine covers at newsstands. Down in the basement at Port Authority bus terminal at two A.M., it was a much different world. Homeless women dragging rags, smelling like barrels of rotted potato peels. A man calmly lighting a crack pipe while waiting for a bus to Jersey. A guy running around waving a needle in his hand, threatening to spike people with AIDS. Realizing there was social chaos beneath all the yuppie pretense, there was no way I'd buy the conservative line of bullshit. In targeting the poor, conservatism pointed a finger at those who weren't to blame. But the liberals eventually lost me, too. They pointed a finger at me, and I wasn't to blame, either.

I started losing faith in liberalism when I began noticing that every liberal who accused me of white privilege seemed to come from a more privileged socioeconomic background than I did. I got sick of their middle-class hypocrisy that shed tears for the black "struggle" while laughing at my white-trash roots. If indigenous Amazonian tribes were subjected to acid rain, the liberals were emotionally devastated. But if a trailer park full of white trash across town all got cancer because they lived atop a toxic dump, it was a joke. I've heard ideological Marxists scream about capitalistic exploitation all while gleefully exploiting their parents' economic generosity. City kids living on their attorney parents' trust funds howling that rural rednecks are the oppressors. I tired of "anarchists" whose mommies paid the bills. They can't even kick their coke habit, and yet they claim to know what's best for the world. They still wear the lobster bibs of cultural entitlement, no matter how they try to hide it. With all the intestine-scrubbing granola they ate, they STILL acted as if there was something stuck up their ass. Could it be that CLASS is what's stuck up their ass?

Let's take a peek inside a coffeehouse full of white liberals. Espresso hipsters. Gentrified radicals. Earth Shoe–wearing, burlap-clad conformist shitheels. Bean-sprout totalitarians. Bleeding hearts. Postnasal drip. Diarrhea pudding. Mealy-mouthed macrobiotic mouse-haired mendicants. Insufferable sufferers. Pinched faces sipping chamomile tea. Each anus clenched tightly enough to cut diamonds. So uptight, it's a wonder their heads don't pop off their shoulders and fly around. Major-league victims. Self-pitying pukes. Unethical moralists. Mean-spirited peaceniks. Doe-eyed, self-important drones. Ideologically as rigid as an ironing board. Just a bore.

CONSCIOUSNESS-RAISING. *Close your eyes and deny everything.* EMPOWERMENT. *Complaining more loudly than usual.* NEW AGE. *Old superstition.* GODDESS IS COMING. *She'd better douche this time.* VISUALIZE WORLD PEACE. *A global lobotomy.* PEOPLE OF COLOR. *Do you mean colored people?* STOP THE HATE. *Honey, I ain't even* STARTED *hatin'.*

It's Liberal Pentecost—everyone in the coffeehouse has a holy flame dancing atop their head. Meek little worms wriggling on a fish hook of sensitivity. A delicate web of frightened arachnids. Crippled Easter bunnies bleeding on the roadside. Skateboarders for racial equality. Surfers against hunger. Mansion-owning crusaders against homelessness. It's all flaky pastry and fine cheese. The bourgeois masquerading as the oppressed. Their little marches and candlelight ceremonies and boycotts. Their false, self-generated sense of stylistic oppression. Sitting there with their thumbs planted in their asses, they've convinced themselves they're making a difference.

Over near a huge glass jar of chocolate-coated coffee beans stands a stack of free alternative weekly newspapers. No doubt there's at least one free alternative weekly in your town—they're identical from San Diego to Maine, Seattle to Miami. It's as if they're all put out by the same company. Same mind. The alternative weekly newspaper encapsulates everything that's wrong with liberalism. As the ink rubs on your fingers and seeps into your bloodstream, you can read about all the toxins in the environment. On newsprint paper that has felled untold forests, you can read about saving the trees. This week (like last week) the editors are outraged that women workers only make seventy cents compared to every dollar that men make. But they never mention that rural workers suffer similar economic disparities compared to city dwellers. Or that Southern incomes have always been much lower than those in the North.

Arbeit macht frei weekly. It's a free weekly, and it's worth every penny. These alternative weeklies thrive on advertising, because it certainly isn't the writing. Futon prices slashed and universal brotherhood. Colonic irrigation while astral-projecting. Ceramic dildos on sale and how to tell if you're a sexist. Pierced nipples and punctured brains. Dull tattoo rebellion. Classified ads for gay cruises and lesbian home furnishings. Nudist bed-and-breakfast weekend retreats. Reiki bodywork for men. A drowning sense of wellness. Anal isometrics. Anti-smoking spirit-channeling hypnotherapists. Voluntary herpes-cream experiments. Holistic veterinary clinics. Marimba benefits for persons with AIDS. High-financed tax-free arts foundations. Giant corporate sponsors spreading good will.

Ballet. Performance art. Modern dance. Pottery class taught by an old woman from Guadalajara. Bulk-grain foods in large cardboard barrels. Forceful coffinlike enclosure in a saline flotation tank with twenty-four hours of feminist folk music pumped in at one hundred twenty decibels. Scented candles, closed minds. Unicorn incense holders and a knife to the throat. Homeopathic herbal remedies and a bullet to the brain. Shiatsu foot therapy and glass fragments rubbed into your skin. Rebirthing and a bloody smear of afterbirth.

So full of their own shit, it's a wonder they don't sprout daisies. So off the mark, radar couldn't find them. So wrong, they've almost rounded the final corner back toward right. So empowered, they'll electrocute themselves. So sensitive, they have to live in an oxygen tent. So enlightened, you have to look away for fear of being blinded. So much pretense, they never get to the main course. So ironic, it's as if they're lost in a hall of mirrors. So fucking cool, they can't even spell their own names.

The artists are clueless. They've never had the slightest idea how to rule the world. That's why they're artists. It's "revolution" as conceived by Hollywood brats rather than the working class. Clove cigarettes and patchouli oil and black lipstick and rubber whips. Smelly armpits and vegetable breath. Tongue piercings and ironic comments about Saturday-morning cartoon shows. The girls with backpacks and Edith Prickley horn-rimmed glasses. The boys with dirty-blond Julius Caesar haircuts and fuzzball-laden old sweaters. Inarticulate slacker pop-culture inbreds. Crumpled tinfoil and a scab on the lip. Stuttering autism as genius. Compassion as fashion. Meaningful emptiness. Scratch-and-sniff attitudinal posturing. All butter, no potato. All frosting, no cake. The hipsters have been entirely subsumed into the *Über*-culture. Their "rebellion" is fashion-ad posery, a million skulls with green crewcuts and no brains inside. Their "culture" is merely a syncretic jumble of received media images. Their ideas of "freedom" are purely a fashion show—freedom to suck cock, smoke crack, and wear loud clothing. Consensual enemas and purple hair and iron cock rings are just dandy, but they're kinda hard to enjoy when you can't put food on the table.

Yessiree, Buffalo Bob, they really have tamed the post-Woodstock kiddies with bread and circuses. For much longer than I care to remember, the "counterculture" has been an empty parade of runway models with needles in their arms. Bratty slackoffs with nothing to say and a lot of costumes in which to say it. The rotted produce of post-World War II prosperity, taking money from their parents with one hand while flipping them off with the other. While the angriest segment of society —and thus the most disillusioned, open to new ideas, and most potentially creative—was stinking up the assembly line with its bone-snapping labor, the leisure-class art geeks tossed out frilly satirical lead balloons, weighted by irony and one-hundred-percent substance-free. And this counterculture congratulated itself on its unbending sympathy for oppressed peoples everywhere—everywhere, that is, but the trailer parks across the tracks on the other side of town.

White liberals will recycle anything but white trash. Their "alternative lifestyles" never include being a redneck. Punk rockers, whose entire shtick rested on making people sick, were themselves nauseated by the hillbillies. After the Sex Pistols toured the South in 1978, guitarist Steve Jones lamented that the experience had been "like *Deliverance.*" Iggy Pop's self-mutilation and G.G. Allin's coprophagy were somehow palatable, but rednecks were just too disgusting. Even though white-liberal Punky Brewsters proposed grotesquerie as an aesthetic paradigm, white trash seemed just too repulsive for them to stomach.

The liberal only goes halfway. Liberal dribbles. Limp noodles. Happy doodles. French poodles. Yolkless eggs. The white liberal wants to be hard-hitting, but he doesn't want to offend the advertisers. He wants to ride the roller coaster, but he doesn't want to muss his hair. He pretends to enjoy trash, but he won't get his hands dirty. He craves excitement, but he doesn't want to get a heart attack. The white liberal eschews all forms of extremism. It's too bad that he lives in an extreme world. I wonder when a five-mile-an-hour wind will come along to blow him away.

Children of pain. The enshrinement of the victim. The victim pinned to velvet-covered cardboard like a butterfly in a science-fair project, unable ever to wriggle free. Pity the young white liberal who tries to sleep atop a stack of twenty mattresses, flapping and flailing about his *Princess and the Pea*–sized problems.

And it's people such as this who've woven the myth of the Angry White Male and have accused him of whining. That's right—white American liberals, one of the whiniest, most protected classes in earth's history, have the Rocky Mountain–sized gallstones to accuse your average Spam-eating ditchdigger of whining. Listen, Bucky Beaver, I'm aware that anyone can whine, including Angry White Males. I've whined. I can bear to hear my own whining for a while, but even I can't stand it after a point. That's why this is the last chapter. But white liberals really are in no place to cast judgment about whininess. They NEVER TIRE of hearing themselves whine.

Liberal muralists will portray the archetypal "whiny white guy" with a fishing rod and a CAT tractor hat. Interesting that you don't hear so much about the whiny entertainment lawyer or the whiny civil-rights activist. Or the whiny alternative-weekly writer. Or the whiny art-gallery owner. Only minorities are allowed to groan under the lash. And, curiously, gentrified whites with the proper political sympathies. They don't think performance artists can whine about being denied NEA grants to stick yams up their asses, but Angry White Males are somehow throwing temper tantrums about being taxed and worked to death. At least the white boys are "whining" about lost jobs and economic exploitation, rather than naughty words and fashion mistakes. Apparently, white liberals aren't complaining about economics because they're doing fine.

Complaining is bad enough. Party-line piety is unforgivable. The white liberal is an unsavory hybrid of Joseph Stalin and Mother Teresa. Too many rules mixing with too much righteousness. Too little to back everything up. Sensitivity by force. Understanding through indoctrination. Brotherhood at gunpoint. The left, like the right, has drawn a clearly perceptible party line, and to wander astray of it immediately makes you a suspect. You disagree with one factoid, and all of a sudden you're the King Kleagle. The white liberal's ideological opponents don't merely disagree with him, they're "sick." White liberals aren't free thinkers, they're ideologues. And they don't possess the wisdom to tell the difference.

They've somehow convinced themselves that if they aren't members of the "Christian right," this makes it IMPOSSIBLE for them to be uptight, censorious meddlers in others' affairs. Liberalism, for all its self-conscious distancing from Bible-thumpers, fulfills the same sort of masochistic impulse as does classic Christianity. The average liberal's intentions are probably no more or less pure than your average idiot Christian's and about equally as misguided. Liberals have their own taboos and sacred cows and "lines" you shouldn't cross. At this point, the Liberal Catechism might even be thicker than the Holy Bible. Liberals are as simplistically fearful of (and naive about) racism, sexism, and homophobia as Christians are about Satanism, communism, and pornography. They're as sensationalistically heart-tugging with their rape and hate-crime scare stories as the Christians are about Satanic abduction rumors. Their fear of "the horrible" is as palpable as any fundamentalist's, although the fundies have more vivid imaginations. The liberal's beliefs, like those of the Jesus freaks, are founded on justice, goodness, and equality. In short, nothing that can be proven.

Liberals are right about one thing: "Politically correct" is a shopworn phrase that implies that only leftists can be humorless ideologues. So instead of the overused "PC," I prefer "self-righteous" or "ideologically constipated," because such terms can apply to any asshole in the cosmos. But like all other starry-eyed Pious Creeps, white liberals will say they're not being self-righteous, they're just DOING THE RIGHT THING. So do the right thing. Go home. Your life is in shambles. Clean up your own nest before you try to save the spotted owl.

It'd help matters if white liberals actually WERE correct. But they blame anger when they should blame frustration. They blame whiteness when they should blame greed. They blame maleness when they should blame power. Instead of dismantling the very architecture of bigotry, they merely slap on a new coat of paint. Their response to a penis-centric culture is Goddess theology and vagina-worship. Their rebuttal to white supremacy is black supremacy. Their rejoinder to gay-bashing is the demonization of hetero "breeders." They say they want to transcend sexism, yet they condemn anything they consider too "male." They want to kill racism, but they shy away from anything too "white." They're against homophobia, yet they want rednecks to stay in the closet. Their response to fascism is their own brand of ideological dictatorship. They only seem able to uplift themselves while stepping on someone else's face. They pin everything on white-male anger, as if there had never been corrupt political regimes in Asia, Africa, or Latin America. As if there had never been anything such as sexism, homophobia, ethnic bigotry, territorial aggression, or police brutality displayed in any of these places.

The most enjoyable thing about analyzing liberalism is watching it run into conflicts of interest—what do they do about black sexism? Latin homophobia? Lesbians who beat their partners? Socialist governments who murder their citizens? Is pedophilia included as a lifestyle choice? Do you ally with the "racism" or the "domestic violence" side of the O.J. Question?

Good intentions often lead to bad moods. For all their rhetorical sweetness, white liberals are some of the bitterest people I've ever met. Judgmental. Intolerant. So stuck up, it'd take the Jaws of Life to pull them back down. As individuals—*tête-à-tête, mano a mano*—many strident liberals I've known are the meanest, lowest, pettiest, most back-stabbing jerkoffs you'd ever want to avoid. The reason they're so irritable is because they constantly face a world that does not fit their beliefs. It's the same way that Christians get all hot and peppery when you start blowing shotgun holes through their arguments. When you begin slicing through a liberal's flimsy cellophane ideology, his true inner meanness—hardly liberal—is revealed.

It would seem strange for a King Crab such as myself to chide ANYONE for being mean. It isn't liberals' meanness per se, it's that they seem entirely unaware of it. Or if aware, they try to bury it under some ennobling excuse. My objection is to their pretense of sweetness. If they came to terms with their meanness, they might actually be fun. But like a stagnant pond is clogged with slime, the liberal is FILLED with hate, because his ideology doesn't allow him to express and release it. There are plenty of things that liberals hate, they just can't bring themselves to use that awful word. The liberal's main problem isn't that he's an asshole, it's that he can't come to terms with it.

Liberals aren't evil, they're merely misguided human beings adhering to a code that denies them their humanity. Amid all this stifling equality, the fundamental human need to feel superior was left unsatisfied. For all the tongue-flapping they do about equality, almost all white liberals act as if they feel superior to white trash. While they accuse rednecks of dehumanizing others, liberals refer to rednecks as "scum," "slime," "vermin," and "subhuman pigs." If whites aren't even equal among themselves—a premise established by the very IDEA of white trash—how can they be equal with others? If equality doesn't exist *within* a race, how can it exist *among* races?

The Angry White Male has become the acceptable dumping receptacle for all the white liberal's prejudicial instincts. The Angry White Male serves all the psychological functions of a debased Cartoon Watermelon Nigger for him. White lib-yoo-ruls dehumanize, marginalize, demonize, and satirize the Angry White Male, and still they wonder why he's angry. But it apparently isn't the anger that disturbs white liberals, it's the fact that a Caucasian penis is attached to it. Without blinking, liberals will celebrate cauterizingly wrathful radical feminists or type A–personality black rappers. Anger only evokes the white liberal's latent class prejudices when a rustic-looking white male is spewing it.

Angry? White? Male? GUILTY on all three charges. I'm angry because every time I open my mouth, I spit blood. I'm white because

243

Negroes don't have freckles on their back. I'm male because I'm able to use a urinal. I'm angry because people think I'm a demon, when I can't find my underwear half the time. I'm white because my nose more resembles a scoop than a shovel. I'm male because my testicles expand and shrink with fluctuations in room temperature. I'm angry because people who angrily accuse others of being angry won't 'fess up to being angry. I'm white because my lips more resemble earthworms than leeches. I'm male because my nipples have no explicable function. I'm very angry, extraordinarily white, and unbearably male. Better an Angry White Male than a guilty one, I say. Better to be misunderstood than self-deceived. I'd rather rule in hell than attend your boring garden party.

Gallons of pus-colored snake venom have been flung at the Angry White Male. So let's talk about his polar opposite, the Guilty White Male. Since I'm EXTREMELY sensitive to accusations of sexism, we'll leave the loudmouth liberal chicks out of it. I'll just deal with the liberal guys for the sake of parity. Innumerable libbie wags have made careers out of condescendingly scrutinizing the Angry White Male's "fears" and "anxieties." As partial payback, allow me to analyze the Guilty White Male's hang-ups. It's only fair. My tit for their tat. Since many liberals diagnose dissenters as being "phobic" about something or other, I'll return the favor. Liberals are redneckaphobic.

There is much that the Guilty White Male fears about the redneck. I think he's dimly aware that there's more to the story; he's just afraid to deal with it. The Guilty White Male fears that the redneck may have legitimate gripes after all. He fears that a lot of the uglier manifestations of white-trash culture aren't signs of degeneracy, they're reactions to a desperate environment. He fears the redneck's crude honesty and lack of pretense. He fears guns because he fears proletarian rage.

The Guilty White Male fears the redneck within himself. He's scared that he might somehow decay into white trash if he isn't constantly vigilant. He fears the fact that rednecks are TRULY tapped into the primitive in a way that white liberals can only vicariously experience through blacks. With all those images of insatiable-appetite Jethros and superbuff Abners, maybe the Guilty White Male fears the redneck's unspoiled countrified sexual prowess. White liberals cynically allege

244

that rednecks hate blacks because they secretly want to *be* black. So is this the same reason why hipsters hate hillbillies?

"I could be wrong" is a four-word sentence that never occurs to the Guilty White Male. Deep down, he has no proof of equality. No hard evidence for how or why our unprecedented multicultural social picnic will actually work. He can't explain all the world's violence beyond the word "hate." Can't account for his opponents' motivations beyond the word "evil." Can't deal with aggression. Can't deal with biology or genetics or logic. Can't deal with death. Can't explain much of history at all. Can't honestly blame all Third World poverty on whiteness. Can't account for natural inequalities. Can't deny that nature has a cruel sense of humor. Can't tell you what governs the world other than force. Can't dodge the fact that all his privilege was purchased with blood. The Guilty White Male is a well-meaning Sugar Bear who's hibernating from reality. His good wishes consistently rub up against a rotten world. So he pretends. He dreams about a different world.

For all his self-touted enlightenment and higher education, the Guilty White Male's argumentative style favors wishful thinking over factual precision. His bowl o' beans is a mix of good intentions and bad comprehension. Of uplifting rhetoric stirred with impossible dreams. Of good wishes muddying sound observations. The Guilty White Male finds nobility in dysfunction, empowerment in weakness, and strength in deformity. He prays for happy endings. He expects something different from what the world has to give. There is no heaven. There is no justice. There is no universal brotherhood. A wish won't make it come true. A dream ends when you awake. There's no reason to be optimistic. Everyone dies and is forgotten. To be a humanist is to ignore most of what humanity has done. If history tells us anything, it's that people are very, very uncool.

Liberalism's only hope is in surgical rewiring of the human brain. It would be nifty if cars cost a dollar and if pet hamsters never died, either. It would be really great if I owned a pony. I always wanted a sleigh with reindeer, too. It'd be ginchy if chocolate didn't make you fat or if you could sprout pterodactyl wings and fly to Maui. It'd be radical if prostate cancer was cured by bubble gum and if all human suffering could be nipped in the bud by more bumper stickers on the backs of VW buses.

The Guilty White Male fears admitting exactly WHERE his heartfelt compassion ends and his instinctual self-preservation begins. Because you know it's somewhere. The Guilty White Male knows that only his car window protects him from rioters. Only a weak lock on the front door. He knows that the world's a dangerous place. And yet he projects this fear of potential violence onto the Angry White Male.

At the bottom of everything, the Guilty White Male fears confronting the fact that rednecks mostly exist in a social class BENEATH him. Hipness is a luxury. Being white trash isn't. Even by using the rules of liberalism—victims are saints—the redneck beats the white liberal.

Ideologically, the Guilty White Male is down with the program; materially, he's still a filthy-rich imperialist Yankee hyena. His "shame of being white" is more a sort of cutesy atavistic role-playing than anything tangible. He'll write bighearted articles about the homeless, but he won't offer his spare bedroom. He's tortured with guilt about his relative leisure and affluence compared to most indigenous peoples worldwide, yet he's not quick to pawn his cozy condo and Pentium chip in order to air-drop corn meal to the starving Pakistani peasantry. He's outraged about the oppression of blacks, but he isn't moving into the black slums, at least not this year. He feels terrible that the land was stolen from the Indians, but it doesn't appear as if he's giving it back anytime soon.

Why doesn't Mr. Multicultural give all his cool toys back to the Injuns? Because that would release him from guilt, and he likes to live in guilt. His guilt serves a definite psychological purpose for him, and he wouldn't ever want to get rid of it. The Guilty White Male takes pride in his own shame. But guilt only serves the guilty. Ever wonder why comfy urban white liberals feel such guilt about history and rural rednecks don't? The white liberal's guilt pangs have little to do with noble contrition; his guilt reflects an uncomfortable sense of his place in the historical order. If he feels so guilty . . . well, maybe he should. Maybe his guilt is real. Maybe that's why rednecks and blacks feel no guilt, while white liberals are stricken with it.

Harriet Beecher Stowe, authoress of *Uncle Tom's Cabin*, would have been a white liberal were she alive today. Her problem wasn't that she criticized black slavery in the South, it was that she was a wealthy New England society chippie who ignored all the mangled white factory workers and bruised white kiddie laborers huddled right outside the debutante ball. She was a Northern aristocrat who scolded Southern aristocrats for how they treated their underclass, yet she defecated on the underclass in her own hometown.

Stowe toured Great Britain in 1853 and was hosted by the Duchess of Sutherland, another wickedly wealthy white salon lady who habitually hoisted tea and crumpets on behalf of Negrowth and Afrocharity. After her trip, Stowe called the Sutherland family "enlightened." [1] This must be what she meant: Starting back in 1811, the Sutherlands had begun a systematic expulsion of the Scottish peasantry who'd lived for centuries on common lands. Out of a disputed 800,000 acres, the Sutherlands claimed 794,000 for themselves. They hired British police to forcibly drive out the aboriginal Scots and burn their homes. One elderly woman was torched alive while still in her hut. Peasants were beaten and set adrift. Many starved to death. The Sutherlands' brand of enlightenment created fifteen thousand homeless people and replaced them with sheep. It was very altruistic for the Duchess of Sutherland to shed tears over black slavery in the American South when she had raped her own peasantry. She would have been a white liberal, too.

Karl Marx called the Duchess of Sutherland's brand of charity "a philanthropy which chooses its objects as far distant from home as possible, and rather on that than on this side of the ocean." Charles Dickens referred to the British Negro Uplift parlor-game societies as "telescopic philanthropy," [2] since they focused overseas while ignoring death and starvation within their own shadows.

The modern white liberal is the same way. He can't get along with the downtrodden among his own race, but he wants to prove how open-minded he is by getting along with blacks. It's suffering as viewed through the thick lens of a society matron's monocle. It's just table-lace art patronage, as it's always been. In their eagerness to help oppressed peoples across the ocean, they leapfrog right over white trash in their own pond. Starving children in India. Starving children in Africa. Starving children everywhere but Appalachia. They think globally, ignore white trash locally. There's a weird upper-class schizophrenia about whose suffering seems most immediate. The plight of indigenous yam-diggers ten thousand miles away draws their tears more than the stinking traumas of trailer trash only ten miles across town. White liberalism's first rule seems to be that charity never begins at home.

At some point during the rise of European class systems, white nobles and white trash must have separated to a degree where they began viewing each other as alien races. There's a lost brotherhood, a fall from grace, an ancient schism between white trash and white cash. They fucked with the white underclass for at least seven hundred years before they ever started exploiting blacks. White trash reminds them of something they'd just rather not think about. It's just too much guilt. They don't like to face their benighted ex-brethren. With all the bounteous liberal sympathy in Hollywood, I'll bet that very few limo libs employ white maids and butlers. They can't bear the image of a white person acting too much like a serf, at least not in their presence.

Oh, these liberal kids and their vicarious oppression. Oceans of compassion from the fat-free hearts of trust-fund babies. Their love for Native Americans extends to buying Navajo jewelry and handbags. Their Holocaust reparations consist of a Sunday-morning bialy roll with butter. Their empathy for blacks is represented by an extensive collection of Motown CDs.

The Guilty White Male seems to believe that blacks will appreciate his benevolent smile and conciliatory attitude and how much he hates his own skin. The Guilty White Male thinks his Michael Jordan posters and Maya Angelou books are all that's needed for appeasement. His negrophilism seems to be nothing beyond a fashion statement, almost a way of accessorizing. It's black pride without ever having to endure the downsides of being black. Ultimately, it's a way for bland white people to feel connected to the oppressed. Not to BE connected, but to feel it. A safe, packaged form of negrophilism. Freeze-dried instant-coffee negrophilism. It's convenient. He can take it along for a snack. And he'd last about five minutes in a black ghetto.

The blunt-edged fact is that most guilty white liberals and proud

American blacks have next to NOTHING in common. Nothing culturally. Nothing economically. Don't live in the same neighborhoods.
Different belief systems. Different sensitivities. They find different
things funny. They don't even breathe the same air most of the time.
The bittersweet truth is that while white liberals may love black people,
one could hardly say the opposite is true. That's the classic joke of
white liberalism: the self-negating, shirt-rending white person making
clumsy entreaties to a crowd of blacks who don't cotton to negrophiles
and might even call him a punk-ass honky to his face. Be careful
whom you wish to uplift, for they may just uplift themselves. Many
black radicals correctly discern the self-serving tenor of most white-
liberal "philanthropy." They're tired of white liberals telling them how
to be black. And I'm tired of white liberals telling me how NOT to be
white.

In hipster argot, "white" has come to mean "empty" in the same
way that "black" used to connote "evil." Standing on a street corner,
the Guilty White Male loudly reminds everyone that whites HAVE no
culture. He utters the word "white" with more hatred than any black
person does. What to make of his curious self-loathing? Why does he
mistake it for enlightenment? He seems unaware that this footloose
doctrine of antiwhite vengeance might one day come stomping toward HIM.

The Guilty White Male has seen who he is, can't stand the idea, and
yet pretends that he can change it. The Guilty White Male is the most
soulless of all white people. That's why he tries so desperately to
connect with the perceived soulfulness of nonwhites. But the Guilty
White Male's wholesale bashing of whiteness will never change the
fact that HE'S WHITE. He'll use "lily-white" as a pejorative, but the
mirror doesn't lie. If he could change his skin color he probably would,
but for now he's stuck. By objectifying whiteness, he's fooled himself
into believing he must be something else.

Racial chameleon boy. It's noteworthy that white liberals identify
themselves merely as liberals, and hardly ever as WHITE liberals, yet
they make a point of the Angry White Male's skin tone. They're
trying to exorcise the whiteness out of them, basking in guilt to give
themselves a cultural tan. Good luck. In the ways that THEY derisively

use the term "white"—narrow-minded, born to economic privilege, bad dancers—most white liberals I've known are whiter than me. Deal with it.

Historically, the Guilty White Male has suffered a lot less than has the Angry White Male. So now it's Mr. Guilty's turn. He whimpers so much about an oppression which seems nonexistent in his life, it almost makes you want to oppress him. Being liberated and empowered has only seemed to make him cranky. Why not punish the Guilty White Male with all the angst he so deeply wants to feel?

The white liberal craves cinematic pain. Literary suffering. I think he deserves better. A bit of true pain to complement his fantasies. The kind I've always known. Pain ain't a thing to me. Beat me up, I wipe myself off and walk away. But pain is something the white liberal either fears (when it's near) or fetishizes (when it's someone else's). I say give him a full taste of the oppression he's jonesin' for. Drag him through all the progressive beauty he finds in the Third World experience. Everyone might be happy that way.

Therefore, I propose that all white liberals should be forced to pick cotton and tobacco. Chain and stuff them together in the holds to galley ships. Send all white liberals to Africa to work on plantations. They should endure all the pains of slave life except forcible rape, because that would only validate their feminist fantasies. I suggest that white liberals be herded into concentration camps in which they're forced NOT to take showers. In a white-liberal prison camp, they'd all feel each other's pain (and body funk) together. They'd love it.

Or just make them WORK for a change. Put them in Moonie jumpsuits and make them pick up trash along the highway. I'd like to see white liberals as apartment-house doormen and elementary-school janitors. White liberals as shoeshine boys and bellhops and migrant workers. The editors of the *Village Voice* working in a chain gang. Force all performance artists to work as sharecroppers and lumberjacks. Make drag queens labor as coal miners in the *true* underground. Make Hollywood liberals DRIVE limousines for a change. They should be forced to live in the hills for a year without electricity and running water before they make fun of hillbillies. Let them plow a farm for a year and then come back with bestiality jokes. Maybe white liberals should be sent off to die in war while rednecks stay at home and protest. Let's have some sensitivity training that makes sense.

And perhaps some humiliating role reversal to complete the treatment. I envision a 1990s version of *Watermelon Man* or *Black Like Me* —an urban liberal yuppie wakes up one morning as a toothless rural hillbilly and finds that he can't change. Maybe white liberals should be forced to perform in whiteface, humiliating themselves to the delight of all-black audiences. I'd like to see a minstrel show where penitent white liberals perform "Puff the Magic Dragon" and other sixties folk songs while rowdy Negro hecklers throw rotted fruit at them. I have nothing against white liberals. Everyone should own one.

Maybe it's wrong to wish that they suffer. Maybe that's just what they want. Maybe the most sadistic thing would be to wish them a long, happy life. Maybe they shouldn't be murdered. Maybe they should just walk around saddled with the living knowledge of what shallow pains in the ass they are. They shouldn't be killed, but dog leashes aren't out of the question. They shouldn't be exterminated. But they HAVE to be sterilized.

Since they're as literal-minded as your average fundamentalist Republican Elks Club member, they'll probably think I'm REALLY calling for the seizure and arrest of anyone with liberal politics. Maybe they'll think my words constitute actual hate speech that directly incites brutality against white liberals. A man can dream, can't he?

In its late-1960s hippie incarnation, liberalism was often funny and irreverent. Now it's reverent to a degree that borders on the comic. I'm not sure exactly when liberals lost their humor, but the loss seems nearly complete. As a man's penis sometimes shifts from one side of his slacks to the other, the pendulum has swung the other way. As sensitive as liberals are, they've become entirely numb to humor. Oh, they'll say that they can appreciate comedy, but that some topics are NEVER FUNNY. They've mastered nuclear fission and chaos theory, but they still get upset with words. How can you trust people who can't even tell when you're kidding? Beware the smiling faces that can't take a joke. And not only are they unable to take a joke, they'll sue you for defamation.

The film *Easy Rider* seemed to define the cultural struggle for a generation: Two drug-gobbling hippie bikers allied themselves with the world's oppressed against THE ESTABLISHMENT, strangely represented by two rural Louisiana hayseeds in a pickup truck. But cultural sensibilities have changed so much since 1969, I'd suggest a contemporary remake of *Easy Rider* with the heroes and villains completely switched. In the spirit of radical right-wing antistatism, the film would be called *Freedom Rider.* Instead of Billy and Captain America, the main characters would be Hillbilly and Corporal Militia. The boys try to smuggle plutonium in their motorcycle gas tanks from a radical, Bigfoot-worshiping religious compound in rural Oregon to a paramilitary tax-protest group on Montana's eastern plains. They fall asleep at night in a public park in Olympia, Washington, where they are savagely clubbed by riot grrrls who scream at them for being racist, sexist, and homophobic assholes. They later wake up in jail next to a Southern-accented lawyer, but instead of Jack Nicholson it's Morris Dees from the Southern Poverty Law Center. Dees befriends Hillbilly and Corporal Militia with the intention of deprogramming them from their racist ways. But one night around a campfire, the boys trick Dees by ripping a page out of a hate-literature magazine and rolling a joint with it. They smoke the Hate Joint with Dees. His mind poisoned by inhaling the superpotent hate literature, Dees instantly becomes racist and starts blurting out lines such as, "This used to be a hell of a country . . . until the NIGGERS took over." Dees is later stabbed to death by a black transvestite whom he'd rejected for a secretarial job. Corporal Militia and Hillbilly split for Oktoberfest outside Coeur d'Alene, Idaho, where they snort crank and perform sadomasochistic acts with a pair of Nazi hookers. After leaving Oktoberfest, Corporal Militia and Hillbilly are shot to death by a truck-driving radical lesbian. The times, they've a-changed.

Liberals have forgotten the value of death. In the early 1970s, zero population growth was a solid plank in the liberal platform. Now they've abandoned it, presumably because they thought it was racist to fret about overpopulation. Bad mistake. Stick around for another fifty years if you don't know what I mean.

Haven't you noticed how crowded it's getting? Redneck individualism grows more difficult as the country branches out into one tentacle-clotted cement suburb. It's harder and harder to run away from the octopus. Rural life will become something from the past, like clean air. The city is no place for a person to do some thinking. So I'm headed out to the piney woods. To flyover country. Across the railroad tracks. Beyond the Pale.

You can stay in the city and keep running away from who you are. I'll run to the hills and stay true to myself. The city walls have always held the power. There's nothing I find distasteful about white liberals that a thousand miles of distance wouldn't cure. You can have your Sodom and Gomorrah. Green Acres is the place to be. I want to get far enough away from the city that I can't see the flames anymore. You know you've had enough of city life when inbreeding starts to sound better than overcrowding.

I want to be
Where the land is free
Of irony.

Some folks just don't want to believe the truth, no matter how hard you slap their faces with it. No matter how deeply you dunk their heads in the toilet with it. No matter how viciously you clobber them with your Buford Pusser stick. The white American liberal stubbornly fails to see that he is a transitory creature. A big boo-boo for each generation is myopically to assume it has reached the final stage of enlightenment, and that its most sacred beliefs won't be disproven within fifty years, if not much sooner. White American liberals seem to think we reached cultural satori sometime in 1966 or '67, and they want to establish a Thousand Year Reich of Haight-Ashbury.

But it isn't the redneck who's running away from himself, it's the white liberal. And sooner or later, he's going to get tired. Self-hatred can be fatiguing. A guilt complex can really poop you out. It would be so easy just to let go of the shame, just to exhale and release all the tension. A few more years, and liberals won't be holding on to their beliefs, they'll be desperately clutching them. The white liberal is a dandelion atop a toxic dump who doesn't realize a bulldozer is crawling up the hill. The white liberal will bury himself. Liberalism will wither from its own nugatory squeakiness. From its own crushing weightlessness. It'll strangle itself to death with the force of its own goodness. It'll lose focus because it never really had any. In fact, it started dying a long time ago. I'm just here to kick it while it's down. Evil doesn't exist. One day, white liberals won't, either. There will be nothing left of the left.

The redneck has never lost his soul. The white liberal has never been able to find his. White liberals like to portray the Angry White Male as an endangered species, but he'll last a lot longer than the Guilty White Male. The roots of the Redneck Sequoia reach much deeper than those of the White Liberal Bonsai. Redneckism isn't a political party, it's a historical inheritance. It's not a philosophy, it's a legacy. White trash has existed ever since class structures arose in Europe, thousands of years ago. The white liberal has been around for, ehh, about forty years. Want to place bets on who's going to last? Methinks that a hardy strain that survived barbarian invasions, feudalism, the Plague, indentured servitude, farm poverty, industrial death, and trench warfare can survive white liberalism. The gene that causes white trash is a hardier sort than the virus that produces white liberals. Liberalism will die before anger or whiteness or maleness will. Rednecks are forever.

So how do I propose to snatch away the oily blanket of cultural misunderstanding that hangs between most of America and this wondrous thing called white trash? Shit, I thought it was enough merely to STATE the problem. Umm, sure . . . let's see . . . maybe a national Hillbilly Holiday. Maybe like everyone's Irish on St. Patty's Day, people should get the chance to be a redneck for twenty-four hours. They might like it. Perhaps we should urge the inbred to form their own victims'-rights groups and antidefamation clubs. Of course I jest. I poke. I nudge. I goad. The last thing this country needs is for the left-handed chicken-choke of campus-fascist speech codes to be tightened around the word "redneck." There are bigger problems than dirty words. The world is collapsing into a stinking shitpile, and the flies buzzing atop it are worried about hurting people's feelings.

The cultural grease drippings of the 1960s will no longer be applicable in the twenty-first century. But class politics will. Anti-industrialism will. Redneck rural individualism, once thought to be a sure sign of mental retardation, will seem wise in the face of seething overpopulation. There are a lot of first-class philosophers hiding in the hills, too smart ever to come down into the city. Exit the white liberal. Enter the redneck. The avant-garde is the Old Guard. The East Village is a dead zone. San Francisco is a bombed-out crater. The Left Bank has slipped into the river. Bohemia is scorched earth. But the hills are still standing.

Up, up, ye mighty trailer park. The hills are alive with the sound of muskets. A stink rises from America like steamin' horse manure wafting through the cornfields. Can you smell it, my friend? A rebel yell echoes from the hills and into the greenish glens. Can you hear it, my friend? The shit's gonna rise one day. The trash is only starting to strike back.

The fog lifts. The sun burns through the clouds. The necks slowly sizzle to red.

MONTANI SEMPER LIBERI

Endnotes

Chapter 1

1. Tad Friend, "White Trash Nation." *The Oregonian* (published in three parts), 11/6/94–11/8/94.

Chapter 2

1. Cantor, *The Medieval World,* pp. 67–69.
2. Information about the Picts is from Waddell, *The Phoenician Origin of the Britons, Scots & Anglo-Saxons.*
3. Bloch, *Feudal Society,* p. 9.
4. Boissonnade, *Life and Work in Medieval Europe,* p. 29.
5. Pirenne, *Economic and Social History of Medieval Europe,* p. 17.
6. Boissonnade, *Life and Work in Medieval Europe,* p. 151.
7. *Ibid.,* p. 326.
8. *Ibid.,* p. 123.
9. *Ibid.,* p. 117.
10. Duby, *The Three Orders,* p. 278.
11. *Ibid.,* p. 136.
12. Bloch, *Feudal Society,* p. 257.
13. Duby, *The Three Orders,* p. 136.
14. *The Oregonian,* 5/28/96, p. C1.
15. Boissonnade, *Life and Work in Medieval Europe,* p. 263.
16. *Ibid.,* p. 262.
17. Duby, *The Three Orders,* p. 352.
18. Schor, *The Overworked American,* p. 61.

19. Boissonnade, *Life and Work in Medieval Europe,* p. 148.
20. Duby, *The Three Orders,* p. 288.
21. *Ibid.,* p. 334.
22. Cheyney, *The Dawn of a New Era,* p. 133.
23. Epstein, *Wage Labor and Guilds in Medieval Europe,* p. 254.
24. Hill, *The World Turned Upside Down,* pp. 50–52.
25. *Ibid.,* pp. 41, 34, 64, 76, 186, 100, 39, and 21, respectively.
26. Foster, *Modern Ireland,* pp. 136–37.
27. Leyburn, *The Scotch-Irish,* p. 138.
28. Foster, *Modern Ireland,* p. 32.
29. Leyburn, *The Scotch-Irish,* p. 125.
30. *Ibid.,* p. 131.

Chapter 3

1. Bailyn, *The Peopling of British North America,* p. 61.
2. Zinn, *A People's History of the United States,* p. 46; also Ekirch, *Bound for America,* p. 58; Leyburn, *The Scotch-Irish,* p. 176; Nash, *Class and Society in Early America,* p. 82; Hofstadter, *America at 1750,* p. 34.
3. Wertenbaker, *The First Americans,* p. 33.
4. Leyburn, *The Scotch-Irish,* p. 178.
5. Kellner, *Moonshine: Its History and Folklore,* p. 34.
6. Hoffman, *They Were White and They Were Slaves,* p. 62, citing George Novack, "Slavery in Colonial America," *America's Revolutionary Heritage,* p. 142.
7. Eric Williams, *From Columbus to Castro,* cited in Usenet newsgroup soc.genealogy.uk + ireland.
8. Hoffman, *They Were White and They Were Slaves,* p. 11, citing "Some Observations on the Island of Barbados," Calendar of State Papers, Colonial Series, p. 528.
9. Hoffman, *They Were White and They Were Slaves,* p. 68, citing Jill Y. Sheppard, *The "Redlegs" of Barbados,* p. 18.
10. Hoffman, *They Were White and They Were Slaves,* pp. 62–63.
11. *Ibid.,* pp. 90–91.
12. Clinton V. Black, *History of Jamaica,* p. 37, cited in Usenet newsgroup soc.genealogy.uk + ireland.

13. Hofstadter, *America at 1750,* p. 37.

14. Nash, *Red, White, and Black,* p. 217.

15. Caudill, *Night Comes to the Cumberlands,* pp. 5–6.

16. Hoffman, *They Were White and They Were Slaves,* p. 15, citing British writer Francis Trollope's estimate that 200,000 or more British children were kidnapped and forced into factory labor.

17. Cash, *The Mind of the South,* p. 7.

18. Wertenbaker, *The First Americans,* p. 63.

19. Steinfeld, *The Invention of Free Labor,* p. 199.

20. *Ibid.,* p. 247.

21. Hoffman, *They Were White and They Were Slaves,* p. 72, citing Robert C. Johnson, "The Transportation of Vagrant Children from London to Virginia, 1618–1622," in *Early Stuart Studies,* p. 139.

22. *Ibid.,* p. 70, citing Egerton Manuscript, British Museum.

23. Nash, *Red, White, and Black,* p. 217, citing Peter Gouldesbrough, "An Attempted Scottish Voyage to New York in 1669," *Scottish Historical Review,* 40 (1961), p. 58.

24. Hoffman, *They Were White and They Were Slaves,* p. 55, citing Edward Channing, *History of the United States,* Vol. II, p. 369.

25. *Ibid.,* p. 77, citing a pamphlet by M. Godwyn, London, 1680.

26. Genovese, *Roll, Jordan, Roll,* p. 5.

27. Kennedy and Kennedy, *The South Was Right!,* p. 67.

28. Mittelberger quotes taken from Zinn, *A People's History of the United States,* p. 43, and Hofstadter, *America at 1750,* pp. 39–40.

29. Hofstadter, *America at 1750,* p. 38.

30. *Ibid.,* p. 42.

31. Ekirch, *Bound for America,* p. 104.

32. *Ibid.,* p. 104.

33. Hoffman, *They Were White and They Were Slaves,* p. 80.

34. Hofstadter, *America at 1750,* p. 48.

35. Ekirch, *Bound for America,* p. 103.

36. *Ibid.,* p. 103.

37. Hofstadter, *America at 1750,* p. 42.

38. Ekirch, *Bound for America,* p. 102.

39. Zinn, *A People's History of the United States,* p. 44.

40. Nash, *Red, White, and Black,* pp. 53–54.

41. Hofstadter, *America at 1750,* p. 34.

42. Ekirch, *Bound for America*, p. 123.

43. *Ibid.*, p. 129.

44. *Ibid.*, p. 129.

45. Steinfeld, *The Invention of Free Labor*, p. 88.

46. Hoffman, *They Were White and They Were Slaves*, p. 40.

47. Steinfeld, *The Invention of Free Labor*, p. 88.

48. Hoffman, *They Were White and They Were Slaves*, p. 99, citing H. White, *Life and Services of Matthew Lyon*, p. 6.

49. *Ibid.*, p. 53, citing Richard Ligon, *A True and Exact History* (1657).

50. *Ibid.*, p. 53.

51. Nash, *Red, White, and Black*, pp. 53–54.

52. Steinfeld, *The Invention of Free Labor*, p. 89.

53. Ekirch, *Bound for America*, p. 146.

54. Zinn, *A People's History of the United States*, p. 44.

55. Hoffman, *They Were White and They Were Slaves*, p. 89.

56. *Ibid.*, p. 89.

57. *Ibid.*, p. 89.

58. *Ibid.*, p. 89.

59. *Ibid.*, p. 91.

60. Wertenbaker, *The First Americans*, p. 227.

61. Hoffman, *They Were White and They Were Slaves*, p. 107.

62. Zinn, *A People's History of the United States*, p. 44.

63. Wertenbaker, *The First Americans*, p. 227.

64. Hoffman, *They Were White and They Were Slaves*, p. 107.

65. *Ibid.*, p. 108.

66. *Ibid.*, p. 113, citing Public Record Office, London, High Court of Admiralty.

67. Ekirch, *Bound for America*, p. 159.

68. Hamrick, *Antient White Slaves*.

69. Higginbotham, *In the Matter of Color*, p. 156.

70. Ekirch, *Bound for America*, p. 147.

71. Steinfeld, *The Invention of Free Labor*, p. 46.

72. Higginbotham, *In the Matter of Color*, p. 214.

73. Steinfeld, *The Invention of Free Labor*, p. 134.

74. Ekirch, *Bound for America*, pp. 196–97.

75. Hamrick, *Antient White Slaves*.

76. Wertenbaker, *The First Americans,* p. 230.

77. Hofstadter, *America at 1750,* p. 55.

78. *Ibid.,* p. 55.

79. Hoffman, *They Were White and They Were Slaves,* p. 88.

80. *Ibid.,* pp. 88–89.

81. Higginbotham, *In the Matter of Color,* p. 22, quoting John Hope Franklin.

82. *Ibid.,* p. 28.

83. *Ibid.,* p. 459.

84. *Ibid.,* p. 280.

85. Hoffman, *They Were White and They Were Slaves,* p. 11, citing Thomas Burton, *Parliamentary Diary: 1656–59,* Vol. IV, pp. 253–74.

86. Higginbotham, *In the Matter of Color,* p. 411.

87. Ekirch, *Bound for America,* p. 227.

88. *Ibid.,* p. 122.

89. "Observations on the Slaves," etc.

90. Caudill, *Night Comes to the Cumberlands,* p. 18.

91. Steinfeld, *The Invention of Free Labor,* p. 101.

92. Ekirch, *Bound for America,* p. 160.

93. Zinn, *A People's History of the United States,* p. 37.

94. Genovese, *Roll, Jordan, Roll,* p. 57.

95. Leyburn, *The Scotch-Irish,* p. 178.

96. Hofstadter, *America at 1750,* p. 46.

97. Genovese, *Roll, Jordan, Roll,* p. 23.

98. Kennedy and Kennedy, *The South Was Right!,* p. 97.

99. Ignatiev, *How the Irish Became White,* p. 42.

100. *Ibid.,* p. 109.

101. Ekirch, *Bound for America,* p. 20.

102. *Ibid.,* p. 226.

103. *Ibid.,* p. 136.

104. Hofstadter, *America at 1750,* p. 49.

105. Ekirch, *Bound for America,* p. 139.

106. *Ibid.,* p. 27.

107. *Ibid.,* p. 38.

108. *Ibid.,* pp. 1–2.

109. *Ibid.,* p. 223.

110. *Ibid.,* p. 31.

111. *Ibid.,* p. 64.

112. *Ibid.,* p. 58.

113. Hoffman, *They Were White and They Were Slaves,* p. 66.

114. Ekirch, *Bound for America,* p. 67.

115. *Ibid.,* p. 29.

116. *Ibid.,* p. 28.

117. Hoffman, *They Were White and They Were Slaves,* p. 71, citing Edward Burt, *Letters from a Gentleman,* Vol. II, pp. 54–55.

118. Higginbotham, *In the Matter of Color,* p. 394.

119. Caudill, *Night Comes to the Cumberlands,* p. 5.

120. Hoffman, *They Were White and They Were Slaves,* p. 79, citing William Stevenson to James Cheston, Sept. 12, 1768 and Dec. 30, 1769, Cheston-Galloway Papers, Maryland Historical Society.

121. Hofstadter, *America at 1750,* p. 45.

122. *Ibid.,* p. 45; also Nash, *Red, White, and Black,* p. 53.

123. Nash, *Class and Society in Early America,* p. 41; also Ekirch, *Bound for America,* p. 133.

124. Bailyn, *The Peopling of British North America,* p. 28; also Wertenbaker, *The First Americans,* p. 25.

125. Perkins, *The Economy of Colonial America,* p. 72.

126. Ekirch, *Bound for America,* p. 202.

127. Hoffman, *They Were White and They Were Slaves,* pp. 85–86.

128. Hofstadter, *America at 1750,* p. 60.

129. Ekirch, *Bound for America,* p. 125.

130. Hofstadter, *America at 1750,* p. 60.

131. Nash, *Red, White, and Black,* p. 220.

132. Zinn, *A People's History of the United States,* p. 47.

133. Ekirch, *Bound for America,* p. 183.

134. Wertenbaker, *The First Americans,* p. 193.

135. Genovese, *Roll, Jordan, Roll,* p. 641.

136. Nash, *Class and Society in Early America,* p. 47.

Chapter 4

1. *Encyclopedia of Southern Culture,* pp. 1126–27, 1398.

2. Leyburn, *The Scotch-Irish,* p. 191.

3. Bailyn, *The Peopling of British North America,* p. 117.

4. Nash, *Red, White, and Black,* p. 235.

5. Ekirch, *Bound for America,* p. 193, citing Anthony Stokes, *A View of the Constitution of the British Colonies.*

6. Helper, *The Impending Crisis of the South,* p. 318.

7. *Ibid.,* p. 322.

8. Hundley quoted in Reed, *Southern Folk, Plain & Fancy,* pp. 43–44.

9. Williamson, *Hillbillyland,* p. 37.

10. Swift, *Gulliver's Travels,* p. 272.

11. Leyburn, *The Scotch-Irish,* p. xvi.

12. Hoffman, *They Were White and They Were Slaves,* p. 111.

13. From the thread "Rednecks" on Usenet newsgroup alt.appalachian, citing D. H. Fischer, *Albion's Seed,* p. 758.

14. From the thread "Rednecks" on Usenet newsgroup alt.appalachian, citing the OED.

15. From the thread "Rednecks" on Usenet newsgroup alt.appalachian.

16. Flynt, *Dixie's Forgotten People,* p. 19.

17. *Encyclopedia of Southern Culture,* p. 885.

18. Helper, *The Impending Crisis of the South,* p. 332.

19. *Encyclopedia of Southern Culture,* p. 864.

20. Reed, *The Enduring South,* p. 83.

21. Shapiro, *Appalachia on Our Mind,* p. xvi.

22. *Ibid.,* p. 80.

23. *Ibid.,* p. 3.

24. *Ibid.,* p. 17.

25. *Ibid.,* p. 79.

26. Kephart, *Our Southern Highlanders,* p. 18.

27. *Encyclopedia of Southern Culture,* p. 948.

28. Blount, *Crackers,* p. 244.

29. *New York Times,* 1/1/12, p. 12:6, cited in Shapiro, *Appalachia on Our Mind,* p. 329.

30. From the fact sheet *Hate Whitey: The Cinema of Defamation,* by Michael A. Hoffman II.

31. *New York Times,* 2/9/94, p. A21.

32. Reed, *Southern Folk, Plain & Fancy,* p. 66.

33. *Ibid.,* p. 100.

34. Kephart, *Our Southern Highlanders,* p. 297.

35. Shapiro, *Appalachia on Our Mind,* p. 306.

36. Capp, *Li'l Abner Dailies,* Vol. I, p. 5.

37. Reed, *Southern Folk, Plain & Fancy,* p. 45.

38. Blount, *Crackers,* p. 108.

39. Adamic, Louis. "The Hill-Billies Come to Detroit." *The Nation,* 2/13/35, cited in Killian, *White Southerners,* p. 98. / Maxwell, James. "Down From the Hills and Into the Slums." *The Reporter,* 1956, cited in Killian, *White Southerners,* p. 99. / Votaw, Albert N. "Hillbillies Invade Chicago." *Harper's,* 2/58, pp. 64–67, cited in Tullos, *Long Journey Home,* p. 199. / Bruno, Hal. "Chicago's Hillbilly Ghetto." *The Reporter,* 6/4/64, pp. 28–31, cited in Tullos, *Long Journey Home,* p. 199. / Adams, James. "Appalachia Transplanted." *Cincinnati Post,* 7/71, cited in Tullos, *Long Journey Home,* p. 199. / Janson, A. "Displaced Southerners Find Chicago an Impersonal Haven." *New York Times,* 8/31/63, cited in Killian, *White Southerners,* p. 101.

40. Killian, *White Southerners,* pp. 103–7.

41. *Ibid.,* p. 99.

42. "Hillbillies Invade Chicago."

43. Killian, *White Southerners,* p. 98.

44. "Hillbillies Invade Chicago."

45. Killian, *White Southerners,* pp. 103–7.

46. *Ibid.,* p. 101.

47. *Ibid.,* p. 108.

48. *Ibid.,* p. 97.

49. *Encyclopedia of Southern Culture,* p. 1129.

50. Information provided by Jessica Morgan, Nitro, WV.

51. Goldstein, Richard. "My Country Music Problem—And Yours." *Mademoiselle,* 6/73, cited in Reed, *Southern Folk, Plain & Fancy,* p. 40.

52. FBI Uniform Crime Reports 1988—of 9,415 interracial rapes, only ten were white-on-black. Statistics cited in American Dissident Voices Tape #585, "Two Nations, Not One," National Vanguard Books, Hillsboro, WV.

Chapter 5

1. Weber quoted in Nash, *Class and Society in Early America,* p. 79.

2. Genovese, *The World the Slaveholders Made,* p. 183.

3. Cook, *Capitalism Unmasked*, p. 9.

4. Binzen, *Whitetown USA*, p. 43.

5. Zinn, *A People's History of the United States*, p. 192.

6. Schor, *The Overworked American*, p. 192.

7. *Encyclopedia of Southern Culture*, p. 1412.

8. *Ibid.*, p. 45.

9. Flynt, *Dixie's Forgotten People*, p. 67.

10. Tullos, *Long Journey Home*, p. 217.

11. *Encyclopedia of Southern Culture*, p. 1390.

12. *Louisville Courier-Journal*, 2/12/1888, cited in Waller, *Feud*, p. 211.

13. *New York Times*, 2/18/1888, cited in Waller, *Feud*, p. 214.

14. Shapiro, *Appalachia on Our Mind*, p. 161.

15. Waller, *Feud*, p. 233.

16. *Encyclopedia of Southern Culture*, p. 1415.

17. Zinn, *A People's History of the United States*, p. 272.

18. *Ibid.*, p. 320.

19. *Ibid.*, p. 373.

20. Appy, *Working-Class War*, p. 7.

21. Parenti, "Hidden Holocaust, USA."

22. *Trucking '95*, 3/95, p. 24.

23. Kelley, *Hammer and Hoe*, p. 174.

24. Lutton and Tanton, *The Immigration Invasion*, pp. 69, 139.

25. Dalton, *Will America Drown?*, p. 32.

26. *Ibid.*, p. 20.

27. Zinn, *A People's History of the United States*, p. 78.

28. Butler, *War Is a Racket*, p. 9.

29. Statistic calculated using estimate that the US had documented 4,739 black lynchings "to the early 1950s, by which time lynching had virtually ended [*Encyclopedia of Southern Culture*, p. 174]," and that at least ten percent of the 58,191 Americans killed in Vietnam were black.

30. Appy, *Working-Class War*, p. 6.

31. *Ibid.*, p. 41.

32. Schor, *The Overworked American*, p. 81.

33. Jim Redden, "Death to the New World Order." *PDXS* [Portland, OR], August 9–22, 1996, p. 2, citing statistics from "It's the Global Economy, Stupid," in *The Nation*, 7/15/96.

34. Schor, *The Overworked American,* p. 151.
35. *Ibid.,* p. 152.
36. *Ibid.,* p. 47.
37. Redden, "Death to the New World Order."
38. Zinn, *A People's History of the United States,* p. 6.
39. *Ibid.,* p. 49.
40. Redden, "Death to the New World Order."
41. Tad Friend, "White Trash Nation," citing the 1990 US Census.

Chapter 6

1. Patterson, *Historical Atlas of the Outlaw West,* p. 154.
2. RF VIDEO Promotional Flyer.
3. Mothers Against Drunk Driving statistics—16,589 alcohol-related motor-vehicle deaths in 1994 and 17,274 in 1995.

Chapter 7

1. Zinn, *A People's History of the United States,* p. 4.
2. *Ibid.,* p. 34.
3. Kimbrough, *Taking Up Serpents,* p. 37.
4. *Ibid.,* p. 111.
5. Strasbaugh, *E: Reflections on the Elvis Faith,* pp. 23, 32.
6. Elvis Impersonator quotes #1–7 were taken from *I Am Elvis.*
7. Frankie "Buttons" Horrocks quoted from the film *Mondo Elvis,* directed by Thomas Corboy; Monticello Productions, 1984.
8. Jesco White quoted from the film *Dancing Outlaw,* directed by Jacob Young; WPNB (Morgantown, WV), 1991.

Chapter 8

1. Parfrey, *Cult Rapture,* p. 326.
2. *Ibid.,* p. 327, citing a *Montgomery Advertiser* series on Dees.
3. Stern, *A Force Upon the Plain,* p. 11.
4. Statistics from Stop Prisoner Rape, New York, NY.
5. *The Nationalist Times,* 1/96, p. 18, citing R. Rummel, *Death by Government.*

6. Parfrey, *Cult Rapture,* p. 334.

7. Martin, *Black vs. White Equals Slavery: The Color Bomb,* p. 9.

8. Reed, *Southern Folk, Plain & Fancy,* p. 68.

9. Stern, *A Force Upon the Plain,* p. 147.

10. Parfrey, *Cult Rapture,* p. 316.

11. James Madison quoted from Federalist Paper No. 46 and 1st Annals of Congress, June 8, 1789. Washington quoted from his address to the 1st Congress. Patrick Henry quoted from Virginia Convention on the U.S. Constitution's ratification. Samuel Adams quoted from the Convention of the Commonwealth of Massachusetts. Alexander Hamilton quoted from the Federalist Papers. George Mason cited in Elliot, *Debates in the Several State Conventions* (1836), 425–26. Jefferson quoted from *Thomas Jefferson Papers* (C. J. Boyd, ed., 1950) and a 1764 letter in which he quoted an essay by Cesare Becca.

12. Freedom Facts Number 7, 2/96, citing R. Rummel's *Death by Government.*

13. Martin, *Black vs. White Equals Slavery: The Color Bomb,* p. 14.

14. "Free the People" newsletter, Huntington Beach, CA.

15. *Keys to Financial Wisdom,* p. 2.

16. Mayer Amschel Rothschild quoted in Martin, *Black vs. White Equals Slavery: The Color Bomb,* p. 10. Letter from Rothschild Bros. quoted in Cook, *Capitalism: Bane to Freedom and Security,* p. 15, citing U.S. Senate Document #23, 76th Congress, 1st Session, p. 99. Josiah Stamp quoted in Cook, *Capitalism (and its Secrets),* p. 9.

17. Jefferson quoted in Emry, *Billions for the Bankers and Debts for the People,* p. 34, and Wade, *Homes: A Casualty of Inflation,* p. 12. Adams quoted in Martin, *Black vs. White Equals Slavery: The Color Bomb,* p. 11. Jackson quoted in Martin, *Black vs. White Equals Slavery: The Color Bomb,* p. 12. Edison quoted in Emry, *Billions for the Bankers and Debts for the People,* p. 33.

18. National Coin Exchange newsletter [Boring, OR], p. 2.

19. Emry, *Billions for the Bankers and Debts for the People,* p. i.

20. Conrad LeBeau, "Is Your Local Banker Involved in: • Check Kiting, • Mail Fraud, • Racketeering?" [flyer distributed by CPA Book Publisher, Boring, OR]. Statistic calculated using quotient of $6 trillion private and public debt divided over 162.9 billion cash dollars circulating in US at time of estimate.

21. Emry, *Billions for the Bankers and Debts for the People,* p. 29.

22. January 1 to May 26 is 40 percent of a year.

23. Statistic from Don McAlvany of the McAlvany Intelligence Advisor on Portland *public-access* TV.

Chapter 9

1. American Dissident Voices tape, citing FBI Uniform Crime Reports; also *The Nationalist Times,* 1/96, p. 3.

2. *The Nationalist Times,* 1/96, p. 5, citing statistics from the Southern Poverty Law Center.

3. *Ibid.,* citing federal crime statistics.

4. See Chapter 5, footnote 29, for lynching estimates. Black-on-black murder rates are calculated using Bureau of Justice Statistics' 1995 estimate that 93 percent of black murder victims are killed by blacks. According to "Violence and the Young," a 1994 seminar at the University of Maryland at College Park, "roughly half of gun homicide victims from 1968 to 1991 were white and half were black." Presuming a similar racial breakdown in other forms of homicide, and assuming an average US yearly murder rate of around 20,000, the number of black-on-black murders within EACH individual year between 1968 and 1991 would easily exceed (and more likely double) the TOTAL number of blacks lynched throughout Southern history.

5. Kirby, *Media-Made Dixie,* p. 149.

6. Hoffman, *They Were White and They Were Slaves,* p. 104. Quoting the author: "Blacks were admitted to the colonial militia responsible for policing White slaves. The aristocratic planters had felt the necessity to 'arm part of their blackmen.' "

7. Genovese, *Roll, Jordan, Roll,* p. 31.

8. Kennedy and Kennedy, *The South Was Right!,* p. 293.

9. There were an estimated 5.3 million whites in the South at 1860, of which an estimated 347,000 were slaveholders.

10. Grayson, *The Horrors of Reconstruction, I and II,* p. 14, citing Dr. G. R. Glenn.

11. Kennedy and Kennedy, *The South Was Right!,* p. 238.

12. Grayson, *The Horrors of Reconstruction, I and II,* p. 6.

13. *Encyclopedia of Southern Culture,* p. 658.

14. Grayson, *The Horrors of Reconstruction, I and II,* p. 6.
15. Zinn, *A People's History of the United States,* p. 285.
16. Riese, *Nashville Babylon,* p. 257.
17. Curtis Mayfield, "(Don't Worry) If There's a Hell Below, We're All Gonna Go," 1971.

Chapter 10

1. Hoffman, *They Were White and They Were Slaves,* p. 123.
2. *Ibid.,* p. 28. quoting *Bleak House.*

Bibliography

Abbey, Edward. *Abbey's Road*. New York: Plume, 1991.

Allen, Gary. *Beware the Trilaterals; The C.F.R.: Conspiracy to Rule the World; Federal Reserve: The Trillion-Dollar Conspiracy; Labor Leaders Must Learn From American Workers; Your Home: Big Brother Wants Control of Housing* (pamphlets distributed by CPA Book Publisher, Boring, OR; years not indicated).

Ankerberg, John, and John Weldon. *The Facts on UFOs and Other Supernatural Phenomena*. Eugene, OR: Harvest House Publishers, 1992.

Appy, Christian G. *Working-Class War: American Combat Soldiers and Vietnam*. Chapel Hill, NC: University of North Carolina Press, 1993.

Bailyn, Bernard. *The Peopling of British North America: An Introduction*. New York: Vintage Books, 1988.

Baumann, Elwood D. *Bigfoot: America's Abominable Snowman*. New York: Dell, 1975.

Binzen, Peter. *Whitetown USA*. New York: Vintage Books, 1970.

Bloch, Marc. *Feudal Society*. Chicago: University of Chicago Press, 1974.

Blount, Roy, Jr. *Crackers*. New York: Ballantine Books, 1982.

Boissonnade, P. *Life and Work in Medieval Europe: The Evolution of Medieval Economy from the Fifth to Fifteenth Centuries*. New York: Harper Torchbooks, 1964.

Butler, Smedley D. *War Is a Racket*. Costa Mesa, CA: Noontide Press, 1991 (originally published 1935).

Cahill, Marie, ed. *I Am Elvis: A Guide to Elvis Impersonators*. New York: Pocket Books, 1991.

Cantor, Norman F., ed. *The Medieval World: 300–1300*. New York: Macmillan, 1964.

Capp, Al. *Li'l Abner Dailies, Volume One: 1934–1935*. Princeton, WI: Kitchen Sink Press, 1988.

Cash, W. J. *The Mind of the South*. New York: Vintage Books, 1991 (originally published 1941).

Caudill, Harry M. *Night Comes to the Cumberlands: A Biography of a Depressed Area*. Boston: Little, Brown, & Co., 1963.

Cheyney, Edward P. *The Dawn of a New Era: 1250–1453*. New York: Harper Torchbooks, 1962.

Comparet, Bertrand L. *The Mark of the Beast: Part One and Two*. San Diego, CA: Your Heritage (year not indicated).

Cook, Peter. *Capitalism (and Its Secrets)*. Wickliffe, OH: Monetary Science Publishing, 1994. Also *Capitalism: Bane to Freedom and Security*. Wickliffe, OH: Monetary Science Publishing, 1994. Also *Capitalism (Socialism for Banks and the Affluent) Unmasked*. Wickliffe, OH: Monetary Science Publishing, 1988.

Crowe, Ray. *The Bigfoot Bar & Grill*. Portland, OR: Ray Crowe, 1991.

Dalton, Humphrey, ed. *Will America Drown?: Immigration and the Third World Population Explosion*. Washington, D.C.: Scott-Townsend Publishers, 1993.

Douglass, Frederick. *My Bondage and My Freedom*. New York, 1855.

Duby, Georges. *The Three Orders: Feudal Society Imagined*. Chicago: University of Chicago Press, 1982.

Eaton, Dian. *Is It True What They Say About Dixie?: A Loving Look at a Colorful, Romantic, and Prideful People, The Southerners*. Secaucus, NJ: Citadel Press, 1988.

Ekirch, A. Roger. *Bound for America: The Transportation of British Convicts to the Colonies, 1718–1775*. Oxford, UK: Clarendon Paperbacks, 1987.

Emry, Sheldon. *Billions for the Bankers and Debts for the People*. Sandpoint, ID: America's Promise Ministries (year not indicated).

Epstein, Steven A. *Wage Labor and Guilds in Medieval Europe*. Chapel Hill, NC: University of North Carolina Press, 1991.

Flynt, J. Wayne. *Dixie's Forgotten People: The South's Poor Whites*. Bloomington, IN: Indiana University Press, 1980.

Foster, R. F. *Modern Ireland: 1600–1972*. London: Penguin Books, 1988.

Frankl, Viktor E. *Man's Search for Meaning: An Introduction to Logotherapy*. Boston: Beacon Press, 1959.

Genovese, Eugene D. *Roll, Jordan, Roll: The World the Slaves Made.* New York: Vintage Books, 1972. Also *The World the Slaveholders Made.* New York: Vintage Books, 1971.

Grayson, Andrew. *The Horrors of Reconstruction, I and II.* Memphis, TN: The Southern National Party (year not indicated).

Grissom, Michael Andrew. *Southern by the Grace of God.* Gretna, LA: Pelican Publishing Company, 1995.

Halbert's Family Heritage. *The World Book of Goads.* Bath, OH: Halbert's Family Heritage, 1996.

Hamrick, Charles L. *Antient White Slaves.* 1996 (via internet).

Helper, Hinton Rowan. *The Impending Crisis of the South.* New York: Collier Books, 1963 (originally published 1857).

Higginbotham, A. Leon Jr. *In the Matter of Color (Race and the American Legal Process: The Colonial Period).* Oxford, UK: Oxford University Press, 1978.

Hill, Christopher. *The World Turned Upside Down: Radical Ideas During the English Revolution.* London: Penguin Books, 1972.

Hoffman, Michael A. II. *They Were White and They Were Slaves: The Untold History of the Enslavement of Whites in Early America.* Dresden, NY: Wiswell Ruffin House, 1992 (fourth edition).

Hofstadter, Richard. *America at 1750: A Social Portrait.* New York: Vintage Books, 1973.

Hoy, Michael, ed. *Loompanics' Golden Records.* Port Townsend, WA: Loompanics Unlimited, 1993.

Ignatiev, Noel. *How the Irish Became White.* New York: Routledge, 1995.

Kelley, Robin D. G. *Hammer and Hoe: Alabama Communists During the Great Depression.* Chapel Hill, NC: University of North Carolina Press, 1990.

Kellner, Esther. *Moonshine: Its History and Folklore.* New York: Weathervane Books, 1971.

Kennedy, Walter Donald, and James Ronald Kennedy. *The South Was Right!* Gretna, LA: Pelican Publishing Company, 1995 (originally published 1991).

Kephart, Horace. *Our Southern Highlanders: A Narrative of Adventure in the Southern Appalachians and a Study of Life Among the Mountaineers.* New York: Macmillan, 1913.

Killian, Lewis M. *White Southerners.* New York: Random House, 1970.

Kimbrough, David L. *Taking Up Serpents: Snake Handlers of Eastern Kentucky.* Chapel Hill, NC: University of North Carolina Press, 1995.

Kirby, Jack Temple. *Media-Made Dixie: The South in the American Imagination.* Baton Rouge, LA: Louisiana State University Press, 1978.

Leyburn, James G. *The Scotch-Irish: A Social History.* Chapel Hill, NC: University of North Carolina Press, 1962.

Logan, N. R. *Children of a Lost Spirit.* Mercer Island, WA: Kideko House Books, 1991.

Lutton, Wayne, and John Tanton. *The Immigration Invasion.* Petoskey, MI: The Social Contract Press, 1994.

McManus, John F. *"A New World Order" Means World Government.* Appleton, WI: The John Birch Society, 1990.

Martin, Len. *Black vs. White Equals Slavery: The Color Bomb.* Boring, OR: CPA Book Publisher, 1994.

Marx, Karl, and Friedrich Engels. *The Communist Manifesto.* New York: International Publishers, 1948 (first English translation 1850).

Marx, Karl. *The Duchess of Sutherland and Slavery.* London, 1853.

Miller, Wilbur R. *Revenuers and Moonshiners: Enforcing Federal Liquor Law in the Mountain South, 1865–1900.* Chapel Hill, NC: University of North Carolina Press, 1991.

Monetary Science Publishing. *Keys to Financial Wisdom.* Wickliffe, Ohio (year not indicated).

Nash, Gary B. *Class and Society in Early America.* Englewood Cliffs, NJ: Prentice-Hall, Inc., 1970. Also *Red, White, and Black: The Peoples of Early America.* Englewood Cliffs, NJ: Prentice-Hall, Inc., 1974.

Newberry, Mike. *The Yahoos.* New York: Marzani and Munsell, 1964.

Parenti, Michael. "Hidden Holocaust, USA." From *Dirty Truths,* Vida Communications and Michael Parenti, 1996 (via internet).

Parfrey, Adam. *Cult Rapture.* Portland, OR: Feral House, 1995.

Patterson, Richard. *Historical Atlas of the Outlaw West.* Boulder, CO: Johnson Publishing Co., 1985.

Paul, Ron. *Ten Myths About Paper Money (and One Myth About Paper Gold).* Lake Jackson, TX: The Foundation for Rational Economics and Education, 1983.

Perkins, Edwin J. *The Economy of Colonial America.* New York: Columbia University Press, 1980.

Pirenne, Henri. *Economic and Social History of Medieval Europe.* New York: Harvest Books, 1933.

Popp, Dr. Edward E. *Money: Bona Fide or Non–Bona Fide.* Port Washington, WI: Wisconsin Education Fund, 1970.

Reed, John Shelton. *Southern Folk, Plain & Fancy: Native White Social Types.* Athens, GA: University of Georgia Press, 1986. Also *The Enduring South: Subcultural Persistence in Mass Society.* Chapel Hill, NC: University of North Carolina Press, 1986 (originally published 1972).

Riese, Randall. *Nashville Babylon: The Uncensored Truth and Private Lives of Country Music's Stars.* New York: Congdon & Weed, 1988.

Schor, Juliet B. *The Overworked American: The Unexpected Decline of Leisure.* New York: Basic Books, 1992.

Shapiro, Henry D. *Appalachia on Our Mind: The Southern Mountains and Mountaineers in the American Consciousness, 1870–1920.* Chapel Hill, NC: University of North Carolina Press, 1986 (originally published 1978).

Slaughter, Thomas P. *The Whiskey Rebellion: Frontier Epilogue to the American Revolution.* New York: Oxford University Press, 1986.

Spooner, Lysander. *No Treason.* Colorado Springs, CO: Ralph Myles Publishers, 1990 (originally published 1868).

St. Johns Review. *Spanning the Decades: St. Johns Bridge Diamond Jubilee.* Portland, OR: Portland Rose Festival, 1991 (originally published 1931).

Steinfeld, Robert J. *The Invention of Free Labor: The Employment Relation in American Law and Culture, 1350–1870.* Chapel Hill, NC: University of North Carolina Press, 1991.

Stern, Kenneth S. *A Force Upon the Plain: The American Militia Movement and the Politics of Hate.* New York: Simon & Schuster, 1996.

Strasbaugh, John. *E: Reflections on the Birth of the Elvis Faith.* New York: Blast Books, 1995.

Styner and Cist, printers. "Observations on the Slaves and the Indented Servants, Inlisted [*sic*] in the Army, and in the Navy of the United States." Philadelphia, 1777 (via internet).

Swift, Jonathan. *Gulliver's Travels.* New York: Washington Square Press, 1961 (originally published 1726).

Tullos, Allen, ed. *Long Journey Home: Folklife in the South.* Chapel Hill, NC: Southern Exposure, 1977.

Waddell, L. A. *The Phoenician Origin of the Britons, Scots & Anglo-Saxons.* Hawthorne, CA: Christian Book Club of America, 1983.

Wade, A. M. *Homes: A Casualty of Inflation.* Wickliffe, OH: Monetary Science Publishing, 1974.

Waller, Altina L. *Feud: Hatfields, McCoys, and Social Change in Appalachia, 1860–1900.* Chapel Hill, NC: University of North Carolina Press, 1988.

Wertenbaker, Thomas J. *The First Americans: 1607–1690.* Chicago: Quadrangle Books, 1971 (originally published 1927).

Whitelock, Dorothy. *The Beginnings of English Society.* London: Penguin Books, 1991 (originally published 1952).

Wilcox, Laird, ed. *Spectrum: A Guide to The Independent Press and Informative Organizations.* Olathe, KS: Editorial Research Service, 1991.

Williamson, J. W. *Hillbillyland: What the Movies Did to the Mountains & What the Mountains Did to the Movies.* Chapel Hill, NC: University of North Carolina Press, 1995.

Woods, Daniel B. *Sixteen Months at the Gold Diggings: An Account of a Journey to the Newly Discovered Gold Regions of California.* Provo, UT: Triton Press, 1989 (originally published 1851).

Zinn, Howard. *A People's History of the United States.* New York: Harper-Perennial, 1990 (originally published 1980).